The Hour That Changes Everything

*How worship forms us
into the people God wants us to be*

By John van de Laar

for Debbie

Sacredise
Cape Town

© Copyright by John van de Laar, 2010

All rights reserved. No portion of this publication may be reproduced, stored in a retrieval system, or transmitted, in any form or by any means, electronic, mechanical, photocopying, recording or otherwise, without the prior permission of the publisher.

SACREDISE PUBLISHING
P.O. Box 27212, Rhine Road
Cape Town, 8050
South Africa
www.sacredise.com

Unless otherwise indicated, all Scripture quotations are taken from the HOLY BIBLE, NEW LIVING TRANSLATION, copyright © 1996. Used by permission of Tyndale House Publishers, Inc., Wheaton, Illinois 60189. All rights reserved.

Additional Scripture quotations (as indicated in the text or footnotes) are taken from the HOLY BIBLE, KING JAMES VERSION

or

The HOLY BIBLE, NEW INTERNATIONAL VERSION®. Copyright © 1973, 1978, 1984 Biblica. Used by permission of Zondervan. All rights reserved.

The "NIV" and "New International Version" trademarks are registered in the United States Patent and Trademark Office by Biblica. Use of either trademark requires the permission of Biblica.

or

THE MESSAGE, Copyright © 1993, 1994, 1995, 1996, 2000, 2001, 2002. Used by permission of NavPress Publishing Group.

Contents

Preface: On Indebtedness	5
Foreword: Rev. Dr. Ross Olivier	9
Introduction: A Roadmap for the Journey	13
Chapter One: An Invitation to Intimacy	27
Chapter Two: Welcome to a New World	43
Chapter Three: Becoming Holy	63
Chapter Four: Becoming True	81
Chapter Five: Becoming Beautiful	99
Chapter Six: Becoming Loving	115
Chapter Seven: Becoming Purposeful	133
Conclusion: Living the Change	153
Appendix A: Guidelines for Daily Devotions	159
Appendix B: Guidelines for Small Groups	227
Appendix C: Guidelines for Sunday Worship	239
Notes:	265

Preface

On Indebtedness

Every time I think of you, I give thanks to my God. Whenever I pray, I make my requests for all of you with joy, for you have been my partners in spreading the Good News about Christ from the time you first heard it until now. (Philippians 1:3-5)

I don't think they will ever know the gift they gave me.

As I read the card, signed by every person in the cast of the musical stage show I had produced, I was amazed that they were thanking me. I was convinced that it was they who deserved my thanks. Apart from my studies, this theatrical production had been the centre of my second year at university. I had learned so much, I had connected deeply with a very special group of people, and I had received the opportunity to stage a show in a 'real theatre'. Even in the midst of the whole gloriously chaotic process, I knew that I would never be the same, and I would be always indebted to those who had joined me in the adventure.

As I trace the course of my life from that time to this, I cannot help but acknowledge the deeply significant role that this experience played in the process that ultimately led to me becoming a liturgist. They will never know it, but I owe my entire life's work to that group of singers, dancers and musicians – that group of friends. In truth, even this book is part of their legacy in my life.

I would love to claim this work as my own, but I know better than that. I know that who I am has been formed by the people who love me; the people whom I love and with whom I share my life. I recognise that I am the product of so many friends, colleagues, authors, musicians, and worship leaders who have influenced my thinking and my faith over the years. I acknowledge that there are no original or new thoughts in these pages. And I appreciate that all I have learned and experienced has been a gift to me from the communities in which I have served and worshipped through the years. I am indebted beyond my ability to repay. My only hope is that in some small way this book will be a fitting testimony to those who have given me so much.

I would love to be able to mention by name every single person whose voice is hidden within my words. Clearly, that would be impossible. However, there are some people who must be named here, who have had an especially important impact on me, and on this book. We all share love for, and eternal gratitude to, the God whose grace and compassion have invited us into divine intimacy.

My wife, Debbie, is my partner-in-life, my teammate, my honest critic and my most faithful believer and encourager. Without her I would accomplish far less than I do, and what I do accomplish would mean nothing. Thank you, Debs, for sharing the process, the pain and the joy of bringing a book like this into being. I love you.

My parents, Ken and Sheila van de Laar, have always been enthusiastic supporters of my ministry and my work. In more ways than I can express, their constant love and care, their interest and practical help has enabled me to develop my work into what it is. Their own relationship of over five decades has been an inspiration to me, and a living example of God's love revealed in human experience. Thank you, Mom and Dad, for all you both are to me.

Within the Methodist Church of Southern Africa there are a number of colleagues and friends who have inspired and supported my work. Chief among them, perhaps, is the Rev. Dr. Ross Olivier. As Executive Secretary of our church, he was the first to give my work 'official' support by inviting me to be

Preface: On Indebtedness

the worship director of three National Conferences. As a friend and a colleague in ministry, he has opened doors for me, he has challenged my thinking, my attitudes and the manner in which I work, and I am a far better minister and person because of him. You will probably never know the extent of your influence on my life, Ross, but it is not small. In writing the foreword for this book, you have, once again, given me a gift I cannot repay. Thank you.

My friend and editor, Greg van der Lingen, began his work long before I sent him the manuscript to this book. Since we first met at Rhodes University in the early eighties, he has always impressed and challenged me with his clear and gracious thinking, his gentle kindness and his dedication to God and God's justice. There is more of him in these pages than simply good grammar and accurate typing. Thank you for sharing in this project, Greg, and for so graciously working to the tight timelines I set for you.

Finally, to every church that has embarked on the journey contained in these pages, to each small group that has explored these chapters together, to everyone who has purchased this book and used it as a personal journey of discovery, I thank you. It is your willingness to listen that gives authors like me a voice. It is your openness to new ideas and creative dialogue that creates the environment in which books like this can be born. I am deeply grateful for the gift of time and attention that your reading gives me.

By now you will have a sense of the immensity of my indebtedness. I must confess, though, that I consider it a privilege to be a participant in a community of faith that includes such grace and generosity. While faith has not always been easy for me, it is the support and love of people of faith that has sustained me and strengthened me. If I have anything of value to offer in these pages, it is not mine. I have simply been the conduit through which the gifts of others have flowed. In writing I have received far more than I have given, and for that, too, I am deeply grateful.

John

Foreword

It is always a privilege to be invited to write a foreword. The immense honour of holding in my hands and poring over the words of a manuscript which embodies many hours of sacrifice, devotion, commitment and sculpted labour by the author, is always a profoundly moving experience. I assess the task of being asked to read the 'about to be published' work of a friend as a sacred charge that demands dedication and integrity.

Exaggeration and hyperbole are regular fare for forewords and 'back of the book' reviews; these are neither helpful nor honourable. Both the author and readers of the book deserve better. Whenever authors entrust the product of their careful and oft draining earnest endeavour to another person, the transaction contains elements of vulnerability and trust, anticipation and completion. I know John well enough to know that he expects me to be honest in my appraisal of his work; whatever else may be said about him, he is a person of utmost integrity and faithfulness, deeply committed to the values of openness, sincerity, truth, and fidelity. It is in this context that I have carefully read - twice - and evaluated this book.

I love to watch television shows of the National Geographic genre; shows which display the wonder, beauty, diversity and adventure of the great outdoors. In particular, I have a fearful fondness and fascination for watching 'white water' river rafting. Generally we are introduced to the adventurers on a stretch of quietly flowing water, easily riding the wind and water, with leisurely opportunity and ease to gently enjoy the sights, smells and sounds of the surrounding vistas. Without warning, imperceptibly, the strength of the river's flow begins to strengthen, the craft's speed increases and the easy-going demeanour of the adventurers gives way to greater attentiveness. Soon thereafter the pace quickens, the waters surge against massive rocks which cause plumes of water to be hurled into the air; the boat rocks and rolls, sometimes perilously perching atop the waves and then crashing into a valley of deep water, disappearing and reappearing midst the turbulence and frenzy of the wild ride. *The Hour That Changes Everything* is that kind of read: reflective and risky, wild and challenging, solemn and adventurous, stirring and soulful, provocative and evocative; never boring, intellectually stimulating, gently soothing, wildly exciting and profoundly spiritual.

The heart of the book articulates John's deeply felt convictions about the acts of Christian worship. It powerfully articulates the premise that worship is never less than the quest to enter into a deeply authentic engagement with God by which we discover, recover, and uncover the soul of our humanity. In worship we find our true identity, begin to more fully comprehend the purpose of life, and become rededicated to our ultimate destiny. As one turns the pages, it becomes ever clearer that none of the above can happen unless we explore, and are explored by, our encounter with God. Worship is the central act by which this takes place because worship is the central act of Christian faith. John leaves us in no doubt that worship, fully understood, embodies, determines and expresses the quality of our spirituality.

The Hour That Changes Everything reminds us that authentic Christian worship seamlessly combines and communicates our quest for faith, the story of salvation and our transformational mission in the world. Furthermore, as the sign of our unity and the guardian of our identity, authentic worship locates us within the fragrance of grace and duty, prayer and protest, tradition and context, laughter and tears, scars and beauty.

It has been so good to again be reminded of the essential truth that transformational spirituality has personal and corporate elements, wherein worship is the primary corporate element. I am challenged by the message that wherever we find a community worshipping within and beyond the precincts of the church building, we will always find a community in mission.

Our communities and churches are richly endowed with wonderfully gifted and resourceful people. Sadly many of them do not develop their full potential; all too often their rich talents are allowed to wither through disuse or misuse. There are few sadder events than observing human potential being wasted or left unfulfilled as a result of indolence, irresponsibility, or poor self-centred choices. It is simple truth that our given aptitude (the talents and opportunities with which we enter this world) must be matched by positive and committed application, discipline and the willingness to learn and grow, if we are to achieve our God-given potential. I am privileged to have known John for many years, as my colleague and friend. I have watched him develop his subject knowledge, skills, artistry and spirit. I shall always remember with sincere and grateful appreciation his acceptance of my invitation to join and assist the congregation I was serving in Mississippi at that particular time. The hours spent in our home, sharing meals and sights, and expertly helping our worship and arts ministry to explore new ways and deepen old ways of designing and leading worship, are a constant rich reminder of John's graciousness and giftedness. It was a special Holy Week pilgrimage in worship that underlined for me the fact that John is both thoughtful theologian and excellent practitioner of *"The Hour That Changes Everything."*

Without any hesitation, I gladly testify to his profound dedication to all of the elements described in this book: God, family, community, hope, service, inclusion, compassion and joy. Furthermore I have enormous regard for his plain-spoken honesty and willingness to take risks for the sake of all that is righteous. He, Debbie and their family exude a sense of wholeness that transcends our universal trials and mishaps. Contained within their wholeness I have observed the courageous love that defines every authentic relationship. In them, the words about worship become a personal witness, and convincing sign, that their shared convictions about the primacy of authentic spirituality and dedication to the cause of Jesus, is tangibly and joyfully real.

John's commitment to excellence is often the source of personal angst yet also the blessing he delivers to all of us. I shall read this book again and again in years to come: to be reminded, instructed, inspired and energised – for worship. As preacher, I shall have to live with a scorching question: do the hours of worship I lead alongside others truly change everything? John - thank you!

Dr Ross Olivier
President: Seth Mokitimi Methodist Seminary,
Pietermaritzburg, South Africa.
July 2010

Introduction

A Roadmap for the Journey

Imitate God, therefore, in everything you do, because you are His dear children. Live a life filled with love, following the example of Christ. He loved us and offered Himself as a sacrifice for us, a pleasing aroma to God. (Ephesians 5:1-2)

My heart sank when I saw the expression on the face of the man walking toward me. He was one of the leaders in the independent Pentecostal church where I was assistant pastor and worship director. He was clearly unhappy, and I was clearly the cause.

"John, I think you need to spend more time in prayer and discernment when you prepare for worship," he said authoritatively, "you really missed God this morning."

As I watched him walk away, I thought to myself, "If you only knew". The truth was that this week had been no different from any other week. I took my work as worship leader to this community very seriously, and I felt the weight of my responsibility keenly. That was why every Thursday I would get to the church early and, taking my guitar, my Bible, a notebook and a pen, I would retreat into the sanctuary (usually the 'cry-room' so I would have more privacy) to pray and prepare for the two Sunday services. I would begin with an extended time of personal prayer and worship, singing, praying and listening for what God might want to say and do among us this week. Then, I would begin to prepare – reading the Bible, forming a structure that would enable the service to flow while opening us to God's Spirit, and selecting music that would give voice to this whole experience.

On this particular week I had felt an overwhelming and disturbing sense that God was calling us to a different journey from the norm. I was captivated by the idea that we needed to spend time in quiet and confession, that we needed to give God 'space' to work, and for people to open to a deep and searching move of God's Spirit in their lives. I also knew that it might be difficult for people to embrace this different 'mode' of worship easily. I had not expected the strong negative reaction that I received from this leader, though.

The following Thursday, as I entered the church to prepare for Sunday, an unformed thought that had been nagging at me became clear in my mind. I found myself questioning how I was being measured. I wondered whether there was real discernment at work, or if people simply judged my success by the level of their excitement and joy in the service. And I realised that I needed to know the answer to these questions. After a short prayer, apologising for my just-made decision not to spend the day in prayer and worship, I began to prepare for Sunday. Laying aside any spiritual considerations, I used my musical awareness to create medleys and transitions that I knew had energy and the capacity to move people emotionally. It did not take long to finish the job.

That Sunday the services were electric. People were literally standing on their chairs and shouting out words and songs of praise. The band played with skill and commitment and the music was powerful and inviting. But, through it all I felt nothing but emptiness and shame. I knew that all I was doing was manipulating people with the music – the only time I have deliberately done so – and I was getting exactly the response I had planned for. But, God seemed somehow distant and removed from me, and the emotional responses from the people felt shallow and unreal.

After the service the same leader who had confronted me a week before came up to me, his face radiant, a huge smile stretching across it.

"Whatever you did this week, John, keep doing it!" he exclaimed. "The worship this week was incredible!" With that he walked away, and I was sure I noticed a spring in his step. But, as I watched his back I thought again, "If you only knew."

The next week I handed in my resignation.

Disillusioned with Worship

Across the globe more and more Christians are asking questions about worship – what it is, what it is for, and how to be most authentic as we participate. It has been regularly noted in the last few years that the Church, pretty much across the board, is in decline. In particular, in North America and Europe there seems to be a growing disillusionment with the Church and its worship. As Sally Morgenthaler observed in her foreword to Dan Kimball's book Emerging Worship:

> When it comes to irony, worship in late twentieth century evangelicalism takes the prize. Just as the world was reenchanting the universe (think Deepak Chopra, *The X-Files*, candle-and-teddy-bear grief vigils, *Final Fantasy* video games, and *Lord of the Rings*), user-friendly Christianity was practicing religious reductionism: shrinking the divine to the size of a three-point outline and four songs in the key of perpetually happy. In denuded corporate temples across America – from strip-mall spaces bathed in eerie green fluorescent lighting to gaping grey warehouses adrift in theatre seats – turn-of-the-millennium "trendy" church is proving anything but trendy in a highly spiritualised culture.[1]

In South Africa we are seeing similar disturbing trends as young people, and older people who are bored with Church-as-usual, leave churches – whether in the suburbs or the townships.[2] One colleague and friend has even taken to referring to the normal structure of worship that most churches follow as *"religious karaoke"*.[3] A lot of this disillusionment with the Church stems from a sense that it is irrelevant, unconcerned for the needs and issues of the world, and selfishly focussed on its own growth and success. In their 2007 study of American young people both within and outside of the Church, David Kinnaman and Gabe Lyons chose as their title the word that best summarised responses to the Church: UnChristian.[4]

However, I suspect that for many people the primary experience of Church is the worship service in the Church building. This is reflected in the language we use – we "go to" church on Sundays. Decline in Church attendance – another Sunday-focussed measurement – must indicate two important realities about our worship, then. Firstly, we, as the Church, have failed to teach and practice worship in ways that lead people into deeper and more life-encompassing spirituality. Secondly, the spiritual encounter that people have come to expect from Christian worship services is unsatisfying and fails to challenge, transform and inspire, as spiritual practices should.

Worship and Lifestyle

In an attempt to address both the disillusionment with worship in our times, and our inadequate practice of worship, it has become common to speak of worship as "a lifestyle". The idea has been to recognise that what we do in Church is not an end in itself, but is intended to lead us into a life of honouring God in all we do. This idea has brought necessary balance to the Church's understanding of worship, leading us to recognise that what we call worship is not simply about singing a few songs and listening to a sermon. Rather, worship must impact every moment, every circumstance, and every interaction in our lives.

My concern, though, is that we may have inadvertently devalued the crucial and transforming work of the sanctuary. Many writers have rightly emphasised that the Church is not a building but the community of people who seek to love and follow Jesus, and reach out to a hurting world in Jesus' name. Many authors have correctly shown how an over-emphasis on the performance of worship services leads to a "consumer" Christianity, in which we come to Church to receive our 'blessing' or 'empowerment' for the week.

Dan Kimball has described it this way:

> Most people view the worship service as a place where we go to get service done to us by "getting our tanks filled up" at the service station. It's a place where someone will give a sermon and serve us with our weekly sustenance. In automobile terms, you could say it is our weekly fill-up. We come to our service station to have a song leader serve us by leading us in singing songs. All so we can feel good when we emotionally connect through mass singing and feel that we did "worship".[5]

This is probably an accurate description of how worship is practiced and perceived around the world. Unfortunately, however, in striving to combat this "worship-consumerism", we too often stray into other, equally unhelpful, views of worship. On the one hand, we devalue the act of worship when we fail to connect it with spiritual formation, with the Church's mission, or with the real work of Christ in people. When we fall into this trap, we find ourselves placing worship last in the work of the Church, and creating a false dichotomy between mission and worship. This is a common reaction to our disillusionment with the Sunday service, but actually operates from the same thinking as the problem we are trying to solve – that the worship service is simply an event that is separate from the daily work of following Christ, growing in spiritual character and participating in missions.

On the other hand, 'lifestyle' language devalues the act of worship by defining it too broadly. Ultimately, if we define something as everything, we end up defining it as nothing. When we speak of worship as a lifestyle, we begin to speak of everything we do as worship, which dilutes the meaning and significance of the communal act of the Church at worship. Certainly there is a sense in which all we do can be seen as an act of worship, in which our work, our play, our loving and our resting are all offered to God and committed to God's service. However, in practice, our daily routines only really become acts of worship when they are formed and informed by an effective, transforming spiritual discipline. And the act of worship is the fountainhead for this worship-filled way of being and living.

The answer to our disillusionment with worship is not to discredit or devalue the Sunday service. On the contrary, it is because we have failed to do the work of understanding and practicing worship well that this disillusionment has crept in. If we seek to change how the Church is viewed and experienced both by those who attend and those who don't, we need to take our Sunday services far more seriously – not merely as ministers and worship leaders who construct and facilitate the experience, but as worshippers who partake of and participate in it.

A new – or ancient – way to think of worship

If possible, then, I'd like to attempt to understand worship in a new way – or rather, return to an ancient understanding of the communal act of worship. To do so, we must begin with the biblical writers, who, it seems, struggled with exactly the same disillusionment that we do today. Isaiah challenged the people of Israel because, although they observed religious feasts, worshipping and fasting regularly, the way they lived failed to change. Because of their continuing injustice, God refused to act on their behalf, in spite of their pleas and complaints.[6] In response to this situation, Isaiah calls the people to a life of worship that overflows into a life of justice, compassion and service. It is important to note that Isaiah's prophecy does not call for less value to be placed on Sabbath day worship, but rather that worship should be more mindfully and rightfully practiced:

> Keep the Sabbath day holy. Don't pursue your own interests on that day, but enjoy the Sabbath and speak of it with delight as the LORD's holy day. Honour the Sabbath in everything you do on that day, and don't follow your own desires or talk idly.[7]

In a similar way, the prophet Amos proclaims God's challenge to people who are religiously zealous, but spiritually dead:

> I hate all your show and pretence—the hypocrisy of your religious festivals and solemn assemblies. I will not accept your burnt offerings and grain offerings. I won't even notice all your choice peace offerings. Away with your noisy hymns of praise! I will not listen to the music of your harps. Instead, I want to see a mighty flood of justice, an endless river of righteous living.[8]

In the New Testament, this pattern continues. In writing to the troublesome Corinthian church, the apostle Paul challenges the believers because their worship practice does not lead them to live more Christ-like, compassionate lives. He draws clear connections between their liturgy (worship) and their spirituality (lives of following Christ).[9]

In none of these examples, or any others that can be drawn from the biblical teachings, is the act of worship in itself seen as the problem. Rather, the problem lies with practicing worship as a self-contained activity that somehow appeases God, or entertains the individual, and that has no connection with spiritual formation and just living. What becomes clear here is that the act of worship is understood in the Scriptures to be a spiritual discipline that is essential to the growth of God's people in faith and righteousness. This understanding addresses both the problem of seeing worship as a weekly "fill up" and the problem of blurring our understanding of worship into everything we do. As Richard Foster explains:

> One reason worship should be considered a Spiritual Discipline is because it is an ordered way of acting and living that sets us before God so he can transform us. Although we are only responding to the liberating touch of the Holy Spirit, there are divinely appointed avenues into this realm.[10]

Throughout the history of the Church worship has been seen in these terms – as a spiritual discipline that transforms us and leads us into a way of living that embodies God's values and purposes. This is especially evident in what has become known as the liturgical tradition of spirituality. Susan White, one contemporary exponent of this tradition, describes this way of viewing worship beautifully:

> The common prayer of the Church provides both the model and the content of the Christian devotional life.[11]
>
> ...[I]t is within the liturgical assembly that one receives the primary spiritual insight, strength, experience of the holy, and nourishment for godly living.[12]

The idea that worship is simply a "filling station", where we come to "get something out" each week, is completely foreign to both the Scriptures and the Church's history. Equally foreign is the idea that worship can be merged into the rest of our daily lives without a regular, intentional, corporate sharing in acts of worship. Although followers of Christ have often fallen short of this ideal, the basic understanding of worship that has always been held by both the biblical writers and the fathers and mothers of the Church is that worship is an act that leads us into a transforming encounter with God from which mission, compassion, and justice flow. **The way we worship defines the way we live.**

To put it another way, we do not strive for a lifestyle of worship – rather **we strive for worship to transform us so that we live lifestyles of Christ-likeness.** It is not the practices and experiences of worship that we should seek to carry into our daily lives. It is **the transformation that worship creates in us** that we seek to bring into our everyday routines. The result of the act of worship, then, is that we find ourselves automatically living in a Cross-carrying, Christ-following, contributing and compassionate way, because we have encountered the crucified, selfless, eternally-loving Christ in our worship, and we are becoming a little more like this Jesus each day.

In this sense, the worship service is at the very heart of the Church's mission, identity and work of spiritual formation. The worship service is the fountainhead from which the life and ministry of the Church flows. Or, to put it the way Bill Hybels, of Willow Creek Community Church, once did: *"As goes the weekend, so goes the Church."*[13]

How Does This Book Fit In?

If worship is to be this transforming spiritual discipline for us, we need to grasp both the meaning and the reality of what happens when we gather for worship. We also need to learn how best to participate in the act in order to open ourselves to God's transforming work. This is the purpose of the book you now hold in your hands.

On the one hand this book is a theology of worship – but don't let that word scare you. In a Church environment in which so much of our understanding and practice of worship is shaped by a market-driven music industry, and by a rather narrow band within the wide spectrum of Christian thought, this book attempts to be a different voice. It seeks to explore the spiritual discipline of worship from a framework of thinking and practice that has been developed over thirty years of worship leading and theological work. It strives to take seriously some of the important questions that are currently being asked of the Christian Faith through movements like the emerging church and writers like Brian McLaren, Phyllis Tickle, Peter Rollins, Matthew Fox, Rob Bell, Marcus Borg and others. In one sense, then, this book can be thought of as a theology of worship for the emerging church.

On the other hand, this book is a practical manual, designed not only to offer ideas about worship, but also to take us on a journey into a new experience of worship. For this reason, the main content of the book must be seen only as a catalyst for the journey that is guided by the resources offered in the final sections – the daily devotional guides, the small group guides and the Sunday service resources. The idea is that entire church communities will embark on this adventure together – reading the chapters, reflecting on them through personal devotional practices, engaging them together in small group worship and conversation, and then sharing in corporate worship gatherings based on the content. The whole experience takes fifty days in total, and promises to lead you into a deeper experience of worship, and a different way of living as a result.

For those who choose to walk this road alone, or with a small group of friends, though, the material can still be used as a guide, perhaps replacing the worship suggestions for small groups with an adapted version of the Sunday service, or making space once a week to practice a personal service of worship. However, since, as we shall see, worship is essentially a corporate activity, I would recommend that you try in some way to find a group to share the journey with.

A Brief Roadmap

When approaching the act of worship as a subject for reflection and discussion, it can be difficult to know where to begin. Many writers have started with the Scriptures and tried to develop definitions and theological frameworks from there. In many ways this is the most obvious course of action. The problem, I have found, however, is that the Bible does not give a simple and clear definition of worship, nor does it offer a structured theological framework. That is not it's purpose, after all.

As a result, I have decided to try a different path. A path which can, perhaps, be thought of as a dialogue between the

Scriptures and the thinking of one particularly helpful scholar. A simple definition from this well-known and respected Church leader has provided the framework for the dialogue. In examining and questioning each part of his five-fold definition, the Bible has offered clarity, direction, wisdom and practical guidance. What I have enjoyed about this process is the way it has taken both the divine and the human activity in worship seriously.

Let me introduce you to the person who will be our guide on this journey. His name is William Temple, and he was ordained as priest in the Anglican Church in Britain in 1910. He went on to become Archbishop of Canterbury from 1942 until his death in 1944. William Temple was a highly respected theologian, preacher and leader throughout his career, the author of a number of influential books, and was deeply committed to challenging the Church to be a positive and transforming influence in society. All of this is reflected in one of his better known statements: *"The Church is the only society that exists for the benefit of those who are not its members."*[14]

It is particularly Temple's understanding of worship, and his practice as a worship leader that is particularly important for us, though. One story from his career can illustrate the sensitivity he had to God's leading in worship, and the high value he placed on the act of worship in the Church's life.

In 1931 William Temple was leading a congregation in the University church of St. Mary the Virgin at the end of what was known as the Oxford Mission. During the singing of the hymn *When I Survey The Wondrous Cross*, he stopped the music just before the last stanza, and encouraged the people to read the words to themselves silently. Then, he invited those who could sing with whole-hearted commitment, to sing the words loudly. Those who did not feel they could commit to the words, he invited to remain silent, and those who felt they could mean the words only a little, and who wanted to grow in their commitment to them, he asked to sing in a whisper.

With that, the organ began to play again, and the whisper of two thousand voices was heard singing:

> Were the whole realm of nature mine
> That were an offering far too small
> Love so amazing, so divine
> Demands my soul, my life, my all.[15]

This experience was not forgotten by those who were present.[16]

Over the years I have encountered Temple's definition of worship many times and in many different forms. It has influenced the thinking and practice of many liturgists over the decades, and, after using it as the foundation for my workshops and training events, it seemed to offer the most natural and helpful framework for this dialogue. Here is how he expressed his understanding of worship:

> To worship is to quicken the conscience by the holiness of God, to feed the mind with the truth of God, to purge the imagination by the beauty of God, to open the heart to the love of God, to devote the will to the purpose of God.[17]

There are five statements in this definition, each of which corresponds with a characteristic of the Church, a facet of the Church's life in the world, and each of which is a window into both God's activity in worship and our response to it. Using these five statements as a framework allows the Scriptures to speak clearly and powerfully to our understanding and practice of worship, and leads us into encounters with God that transform us and the way we live.

Before we tackle the definition, though, there is some groundwork that needs to be laid. We need first to attempt to understand what we mean by the word 'worship' and how our Sunday activity seeks to embody this meaning. This is the work of Chapter One. Then we need to understand the difference our worship makes to how we inhabit our world, and how we relate to the people in it. In other words, we need to recognise that when we commit to being whole-hearted worshippers, our world is changed – or at least our perceptions and experience of it. I think of this as the 'external' change that worship brings. This is the work of Chapter Two.

Then, from Chapter Three to Seven, we explore in turn the five statements of Temple's definition, recognising how worship facilitates the changes within us that he describes. This is what I think of as the 'internal' change that worship brings. In reality there is no clear way to separate the internal changes from the external. They overlap and feed into each other. It is helpful, though, to recognise that worship is neither a purely internal activity, nor a purely individual one.

A Final Invitation

You may feel that you have already begun the 'work' of this journey into worship – and you'll be right. But, this was only the necessary preparation for starting out. It was the packing, the gathering of resources and information, the planning of the trip. What lies ahead now is the adventure of the journey itself.

I can guarantee that this will be a challenging quest. There will be times of refreshment and rest, times of play and silent reflection. But, there will also be times of turbulence, times of surprising and perhaps frustrating detours, times of uncertainty and questioning. This is an inevitable part of seeking to know God – ask any prophets – but it is also where the greatest value will be found. Fortunately, you do not have to undertake this adventure alone. At times you will travel in solitude, but at other times you will be in conversation with a small band of companions who share the road with you, and at still other times you will be part of a larger community that is celebrating together.

It may be helpful to remember a parable that Jesus told for anyone who earnestly desires to enter God's Kingdom – which is, after all, what this quest is all about.

"The Kingdom of Heaven is like a treasure that a man discovered hidden in a field. In his excitement, he hid it again and sold everything he owned to get enough money to buy the field. Again, the Kingdom of Heaven is like a merchant on the lookout for choice pearls. When he discovered a pearl of great value, he sold everything he owned and bought it!"[18]

I pray that in these pages you may find some treasure, some pearls of great value. I pray that you will feel that the work and the journey, the wrestling and the searching have been worth the effort. But, most of all, I pray that as a result of this quest, your experience and participation in worship will be deeper and more transforming, and that you will enter the daily details of your life and relationships with a new passion, and new commitment to compassion and grace. And I pray, that as a result of the change in you, your world will be a little more whole.

It's time. Let's get started.

Chapter One

An Invitation to Intimacy

I pray that they will all be one, just as You and I are one—as You are in Me, Father, and I am in You. And may they be in Us so that the world will believe You sent Me. I have given them the glory You gave Me, so they may be one as We are one. I am in them and You are in Me. May they experience such perfect unity that the world will know that You sent Me and that You love them as much as You love Me. (John 17:21-23)

The first thing that struck me as I walked into the room was how cramped it was. Within minutes I didn't care. I joined the fifty or sixty young people pouring into a space the size of a bedroom, and squeezed onto a tiny square of floor next to the friend who had invited me to this independent, non-denominational youth group. And then the music began. The songs were led by a young, bearded man in his twenties – clearly the leader of the group – playing a 12-string guitar, a tomboyish girl in her late teens on a bass guitar that looked exactly like the one Paul McCartney used to play, and a Mediterranean-looking boy playing a small pair of bongo drums. There were no words displayed or available in any way, but every person in the room was singing.

What really captured my attention, though, was the obvious passion and devotion I saw on the faces of the teenagers around me. They meant every word, using the songs to express the love and joy that was clearly in their hearts. And every ounce of emotion being poured out was being offered to God – a God who was clearly present and very real to each one.

As I allowed myself to be drawn into the act of worship, I recognised the experience as an echo of the night when I had made my first conscious commitment to Christ. I had prayed a simple prayer, kneeling alone at the communion rail in my home church, and I had known this same overwhelming awareness of the divine presence, had been overcome by the same warm wave of emotion. I had thought this was a once-off occurrence related to the significance of the decision I had made a moment ago – a gift from the God I had given myself to confirming that what I had done was real, and inspiring me to continue the journey I had just begun. But, now I realised that initial encounter with God was repeatable, that worship could open the doors of my awareness to God's presence, that God was accessible to me any time I chose to offer my love and devotion in the simple acts of music, prayer and Scripture reading.

That night, cramped into a tiny room with a crowd of passionate teenagers, I gave myself over to the act of worship for the first time. I have never been the same.

Longings and 'Thin Places'

Bill Gates, the founder of Microsoft, is reported to have said this about religion:

> Just in terms of allocation of time resources, religion is not very efficient. There's a lot more I could be doing on a Sunday morning.[19]

I must confess that I am often tempted to agree with him. I am also tempted to believe that I am not alone. In churches across the world, the way we approach Sundays reveals our commitment to efficiency and our struggle with what our worship gatherings are really meant to be. In a desperate attempt to keep people coming back each week, and in a scramble to use the one moment when we know we have the whole community's attention, we fill our services with techniques, information, gimmicks and strategies. We want Sundays to matter, and we long for measurable results, and so we fall into the efficiency trap of trying to get the 'best return' on our 'investment' of time, resources and people power.

But, for those of us who fill the pews each week, we have an uneasy sense that in all this striving, this measuring, this reaching for 'success' we have lost something important. We may not be able to voice exactly what it is, but we know that each week we leave feeling a little disappointed, a little empty and a little less hopeful. At times, when we experience a new way of 'doing worship' or a new musical style, or a new church movement, we may get excited and feel that we've touched something real, but once the novelty has worn off, we discover that all we've done is silence our longing with goose bumps, while our souls remain dry and thirsty. Over a decade ago Sally Morgenthaler, in her book *Worship Evangelism*, bravely blew the whistle on this unspoken crisis:

> We are not producing worshippers... Rather, we are producing a generation of spectators, religious onlookers lacking, in many cases, any memory of a true encounter with God, deprived of both the tangible sense of God's presence and the supernatural relationship their inmost spirits crave. A sickening emptiness pervades much of the born-again experiencing of the 90s, and the hollow rituals played out week after week in so many of our worship centres attest to it.[20]

Unfortunately, very little has changed since those words were written, and Morgenthaler herself has recognised with great disappointment that, rather than heed her warning, many churches simply used her book as the next 'efficient' strategy to 'make church work'.[21] It's as if we have developed a functional atheism, ignoring the reality of which we sing and speak, while embracing corporate strategies that we hope will bring us worldly success. But for all our efforts, we are unable to silence the cry of our hearts for the reality that we sense is at the heart of worship – genuine, transforming, encounter with a living, loving God.

> What we seek on our journey is not a solution to a problem, not the answer to a question, but an encounter with the mystery of hope that will by very definition far exceed the best efforts of our mind, the utmost limits of our imagination.[22]

The quest for this divine confrontation has always been the centre around which the life of faith is built. Throughout the Scriptures, through every age of the Church, prophets, mystics and apostles have testified to God's availability and have encouraged spiritual seekers to settle for nothing less. The yearning of the Psalmist for God is echoed in every human heart:

> As the deer longs for streams of water, so I long for You, O God. I thirst for God, the living God. When can I go and stand before Him?[23]

It is repeated by the prophets:

> For My people have done two evil things: They have abandoned Me—the fountain of living water. And they have dug for themselves cracked cisterns that can hold no water at all![24]

> No, O people, the LORD has told you what is good, and this is what He requires of you: to do what is right, to love mercy, and to walk humbly with your God.[25]

It is proclaimed by Jesus – as demonstrated by his prayer in John 17:21:

> "...as You are in Me, Father, and I am in You. And may they be in Us so that the world will believe You sent Me."

And by the apostles of the New Testament Church:

> That I may know him, and the power of his resurrection, and the fellowship of his sufferings, being made conformable unto his death; If by any means I might attain unto the resurrection of the dead.[26]

This same longing to know God as a lived reality has been consistently expressed through mystics and theologians in the history of the Church. St. Augustine describes a moving encounter with Christ that resulted in his conversion.[27] The eleventh century mystic, Hildegarde of Bingen, spoke about our response to God's availability as *"yielding ourselves to the Word's brightness and wetness"*.[28] The seventeenth century monk, Brother Lawrence, has become well known for his "practicing of the presence of God", and his affirmation that God's presence is available for us to encounter and enjoy at all times.[29] In the Methodist tradition of which I am part, John Wesley's 'heart warming' experience has always been considered to be available for anyone who seeks relationship with God, and not as a unique experience available to Wesley alone. This is simply a small selection of spiritual pioneers from a long and rich tradition.[30]

The longing that we feel in the Church today is simply the most recent expression of this ancient human need, and there is no shortage of voices calling us to listen to our own hearts and set out on the journey to encounter God. It is in answer to this call that our worship becomes most powerful and most transforming. What we do on Sunday is intended for one purpose, and one purpose only – to bring human beings into deep, passionate, life-changing encounters with the God who made us and to whom we long to return.

For Marcus Borg worship *"is about creating a sense of the sacred, a thin place"*. A thin place is a term used in Celtic Christianity to refer to moments, activities and places where the visible world of our daily lives and the reality of God's presence intersect. A thin place is a place in which we become aware of the reality of God within and beyond our physical world, and in which we are opened up to encounter with this divine reality.

In expanding this idea, Borg continues:

> The diverse forms of Christian worship do this in different ways. At one end of the spectrum, the enthusiasm of Pentecostal worship can become a thin place by mediating an almost palpable sense of the presence of the Spirit. At the other end of the spectrum, Quaker silence serves the same purpose. In liturgical and sacramental forms of worship, the use of sacred words and rituals creates a sense of another world.[31]

Worship and Sex

It is this encounter with the reality of God that we know our worship should provide – even if we don't have the words to express it – and for which we constantly seek. The drive within us to find union with God is so powerful that the Scriptures are surprisingly comfortable using sexual language to describe it. The psalmist, for example, offers this directive: *"Kiss the Son, lest he be angry and you be destroyed in your way."*[32] In Paul's writings the comparison between sex and spirituality becomes even clearer. He contrasts our relationship with God with sexual union with a prostitute[33], and compares it to the sexual union of husband and wife.[34]

This is just a small sample of the biblical testimony, but the message is clear. Worship is, essentially, a union with God, which can be understood by comparing it to the intimate union of human beings. As Rob Bells explains:

> You can't talk about sexuality without talking about how we're made. And that will inevitably lead you to who made us. At some point you have to talk about God.
>
> Sex. God. They're connected. And they can't be separated. Where the one is, you will always find the other.[35]

Chapter One: An Invitation to Intimacy

How does the connection between sexuality and spirituality help us to understand our worship as a quest for encounter with God? Quite simply, the sexual act is not complete in itself. Rather, the act of intercourse between human lovers is fulfilled only when it is the outward expression of the inner, intimate connection of their hearts and souls. In the same way, our singing, praying, sacraments, rituals, music, banners, Scripture reading and other worship acts are not complete in themselves. These actions are simply the outward expressions of our inner, intimate, spiritual connection with God.

The problem is that all too often we mistake the expression for the reality it is supposed to point to. We make the same mistake in worship that we make with sex. It has become common in our world to use sex as a commodity. Sex sells. Sex is recreation. We even speak about the "sex industry". Somehow the act of sex has become completely disconnected from the intimate longing for union with another person. We no longer yearn for deep, whole-person connection. Monogamy, it seems, has become a rather quaint, but outdated social construction. All we need – or think we need – is a willing partner to help us scratch the physical itch, and then we can go our separate ways with no further responsibility to each other.

But, if you live that way for long enough, you discover an emptiness in your soul, and you realise that sex doesn't work on its own. Without the connection, the intimacy, the giving of your whole self to another, and receiving their whole self in return, the act gets meaningless and unsatisfying – or even destructive – very quickly. And so, too many of us find ourselves on a treadmill, going from partner to partner seeking, unsuccessfully, to fill the hollow inside of us.

This same pattern is played out in our worship every week. We see worship as a commodity. Worship sells (as many Christian artists who have turned to recording 'worship music' have discovered). Worship is recreation (just go to any worship 'concert' to confirm the truth of this). We even have a "worship industry" (which is worth millions of dollars a year). Somehow the act of worship has become completely disconnected from a whole-person commitment to God, and to God's people. Faithfulness to a faith community has become a quaint and outdated social construct. All we need – or think we need – is a willing group to help us get the emotional high we want, and then we can go our separate ways with no further responsibility to each other.

But, if you live that way for long enough, you discover an emptiness in your soul, and you realise that worship – or the outward expression of it – doesn't work on its own. Without the connection, the intimacy, the giving of your whole self to God and God's people, and the receiving of God's Spirit, and the love of a community in return, the act gets meaningless and unsatisfying – or even destructive – very quickly. And so, too many of us find ourselves on a treadmill, going from church to church seeking, unsuccessfully, to fill the hollow inside of us.

It's like we've become focussed on the packaging and forgotten the gift inside. This is why we spend so much time arguing over musical styles and instruments, or over structure versus spontaneity. Ultimately, if we allow ourselves to become obsessed with packaging, we will be trapped by our own preferences, by the fashions of the day, or by both. This has always been the Church's temptation. When Isaac Watts and Charles Wesley were writing their great hymns of faith, there were church leaders that objected strongly to this 'new' music.[36] The great reformer, John Calvin, was so strongly opposed to the organ (known in his day as "the devil's pipes") that he would melt down the pipes in order to use them for other purposes![37] When packaging becomes the focus – whether in the liturgy of traditional worship, the spontaneity of contemporary worship or the creativity of the emerging church – we find we have traded intimacy with God for a good feeling, and we have changed from worshipers to consumers of entertainment.

This is why the Bible uses sexual language to describe our worship. Both the act of sex and the act of worship are only meaningful when they are an outward expression of an inner, intimate reality. C.S. Lewis points to that reality in a beautiful and poetic way:

> I think all Christians would agree with me if I said that though Christianity seems at first to be all about morality, all about duties and rules and guilt and virtue, yet it leads you on, out of all that, into something beyond. One has a glimpse of a country where they do not talk of those things, except perhaps as a joke. Every one there is filled with what we should call goodness as a mirror is filled with light. But they do not call it goodness. They do not call it anything. They are not thinking of it. They are too busy looking at the source from which it comes.[38]

The Experience of Intimacy – Worship Practices

Once we have identified the longing for God in our hearts, and have realised that God longs to fill our desire with God's self, we inevitably begin to ask how we can make intimacy with God a real, lived experience. It is all very well to speak about worship as intimate union with God, but we cannot help but wonder how this connection is practically experienced. This brings us face to face with the reality that these questions move us into a realm beyond words.

As Peter Rollins explains, when we seek intimacy with God, we must recognise that the God we are dealing with is beyond our ability to understand. Christianity is rooted in the belief that God can be known, that God reveals God's self to human beings, but if God is God, even this revelation leads us into 'unknowing', into recognising that God can never really be 'known'. But, at the same time, our hope is that, through God's revelation, we embark on an eternal journey into knowing, and – more importantly – being known by, God. As Rollins explains:

Hence revelation ought not to be thought of either as that which makes God known or as that which leaves God unknown, but rather as the overpowering light that renders God known as unknown. This is not dissimilar to a baby being held by her mother – the baby does not understand the mother but rather experiences being known by the mother.[39]

Intimacy with God, then, is the experience of growing in our awareness of God's knowing of us. Go back and read that sentence again slowly. Worship invites us into particular actions and practices that enable us to know and express this intimacy with God. Many of these worship practices are ancient and have been used by lovers of God for thousands of years. And, not surprisingly, they tend to correspond to similar practices that human lovers have used to enjoy and express their intimacy with one another for thousands of years.

The power in these practices is in their ability to form us, to shape us in certain ways. Worship practices work in our hearts to point our longings and desires toward God and God's Kingdom the same way that acts of human intimacy work on our hearts to point our longings and desires to our lover. As James Smith puts it:

> [T]he way our love or desire gets aimed in specific directions is through practices that shape, mould, and direct our love.[40]

All intimacy – whether with God or with another human being – is really only mutual self-disclosure – the honest and vulnerable opening of our true selves to each other. The practices of love making in the human realm, and the practices of worship in the divine one, are designed to help us achieve this revealing, this disclosing of ourselves to one another, or of ourselves to God. Three 'movements' in intimacy can give us a framework to understand how different practices work to lead us to the goal of intimacy.

God's Story

The first movement in the process of becoming intimate is **attentive listening** – or what I like to call **"your story"**. In order for two people to find a deep connection, their 'stories' must be told. As the details of family, schooling, friendships, achievements, failures, celebrations, losses, hopes, dreams, griefs, fears and a myriad other facets of personal experience are shared, the one seeking connection must listen carefully and attentively, openly and with active participation. The act of listening is an act of faith, believing that the 'story' is more than merely a container for information or words, but rather is the vehicle through which the other person's deepest self is being shared. We all know those moments when we've met someone and, as we have engaged in conversation, we have 'clicked'. I would suggest that this is a spiritual connection that is made, for which the conversation was merely the facilitator.

In a similar way, worship invites us into the movement of attentive listening to **God's story.** Each week as we gather, there are certain practices that are designed to draw us into God's story, not so that we can know lots of verses from the Bible, or win religious general knowledge quizzes, but so that we can experience the 'click' of God's Spirit connecting with ours through the 'story'. As the Psalmist expresses it:

> "Deep calls to deep in the roar of your waterfalls; all your waves and breakers have swept over me. By day the LORD directs his love, at night his song is with me – a prayer to the God of my life."[41]

As we gather, the ancient practices of our liturgy open us to God's story. The first half of the liturgical calendar – from Advent Sunday to Trinity Sunday – is an annual retelling of the story of God's activity in our human world that draws us into a contemporary experience of God's activity in our lives. This is an extended opportunity each year to listen attentively to God's story. In addition, each week, when we offer adoration and thanksgiving, we celebrate who God is and what God has done – this is God's story. When we read the Scriptures and enact the sacraments we remember God's story among us. As we reflect on ancient symbols and rituals we find the deep truths of God's story hidden there. As Robert Webber explains:

> ...[W]orship tells and acts out the life, death, resurrection, and coming again of Christ through the proclamation of the Word and the Table.[42]

And again, as we participate in these words and acts, God's Spirit reaches out to our spirits seeking union.

Our Story

The second movement in the process of becoming intimate is **vulnerable sharing** – or what I like to call **"my story"**. Intimacy is a two-way process, a dialogue, and so intimacy-seekers need to share themselves through their stories, even as they have listened to the story of the other person. Again, through the words, body language and tone of voice, through actions and gestures, there is more than information being shared – it is the sharing of the self. This means that the depth of intimacy is limited by the depth and vulnerability of the sharing. The deeper and more honest the sharing, the deeper the intimacy. The more that is held back, the more shallow the intimacy becomes.

The same movement is part of our journey into intimacy with God. As we gather, we come to share **our story** with God. It is not that God doesn't know our story. It is, rather, that we need to **know** that God knows our story. Throughout the centuries, certain worship practices have been designed to enable us to do this work of sharing our story in worship.

Every year, the second half of the liturgical calendar – known as Ordinary Time or Kingdom Time – explores how we can live as authentic followers of Christ. This means that we have an extended opportunity to bring our story into the sanctuary and offer ourselves to God. When we come in confession and intercession we share our story. When we baptise our children, join our lovers in marriage and grieve with the bereaved, we express our story. In our preaching, banners, testimonies and pulpit notices, we tell our story.

We have moments when we tell the universal story of our human condition – the story we all share – of life, growth, love, suffering, rejoicing, weakness and death. We also have moments when we tell our own unique stories. But, whether personal or communal, the telling of our story leads us into intimacy with God, because our spirits reach out to God's Spirit through the words, actions and symbols.

This is why the Scriptures and hymns of Israel, and of the church, are filled with the stories of human beings.[43] If we are to encounter God intimately, we need to bring our true selves into the sanctuary, and allow our worship to facilitate the telling of our stories, because when we do this, our stories are transformed by the God who always chooses to enter – to be incarnated – into them.

> I have come to believe that, essentially, worship cannot take place without our response to God himself, wherein our innermost selves reach out to him. For example, in worship we aren't responding to circumstances and situations in the church or in the world, or to values such as goodness and mercy. As a matter of fact, we are not even responding to life itself. Rather, our response is to God – God the Father, God the son, and God the Holy Spirit. And for me, this response is an awesome and holy aspect of worship.[44]

History

The final movement in the process of intimacy is the element of time – what I like to call **"history"**. Intimacy takes time to develop, and as the sharing of stories continues over the years so intimacy grows. In the twenty-four years that my wife, Debbie, and I have been married, we have given an immense amount of time and energy to this sharing of stories, and our intimacy now is far deeper than it was when we first started dating as students at university. This is not because we have continually created amazing experiences, or even had mind-blowing sex at all times. It's because we have continued the work of sharing through both the extraordinary and the mundane.

In the same way, worship is not about creating stirring experiences each week. When we fall into the trap of competing with movies and sports events, we end up being tyrannised by the novel, the exciting, the theatrical, and we lose the heart of the intimacy we seek. Worship is not about goose bump raising experiences so much as it is about the routine – the discipline – of continually sharing with God, and growing gradually deeper in intimacy with the divine. As Craig Groeschel expresses it:

> When we are thirsty for God, God will satisfy that longing. And as we continue to seek God, we'll grow to know Him more and more intimately. When we hear God's voice, we'll recognise it instantly. We'll talk to God all the time and miss him when circumstances distract us from his presence. We'll be a history together, storing up story after story of shared experiences.[45]

The practice of history, of showing up week after week to participate in the act of worship, is what moves our intimacy with God ever deeper. This is why we return to worship again and again. This is why the healthiest worship is when we commit to a community and stay faithful to our companions in the journey, worshipping regularly with the same people through good times and bad.

> In a life of faithful worship, our life is not about us. It's about God.
>
> This kind of radical awakening does not occur overnight. It takes time. It is the work of our whole life and is only

fully accomplished in eternity. It's the gradual unveiling of what is true, so we are not equipped to move there in just one step. We will move ahead and then back, again and again...

Central to this process is communion not only with the Father, Son and Spirit, but also with the community of God's people, the Church.[46]

A Commitment to Intimacy

In the light of God's invitation to intimacy – to fill the longing in our souls with real experiences of encounter with God – we are faced with a choice. We can decide that this is all too much work, and we can continue to attend worship as an act of going through the motions – or walk away from Sunday services all together. Or we can choose to answer the call, and embrace the journey of worship as the most significant act of our lives, allowing intimacy with God to be our primary quest, and seeking for all that we do and are to be an expression of this intimacy. As Robert Webber describes it:

Worship is central to all that we do. And for that reason our whole life is both a procession toward worship and a procession out of worship. Life is a cycle of constant return to the source of our new life and to the empowerment for life that we receive from the Christ we meet and celebrate in worship.[47]

If we have the courage to choose intimacy, we will find that Sundays become a very different day for us. In place of the longing, the desperation, the emptiness and frustration, we will be consumed by what Richard Foster calls a 'holy expectancy'. We will gather in the church grateful for these companions who challenge and support us. We will enter the sanctuary with excitement and openness, waiting to see what God has in store. And we will leave, knowing that we are different because we have intentionally basked in God's presence, and have heard God speak. In describing this expectancy, Richard Foster reflects on the way the New Testament Church approached worship:

> As those early believers gathered they were keenly aware that the veil had been ripped in two, and, like Moses and Aaron, they were entering the Holy of Holies. No intermediaries were needed. They were coming into the awful, glorious, gracious presence of the living God. They gathered with anticipation, knowing that Christ was present among them and would teach them and touch them with his living power.[48]

I hope that you will make the commitment to intimacy. I believe Jesus when he said that God seeks worshippers who will make this commitment.[49] And I know that the world needs people who will allow the spiritual discipline of worship to change them into Christ-like servants. This transformation is what the spiritual life is all about – it's what worship is all about. And it's what the rest of this book is all about. I hope you're ready to be changed.

Chapter Two

Welcome to a New World

I, John, am your brother and your partner in suffering and in God's Kingdom and in the patient endurance to which Jesus calls us. I was exiled to the island of Patmos for preaching the word of God and for my testimony about Jesus. It was the Lord's Day, and I was worshiping in the Spirit. Suddenly, I heard behind me a loud voice like a trumpet blast... When I turned to see who was speaking to me, I saw seven gold lampstands. And standing in the middle of the lampstands was someone like the Son of Man. (Revelation 1:9-10,12-13a)

The young man who approached me was breathless with excitement, his face glowing and his eyes alive and intense.

"As we sang and prayed, it was like I was living the vision from Revelation where people from every tribe and language and nation gather around God's throne," he enthused. "The worship this morning was awesome!"

I watched him walk away with a warmth in my heart, and a sense of excitement that resonated with his. I had been the 'worship leader' that morning, but it was the first time I had ever experienced what we had shared. What made the experience even more significant was that it had happened in what for me was a rather unexpected place: the National Conference of the Methodist Church of Southern Africa – the largest, most important, and, by reputation, most contentious 'business' meeting in my denomination.

I had been approached by our Executive Secretary, Rev. Ross Olivier, who was responsible for the administration and organisation, to be worship leader for the first Conference of the new millennium to be held in Port Elizabeth in 2001. The delegates were Methodist clergy and lay people, men and women, representing all of the diverse generations, races, language groups, worship styles and theological viewpoints in our church. My job was to facilitate moments of worship each day that would enable us to offer ourselves to God while expressing the unity within our diversity. It was a daunting task to accomplish in only forty-five minutes, but, with the help of a gifted and creative team drawn from the various groups, we managed to pull it off. The relief this brought me was expected. The way it changed me was not.

On the third morning, immediately before the worship was to begin, we received news of a 'land grab' in an area called Bredell on the East Rand of Gauteng. With many South Africans still nervous after reports of violent land invasions in Zimbabwe not long before, this was a tense and volatile moment for our gathering. It had the potential to drag the entire Conference into fear and despair.

Yet, amazingly, the theme around which our worship had been built that morning was 'hope'. As we sang together in our various languages and styles, prayed in silence and out loud, and lit candles to demonstrate our faith in, and commitment to, hope, I felt the tension slowly seep away. When we finally got to the business of the day, the sense of togetherness and determination to maintain our relationships was palpable. If I had ever had any doubt, I knew then that the act of worship has the capacity to change those who embrace it, and, more than that, to change the world in which they live.

The Need for Transformation

The inherent human longing for God, which we explored in the last chapter, is coupled with an equally strong yearning to remember ourselves. As startling as it appears when we first realise it, much of the way human society is organised has the effect of putting us to sleep. It is often easier to shut down our dreams and hopes and simply go through the daily motions of living, rather than risk being hurt, mocked or disappointed when our aspirations fail to materialise. The busyness, the weight of responsibility, the sense of being buffeted by economic and political forces that are beyond our control, all tempt us to switch off, to stop caring, and to settle for little more than mere survival. At best, we might find a hobby or leisure activity that gives us joy in our spare time. At worst, we live what Henry David Thoreau called *"lives of quiet desperation"*.[50] As Scott Peck famously stated in the first chapter of his book, *The Road Less Travelled*, life is difficult.

> Most do not fully see this truth that life is difficult. Instead they moan more or less incessantly, noisily or subtly, about the enormity of their problems, their burdens, and their difficulties as if life were generally easy, as if life *should* be easy. They voice their belief, noisily or subtly, that their difficulties represent a unique kind of affliction that should not be and that has somehow been especially visited upon them, or else upon their families, their tribe, their class, their nation, their race or even their species, and not upon others. I know about this moaning because I have done my share.[51]

As Peck indicates, we find it rather difficult to resign ourselves to the way things are. Even as we lament the hardships of contemporary living, we continue to long for more, for a better world, for a better self. Once we have accepted that life is tough, though, we discover a gift awaiting us – the ability to choose the difficulties we will face. We can continue to go through the motions, reactively navigating the struggles that life throws at us, or we can choose to embrace the difficult work of spiritual development, tackling life head on and working with it to create, in some small way, a better world, and of ourselves, better people. Whichever we choose, we will never lose the inner conviction that we need, and are capable of, real transformation.

> ...[S]omehow inside all of us, and in spite of toxic teachings we have inherited, there lies deep within a creative force that wants to give life and taste life in abundance.[52]

The Transforming Power of Worship

The good news is that the abundant life we long for is exactly what Jesus claimed to be offering,[53] and so, ultimately the response to our longing is also a response to Christ's call for us to follow him. The spiritual quest, then, is the quest to follow Jesus into change, into personal and shared transformation, into the wisdom, insight, empowerment and resources we need to find and share abundant life. And, as we have seen, the fountainhead of this spiritual quest is the act of worship.

> The business of religions and their rituals, then, is to effect transformations, not only of persons' individual subjectivities but also transformations of society and the natural world.[54]

In his solitary imprisonment on the Isle of Patmos, St. John found himself "worshipping in the Spirit" on "the Lord's Day". The vision that follows gave John, and the churches to which he wrote, a completely new, God-oriented perspective on the world and the events playing out in it. This worship day experience of John, shared with believers all over the Christian world as it was then, changed him and his readers. It opened their eyes to a reality that was beyond their daily suffering, to a divine process at work in the world, and to God's invitation for them to participate in bringing salvation to all creation.[55]

In a similar way Paul describes the transformation that comes from encounter with God, using the Old Testament story of Moses, whose radiant face had to be hidden beneath a veil after spending time in communion with God:

> But whenever someone turns to the Lord, the veil is taken away. For the Lord is the Spirit, and wherever the Spirit of the Lord is, there is freedom. So all of us who have had that veil removed can see and reflect the glory of the Lord. **And the Lord – who is the Spirit – makes us more and more like Him as we are changed into His glorious image.**[56]

If the quest of worship is to encounter God intimately, the consequence is that we leave the sanctuary different from the way we entered it. We cannot spend time consciously opening ourselves to the presence of God without being changed, and this transformation must overflow into every facet of our lives. As Richard Foster boldly states:

> To stand before the Holy One of eternity is to change. Resentments cannot be held with the same tenacity when we enter his gracious light... In worship an increased power steals its way into the heart sanctuary, an increased compassion grows in the soul. To worship is to change.[57]

This book is all about the changes that God works in us as we worship. It deals with the way our inner world is completely remade as a result of encounter with God, leading to different behaviour, relationships and attitudes. It challenges us to embrace, in particular, the five significant changes that William Temple outlines in his definition of worship. However, it is not only worshippers who are changed by the act of worship. As Anaïs Nin is reputed to have said, *"We don't see things as they are, we see things as we are."*[58] This means that worship changes us **and** our world; not only our **inner** environment, but our **outer** one as well.

John and those who received the written record of his revelation were changed by his encounter with God. But, they also perceived and inhabited the world differently as a result, leading to significant changes in the political and social realities of their day. Part of the wrestling we must embrace if we are to embark on a spiritual quest, if we are to risk entering worship with open and sincere hearts, is this altered perception of the world, and the alternative way of living in it that results. There are at least four major shifts that happen in our world when we become committed worshippers of God.

A Change in Context

Every single person on our planet lives within a particular worldview – a way of understanding the world, the forces in it, the people who inhabit it (including him or herself), and the vision of how it 'should' be. This worldview is often unrecognised, but it infiltrates every thought, every action, every relationship and every decision we make. As Christians we strive for our view of the world to be formed by Jesus' teaching about God's reign.

> Everybody looks at the world through their own lens, a matrix of culturally inherited qualities, family influences and other life experiences. This lens, or worldview, truly determines what you bring to every discussion. When Jesus spoke of the coming of the Reign of God, he was trying to change people's foundational worldview.[59]

While I agree with Rohr about the realities of worldview, I am not convinced that this was what Jesus was primarily trying to change. This is because I have become convinced that our worldview is only a part of much bigger and more important framework or context for our lives. The problem with worldview discussions, as James Smith points out, is that they focus primarily on our thinking, as if human beings are mainly cognitive, thought-based beings, and Christian faith is first and foremost about getting our thinking "right".

However, as Smith points out, we are not primarily thinking creatures, so much as we are beings that **act in and interact with the world.**

> Being a disciple of Jesus is not primarily a matter of getting the right ideas and doctrines and beliefs into your head in order to guarantee proper behaviour; rather, it's a matter of being the kind of person who loves rightly – who loves God and neighbour and is oriented to the world by the primacy of that love. [60]

For this reason, I prefer to speak about the change that worship brings as a change of **context**, which includes, but goes beyond, a change in worldview only. What I mean by this is that in worship the world we inhabit changes not just because we are made to see and understand it differently, but because the overarching framework for our lives – that which guides our ethical, political, economic, and sexual thinking, motivation **and** behaviour – has been completely remade. Ultimately, one of the most important questions any person will face is that of what **context** – what overarching framework for thinking, believing, relating and loving – he or she will choose.

The nature of this change is of the utmost importance, because we influence and respond to the world out of this context in every moment. Sometimes the context we choose for ourselves helps us, and enables us to make a positive contribution to the world. Often, though, it becomes a hindrance to us, causing relationships to break down through misunderstanding, leading us to act out of fear or self-interest, or giving us inadequate information resulting in bad choices. Sometimes it is even our faith that creates this destructive context. William Temple once provocatively remarked that when people live with a wrong view of God, the more religious they become, the worse the consequences are, so that eventually it would be better if they were atheists.[61] If we are to live vibrant, contributing lives, we need a transformation of context.

For many of us, even in the Church, our context is far less robust and vibrant than the one Jesus demonstrated and calls us to. Most of us still find ourselves living in a world which is essentially Godless – without God's constant presence – and with God removed from it, outside of it, and largely uninvolved in it, unless, or until, we pray and God comes swooping in to save the day.[62] Most of us tend to see the world as an inanimate place for us to live in, and a source of resources and commodities for us to possess, refine and resell in order to make money and satisfy our needs and wants.[63] Most of us think of ourselves as independent individuals, as separate and disconnected from (or even threatened by) other people, particularly those who look, believe or behave differently from us.[64] Most of us, even though we may speak passionately about heaven and hell, find our material world far too real, and the spiritual realm we find to be little more than a dream – as evidenced by the fact that behaviour patterns, levels of consumption and broken relationships are no different among Christians than among those who claim no faith.[65] We may speak as if we live in the context of God's reign, as if our thinking, believing and behaving is utterly shaped by the Gospel of Christ, but the fruits of our lives, the impact of our words and actions on our world and the people in it tell a very different story.

So what kind of change to our context does worship offer? As James Smith explains, the actions of worship are designed to transform us into people for whom the primary context of life is love for God and neighbour.[66] But it goes even further than this. The primary, and most profound change that worship brings about is in our relationship with God. Because worship is primarily the act of intimacy with God, the context for our lives is created by our understanding and experience of the God with whom we connect. As Richard Rohr notes, *"You become the God you worship"*.[67] When worship is a true encounter as described in chapter one, the God we love changes (or, if you prefer, our perception of God changes) from the distant, separate deity of the theist, to the present, connected and creation-filling God of what Matthew Fox describes as *panentheism*.

> Now panentheism is not pantheism. Pantheism, which is declared a heresy because it robs God of transcendence, states that "everything is God and God is everything." Panentheism, on the other hand, is altogether orthodox and very fit for orthopraxis as well, for it slips in the little Greek word *en* and thus means, "God is in everything and everything is in God."[68]

The reality of God in everything and everything in God is what the Apostle Paul refers to in his sermon to the people of Athens when he says that it is in God that *"we live, and move, and have our being."*[69] It is also reflected in his beautiful prayer for the Ephesian Church:

> Now [Christ] is far above any ruler or authority or power or leader or anything else – not only in this world but also in the world to come. God has put all things under the authority of Christ and has made Him head over all things for the benefit of the church. And the church is His body; it is made full and complete by Christ, **who fills all things everywhere with Himself.** (Emphasis mine)[70]

Once we begin to recognise the world as contained in and filled with God, everything changes for us – it becomes a whole different world. God is not separate from creation, but expressed through it. The different parts of creation are not separate from each other but connected, dependent on one another and *"held together"* by God.[71] In this God-filled world, our use of the world and its resources is affected, and our treatment of other human beings is affected, which means that our political, economic and sexual attitudes and behaviour are all changed. Worship transforms us by giving us a different context for our lives, and this flows into specific changes in at least three elements of our context.

A Change in Space

A significant part of the context for our lives is the physical environment in which we operate. Our view of the world, of the earth and its resources, of human communities and habitations all impacts the way we inhabit and interact with our environment. If we view and experience the world as a machine, we will tend to live mechanically, unemotionally and with little regard for the world as a living organism.[72] If however, we begin to see the world, not only as a place for us to live for a while, but as also the dwelling place of God, as a sacred creation that is filled with the presence of God, we begin to live differently in it. We begin to tread more lightly, and consider the impact of our choices on the world. We begin to respect the earth, and take seriously both God's call for us to be caretakers of the earth,[73] and also the inherent nature of the earth as an eternal, spiritual reality, as well as a temporal physical one.[74]

The act – and the environment – of worship is what creates this change in our understanding and experience of the spaces in which we live. Worship is always connected to the gathering of a community, and for this gathering to happen, a place needs to be set aside. For centuries the Church has taken seriously the use of dedicated buildings for this purpose, and there is good reason for this.

There seems to be some struggle in the Church today about what to do with our buildings. It is common to hear preachers proclaim that "We don't go to church, we **are** the Church," and many faithful worshippers have chosen to move out of church buildings to worship in homes, warehouses or the open air. I understand the concern that our identity can get too wrapped up in our buildings, and I share the fear that we can too easily see church simply as a place to go to once a week, with no impact on our lives. But we must be careful to ensure that our fear does not rob us of the value that our buildings can offer.

James White explains the importance of space for those of us who seek to follow Christ:

It should not surprise us that a religion whose fundamental doctrine is the incarnation should take space seriously in its worship. Not only did Christ enter human time but he also came to dwell among us, occupying a specific place on earth in Judea. The New Testament is full of place names: Jesus was at Jerusalem, Bethany, the Sea of Galilee, the River Jordan, and so on.[75]

Every time someone has encountered God it has been in a particular place. The sanctuary – the place of worship in a church building – is meant to remind us of this truth. Although our sanctuaries are sometimes less than helpful in facilitating our encounters with God, the fact remains, that the space in which we gather for worship holds special significance. Our sanctuaries can speak to us about the God who meets us in the ordinary, geographical spaces of our lives. For this reason, it is crucial that we take our buildings and meeting places seriously, asking ourselves what effect they are having on our faith and our community. As Brian McLaren notes:

> A friend of mine, referring to how groups form and behave, says, "Architecture always wins," meaning that people's behaviour is always shaped by the spaces in which they gather.[76]

An awareness of our worship spaces is not so much about changing the physical architecture (although, when possible, this may sometimes be a useful thing to do). Rather, it is about understanding the role that our spaces play, and the way they are intended to facilitate and inform our worship. Everything about the sanctuary – the furnishings, the architecture, the décor – is familiar, but enhanced. The Sacraments are performed with ordinary bread and wine and water – basic necessities that we use every day. And in this familiar, but different place, we learn to expect God's transforming presence to meet with us, and we begin to recognise every place as sacred – a place filled with God's presence and the potential for divine encounter.

As David, in a song that would almost certainly have been sung in the Tabernacle worship of Israel, so beautifully sang:

> I can never escape from Your Spirit! I can never get away from Your presence! If I go up to heaven, You are there; if I go down to the grave, You are there. If I ride the wings of the morning, if I dwell by the farthest oceans, even there Your hand will guide me, and Your strength will support me.[77]

The place of worship has the potential to be for us like the ordinary field in which Moses encountered God through the burning bush.[78] We gather in what is simply an ordinary piece of real estate, and it is transformed into holy ground as we encounter God there. Then, as we leave the sanctuary we enter the world with the knowledge that every space is sacred space. Once we have understood this, we can't help but be more careful of this amazing creation that God has given us as our home. We can't help but be more respectful of the personal space of others, and more nurturing of our own. We can't help but see the fingerprint of God in every place, including the darkest, most pain-filled places in the world.

Worship changes the spaces in which we live.

A Change in Time

The next important facet of the context in which we choose to live, is time. Contemporary society has a rather ambivalent relationship with time. Our language is telling: "Time is money," we say, even as we create demanding "deadlines," and strain under the pressure of our "race against the clock." Heaven forbid we should ever be caught "wasting time," – or worse, "killing time" – since it is a hard and unforgiving taskmaster.

This pressure-cooker way of living arises from what the ancient Greeks would call a *chronos* sense of time.[79] *Chronos* is linear time – hours slipping by as events follow one another in sequence, with each moment equal in value to the next. In this sense, once passed, time is forever lost. Inevitably, we find ourselves cramming as much into each second as we can, and rationing time for each part of our lives according to how important we feel each activity is. Unfortunately, we are too often deceived by the tyranny of *chronos*, and we lose the relationships and experiences that we wrongly pushed to the bottom of our list of priorities.

But, Christian worship proclaims confidently that time is also where we encounter God. As James White explains:

> Without time, there is no knowledge of the Christian God. For it is through actual events happening in historical time that this God is revealed. God chooses to make the divine nature and will known by events that take place within the same calendar that measures the daily lives of ordinary women and men.[80]

The gift of worship is that it opens us to this God who is encountered in time, and simultaneously offers us a completely different filter through which to experience time – what the Scriptures call *kairos*. The *kairos* is time with significance, appointed time, time when God's purpose and presence break into our time-enslaved world. It is a moment in which eternity takes centre stage and the ticking of the clock ceases, for a while, to matter.

It was this attention to *kairos* that urged Jesus to stop racing to reach Jairus's daughter before she died and engage a poor woman seeking healing from years of bleeding and the public shame it had brought.[81] Although Jairus's anxiety must have been blatantly obvious, and his grief, on hearing that they had delayed too long, raw and overwhelming, Jesus is somehow released from these pressures, and still manages to minister to each person according to their need. Clearly, Jesus knew how to shift his gaze away from the clock and toward the wind-like movement of God's Spirit.

An encounter with *kairos* is inevitably a startling and healing experience. Somehow, even only a peripheral awareness of the ever-present potential for God to interrupt our experience loosens the hold of *chronos* on our lives. Worship teaches us to move our mindfulness of eternity from the edges of our being to its very heart; to begin to honour the time we have as a gift, and to be open to its flexibility in order to readily make space when eternity chooses to "break in".

Closely aligned with this *kairos* sense of time, is the practice of Sabbath. Although the word is familiar to most people, its meaning is often misconstrued to mean nothing more than a "day off". As Christians we no longer worship on the Sabbath – which is Saturday, the last day of the week. Rather, our worship is on Sunday, the first day of the week, the day of resurrection, ensuring that each week begins with a "little Easter", a remembrance of Christ's saving work, and the hope of resurrection no matter what we may be facing. Our Sunday worship, though, carries much of the same meaning as Sabbath did for the Jews.

A significant part of the practice of Sabbath is aligning ourselves with God's rhythm. As rhythm organises a piece of music in time according to speed and pattern, so Sabbath organises our lives according to God's sense of time – God's tempo and pattern. This is more than simply giving ourselves a breather, or allowing ourselves time to rest so that we can launch back into our busyness with renewed vigour. Sabbath is about learning to recognise the significance of moments in time. It is about learning to recognise God's tempo and pattern for us, our community and our world, and it is about matching our pace with these eternal rhythms.

Eugene Peterson describes the impact of this by reflecting on the Genesis creation week, from which the idea of Sabbath comes. He notes that the Scriptures measure the passing of time through a peculiar phrase: *"And there was evening, and there was morning"*. This view of time's passing is foreign to us he says. As we count our days, we tend to ignore the night while we are asleep and unproductive, and we think of the day starting as we wake up and enter our activity.

> Then I wake up, rested, jump out of bed full of energy, grab a cup of coffee, and rush out the door to get things started. The first thing I discover (a great blow to the ego) is that everything was started hours ago. All the important things got underway while I was fast asleep...
>
> The Hebrew evening/morning sequence conditions us to the rhythms of grace. We go to sleep, and God begins his work. As we sleep he develops his covenant. We wake and are called out to participate in God's creative action. We respond in faith, in work. But grace is always previous. Grace is primary. We wake into a world we didn't make, into a salvation we didn't earn.[82]

This *kairos*/Sabbath view of time ultimately enables us to be more creative and caring people. It frees us from the tyranny of the expedient in which we do things as quickly as possible in order to get the best return on our investment. It frees us from the impatience that characterises much of our lives, and from the temptation to measure everything, from success to relationships, according to short-term criteria. It leads us gently away from the competitive, consumerist values of our world in which whoever accumulates the most "toys" in the shortest possible time wins. Instead, this God-changed view of time, leads us into the gracious rhythms of patience, simplicity, authenticity and collaboration.

Worship calls us into this *kairos*/Sabbath way of living in time. Through setting aside a special (holy) time each week, following the rhythms of the liturgical calendar, and of the worship service, we are moved out of our dependence on *chronos* and made more aware of God's *kairos* activity in us and our world. We begin to see and understand time differently, and we are more able to be present to the people around us, and to fully experience the places and circumstances we find ourselves in. We also discover a new ability to recognise the special *kairos* moments of our lives when they appear, and to cooperate with God's unexpected activity.

Worship changes the time according to which we order our lives.

A Change in People

While it may be preferable to some of us to think of the context of our lives as our own personal realm in which other people have no part or say, we know all too well that the reality is the opposite. The people we interact with, pass by, love and wrestle with all contribute to and shape the world in which we live. There is no shortage of evidence, however, to indicate that our connections with others are ambivalent at best, and dysfunctional at worst. Western individualism, often incorrectly assumed to be the only biblical view of humanity,[83] has left a trail of devastated lives in its wake.[84] From personal and relational breakdown to the huge social crises of our time, the way we see and relate to one another has to change significantly.

It is a mark of the sense of disconnection that we live with in the world that one of the primary questions that troubles people of faith today is what to do with people who believe different things or who belong to other religions. As Brian McLaren notes:

> We all woke up again today in a world where Christians, Muslims, and Jews (along with adherents of many other religions) are either killing one another or planning new ways to kill one another, and many believe that in doing so they are obeying and even pleasing and honouring God.[85]

It is far too easy to use religion, race, language, gender, sexual orientation or any other human trait as an excuse to stereotype, judge, exclude and harm other people, and this is exactly what happens all over the world every day. If we need anything, we need a new way of seeing, understanding and interacting with one another, or we might actually cause our own extinction.[86]

So, the need for worship to transform our relationships as people, then, goes beyond merely teaching us to get along with other people in our home church. It impacts the whole we relate to one another as people with different nationalities, religions, values and priorities. The miracle of worship, though, is that, starting with a small community of people, we are changed in how we experience and relate to all people.

The Christian faith has always been a communal faith. While we speak rightly about the need for personal commitment to Christ, and to taking personal responsibility for our faith and worship, the Scriptures make it clear that this personal journey is always only one aspect of a shared pilgrimage. We are always in this together, or, as a friend of mine, Trevor Hudson, once wrote: *"When we open our lives to [Jesus], he enters with arms around his brothers and sisters."*[87]

The Scriptures are clear about the way God encounters us in community. In Matthew's Gospel, as Jesus teaches about prayer, he offers the following instructions:

> When you pray, don't be like the hypocrites who love to pray publicly on street corners and in the synagogues where everyone can see them. I tell you the truth, that is all the reward they will ever get. But when you pray, go away by yourself, shut the door behind you, and pray to your Father in private. Then your Father, who sees everything, will reward you.[88]

Then, with this personal, private setting as the context, Jesus offers his model prayer for us to use, and the first words are not *"my Father"* but *"our Father"*.[89] Even when we are alone in prayer, we are instructed to remember that we are part of a community of faith. This is further emphasised when Jesus speaks about gathering and prayer.

> I also tell you this: If two of you agree here on earth concerning anything you ask, My Father in heaven will do it for you. For where two or three gather together as My followers, I am there among them.[90]

For Jesus, there is no solitary faith. We are called not simply to follow Jesus, but to become part of a community – a body, as Paul calls it[91] – of diverse people. For many people the decision to join a community of faith is a most profound act, and as George Hacker explains, is often the doorway to significant inner change.[92]

If we look carefully at the people Jesus chose to be his apostles[93], we can begin to understand exactly what kind of community Jesus is thinking of. Jesus did not go out of his way to create a band of followers that was uniform or that would easily get along together. On the contrary, he seems to have gone out of his way to create the most diverse and contentious group he could. He called a bunch of fisherman, including the brothers, James and John, who had such a bad case of sibling rivalry that Jesus called them "the Sons of Thunder." Added to this was Matthew, a tax collector – a hated employee of the Roman Empire, who would have been seen as a traitor by his fellow Jews. Then, just for good measure, Jesus adds Simon, a zealot – a freedom fighter, seeking to overthrow the Romans and their collaborators through guerrilla warfare, and civil unrest. It's as if Jesus wants to make it clear that if he can get this group to work together and love each other, then we have no excuse.

In worship, then, we can expect to find ourselves alongside those who look different, think differently, believe differently and worship differently from us. All too often we are tempted to create churches of people that are "demographically uniform" – defined along generational, linguistic, theological or stylistic lines. Jesus, however, does not allow this luxury. Rather he calls us into a diverse band of followers, some of whom we will easily love, and some who will test our capacity for grace.

But, as we are forced into relationship with these others, we begin to recognise that every person is created in the image of God, and that every person is loved by God. Then, mysteriously this awareness spreads out to include not only those of our own church or denomination or religion, but all God-imaged and God-loved people. And finally we begin to recognise that we are all connected through our common humanity and our common status as recipients of God's love.

Worship transforms us, then, by changing the people (or our understanding and experience of them) who inhabit our world.

Worship that Changes the World

In a world where ideologies so often divide us, where our relationships with ourselves, with others, with the world and with God so easily get out of balance, worship presents itself as a healing balm. Where ideas have failed to unite us, prayer, ritual and hymnody can bring us together. Where ideas have failed to change us, the regular practice of gathering for worship in purpose-designed spaces, in intentionally designated times, with people who share only the desire to encounter God and become more abundantly alive can re-form us into completely different people, living in a completely different world.

If we know anything about God from the Scriptures, it is that this is what God desires for us, and it is what any authentic encounter with God must do for us. I would suggest that the only valid measurement of authentic worship is the extent to which we are changed into people who reflect Christ's values, Christ's attitudes and Christ's gracious activity in the world.

While much of this transformation happens "externally" as a change of the context – the time, space and people that create our world – this external change must create and be created by a corresponding internal one. It is to this internal transformation that William Temple points in his definition. And that is what the rest of this book is all about.

Chapter Three

Becoming Holy

It was in the year King Uzziah died that I saw the Lord. He was sitting on a lofty throne, and the train of His robe filled the Temple. Attending Him were mighty seraphim, each having six wings. With two wings they covered their faces, with two they covered their feet, and with two they flew. They were calling out to each other, "Holy, holy, holy is the LORD of Heaven's Armies! The whole earth is filled with His glory!" Their voices shook the Temple to its foundations, and the entire building was filled with smoke. Then I said, "It's all over! I am doomed, for I am a sinful man. I have filthy lips, and I live among a people with filthy lips. Yet I have seen the King, the LORD of Heaven's Armies." (Isaiah 6:1-5)

I had noticed him sitting in the service. It was obvious that he was facing tough times, so when he shook my hand at the door after the gathering, I was not surprised that he asked to speak to me. As we sat down on a bench, his eyes filled with tears and he began to relate a tale of abandonment by his only surviving sibling, loss of work (which was a common experience after the recession hit South Africa) and his struggle to get home. More than once he assured me that he was an honest person, a genuine follower of Christ and that his story was true.

In spite of my usual suspicion of people with woeful tales such as this, I found myself growing more convinced that he had a genuine need, and so I asked him what he wanted. He refused to ask for money, but said he could use some food, so I took him to a local grocery store and bought him a few staples to last for the next few days. Then, against my better judgment, I gave him some money to help him pay for his journey home. He asked for my contact details promising that, within a week or two, he would repay me.

Needless to say, I never heard from him again.

A Crisis of Conscience

This story is only one of myriads in our world today. The golden rule, it seems, has changed to "do unto others, but don't get caught." The shock we experience when stories break of corruption, abuse, and deceit simply confirms our sense that conscience is a limited resource in our society. Scandals like the Enron saga, and the greed-driven practices of the investment firms and banks that contributed to the global recession, leave us bewildered and angry. The ongoing revelations of sexual abuse and misbehaviour by clerics and pastors in more than one church organisation is a challenge to our faith, and malpractice by those we have trusted enough to vote into public office, can drag us down into suspicion, cynicism and despair.[94]

But, in our hearts, we know that this malady of the conscience affects every one of us. We all know the shame of betraying our convictions, of being "caught out" in deception, or of hurting those we love. In South Africa, we are famous for criticising the corruption and crime that we see in our nation. Yet, at the same time, we fail to recognise the many ways that we contribute to the problem. Our disregard for traffic laws, for the rights and property of others, and for our responsibility to get involved when others are maltreated makes us culpable.

A friend of mine once reflected on his blog about the shock he felt when a truck carrying sugar lost its load on one of our national highways. In spite of the driver doing his utmost to protect his cargo, passers-by – many in expensive vehicles –

quickly looted the goods lying on the road, and cleaned him out. No one seemed to care that this man would probably have to cover the cost of the losses from his own meagre salary.[95]

While popular wisdom may advise us that guilt and regret are useless emotions, we know that we need to change, that our world needs to change, if we are to become the people we long to be, that we know we are capable of being. The big question is how we are to resurrect our conscience. We know, all too well, our need for a clear guide to lead us into ways of life and goodness. We feel the pain and brokenness that arises when we silence the voice of our conscience. We experience the longing that our world should be a safe, equitable and creative place. What we struggle with is how to develop within us a sense of right and wrong that is trustworthy; an ethical framework that is neither cold, lifeless and legalistic, nor lax, inconsistent and "anything goes".

Quickening The Conscience

William Temple offers us a way to reclaim our conscience, and by it, become those who contribute positively to our world. The first part of his famous definition of worship states:

To worship, is to quicken the conscience by the holiness of God.

The word quicken is used here in the sense of "making alive". If we want to awaken our consciences – bring them back to vibrant life – we need a vision of God's holiness. This is, in essence, what happened to Isaiah that day in the Temple.[96] In a time of major political upheaval and uncertainty, Isaiah finds himself in the place of worship. It is in this place that God confronts the man, who is not yet a prophet, with a vision of God's holiness.

Seraphim – the word is plural and means "burning ones" or "fiery ones", and is commonly understood as some kind of angelic being – are flying and crying out their praises: *"Holy,*

holy, holy is the Lord of Heaven's Armies." Isaiah's immediate reaction in response to this vision is to cry out in confession: *"It's all over! I am doomed, for I am a sinful man. I have filthy lips, and I live among a people with filthy lips. Yet I have seen the King, the LORD of Heaven's Armies."* In the face of God's holiness, Isaiah experiences a quickening of his conscience.

The Problem With Holiness

Beneath this conscience quickening encounter with God's holiness hides a deeper question: What is God's holiness, and how does it awaken our sense of goodness and rightness? As Matthew Fox points out, how we answer that question is crucially important, not simply for our worship, but for every part of our lives.

> One of the most telling questions that can be asked about a period's spirituality is, what is its understanding of holiness? A people's grasp of what constitutes holiness will affect its entire way of living, of question, of celebrating.[97]

Holiness can be a tricky word, and can have strongly negative connotations. All too often when we speak of holiness, we find ourselves referring to something that is very far removed from it – being "holier than thou". This may perhaps have something to do with our tendency to view holiness in legalistic terms, as in obeying a set of puritanical, God-ordained laws.

Two decades ago, I joined thousands of excited and expectant spiritual seekers at a large church in Durban to see an internationally prominent evangelist at work. I was accompanied by friends from the brand new church I attended and members of the small youth group I had helped to establish. After an extended time of worship and a lengthy message, the "power ministry" that we had all come to witness began. People were pulled out of the crowd and ushered up on stage to have hands laid on them as they fell enraptured to

Chapter Three: Becoming Holy

the floor under the Spirit's power. Testimonies of supernatural encounters with God were proclaimed emotionally through microphones held in shaking hands. Gentle music led the onlookers in quiet but stirring songs of worship.

In the midst of this holy confusion, the evangelist suddenly pointed to a young couple that were part of our group. Both in their late teens, they shared a passionate longing for God and a passionate love for each other. And it required no word of knowledge to see that they were extremely comfortable with one another's bodies. The preacher looked sternly at them and proclaimed loudly to the crowd, "This young couple are sinning together!" Then he looked at the young woman (he almost ignored the young man), and in hushed tones, which remained crystal clear through the sound system of the church, he told her, "God has shown me a red car in your future. And He has said to me that unless you repent and stop your wickedness, this car will take your life! God is telling you this because He loves you. So, now pray with me, and repent of your sin." He then proceeded to pray enthusiastically for her, becoming a little agitated when she remained on her feet. Over the next few weeks our little church community was turned upside down as we witnessed the trauma and grief that this couple endured as a result of this experience. Even then I found this evangelist's version of holiness impossible to swallow.

The way we understand the God we worship, and the vision of holiness our worship offers, is crucial to our faith and our lives. Over the years I have become convinced that holiness is far more than merely following a set of rules – even if the rules are the Ten Commandments – because God is more than a mere rule-maker.

To go even further, Jesus, it must be said, was a rule-breaker. If you're looking for the ultimate law-people of the Bible, you'll be disappointed with Jesus and his disciples. For law-abiding 'holiness', you need to look at the Pharisees. When it comes to Jesus, we see a different picture. Jesus did all sorts of things he wasn't supposed to – he touched dead bodies and menstruating women[98]; he talked to a gentile woman (to whom he was not married)[99]; he refused to stone an adulteress[100]; he failed to insist that his disciples washed their hands before eating[101]; he did work (healing) on the Sabbath[102]; he visited gentiles, tax collectors and prostitutes in their homes[103]; and he "desecrated" the temple[104]. If holiness is about following a system of laws, then Jesus fell dreadfully short. But, of course, his whole point was that holiness was about something else entirely.

Simply following a set of rules does not quicken the conscience, it does not awaken in us a deeper sense of what is right and good, and it does not make us into the kind of people that reflect God's character and purposes. On the contrary, an emphasis on obeying laws often leads to inaction, to callous aloofness, and to judgemental rejection of anything that falls short of the 'perfection' we seek.

> More and more psychological thinkers are pointing out how superficial and indeed destructive the quest for perfection is. Otto Rank talks about "the disease of perfection" (*Art and Artist*, Agathon Press, 1975, p.199f) and how a perfection quest is an ego quest and not a spiritual quest of the human person.[105]

However, we cannot avoid the call of the Scriptures: *"But now you must be holy in everything you do, just as God who chose you is holy. For the Scriptures say, "You must be holy because I am holy.""*[106] If we are to follow Christ faithfully, and if we are to worship authentically and wholeheartedly, we must wrestle with God's holiness and seek for a true vision that will thoroughly quicken our conscience.

Coming To Grips With Holiness

If we begin with the original languages we discover an interesting thing about holiness. It doesn't refer to obeying rules at all. The literal meaning of both the Greek and Hebrew words for holiness, or to be holy, is to be **set apart**.[107] The meaning is best described by our English term to **sanctify**, and the idea is to separate the holy object or person out **for a special purpose**. Ironically, we have tended to view holiness as being set apart **from**, not **for**. As Floyd McClung writes:

> Reduced to its simplest definition, holiness means to be separate **from the world and its sin**. (Emphasis mine)[108]

There are a few difficulties with thinking of holiness in this way, though. Firstly, if we are to *"be holy as God is holy"* then we face an impossible task. When we think of God as "set apart", the best way to describe what we mean is to say that God is **other**. In other words, God is holy because God is altogether different, in love, in character, in power, in moral altitude from us lowly humans and our world.

In the words of Isaiah:

> "My thoughts are completely different from yours," says the Lord. "And my ways are far beyond anything you could imagine. For just as the heavens are higher than the earth, so are my ways higher than your ways and my thoughts higher than your thoughts."[109]

A vision of holiness that is 'otherness' cannot quicken our conscience, because it is, quite simply, unattainable for us. We cannot be **other** than created human beings. We cannot have thoughts that are higher than our thoughts or ways that are higher than our ways. To even attempt such 'holiness' would only lead us into the grave error of arrogantly believing we could actually become like God. Even if this "apart-from-ness" only refers to "the world and its sin", we still run into difficulties, because it simply leads us back to an individualist and isolationist quest for perfection and all of the accompanying griefs which we have already identified.

Jesus made it clear that if we seek to understand God, we must look to him,[110] and this must include our quest for a vision of God's holiness. The central truth of the Christian faith – that God chose to be incarnated in human flesh as the man, Jesus – makes it clear that holiness is not a separation from anything – not the world, and not even its sin. The incarnation boldly proclaims that God has always chosen to be intimately engaged with us and with the world. Rather than separating himself from sin, Jesus spent most of his time with 'sinners', ultimately even taking on the full brunt of our sinfulness on the Cross. Yet, even as Jesus did this, he remained holy the entire time.

It is far more common in the Bible to speak of things being set apart **for** than set apart **from**. All the furnishings of the Tabernacle and Temple, which were referred to as holy,[111] all the people who are said to be sanctified (or saints) in the Scriptures,[112] are said to be so because they have set themselves apart **for** God and God's purposes.

In what sense, then, is God set apart **for**? And in what sense can we seek to *"be holy as God is holy"*? If the Scriptures tell us anything about God, it is that God is always, and completely, committed to God's purposes and character. God is always who God is, and God always does what God does. Nothing can deter God from God's purpose, and nothing can change God's essential nature. We could, perhaps, put it his way: **God is set apart for Godness.**

Another way to express this is in the words of Jesus: *"be perfect, even as your Father in heaven is perfect."*[113] This may appear to contradict our earlier conversation about perfection, until we recognise that the word Jesus uses here is more accurately translated as "complete" or "whole"[114]. In other words, Jesus is saying "be whole, as God is whole". This is further reinforced when we realise that the English word the translators chose to describe this "set apartness" – holiness – comes from the same root as the word "wholeness".[115] This means that we could talk about holiness as "whole-iness".

To receive a vision of God being "set apart for Godness", or God's "whole-iness", means to recognise that everything God is, does, says, or thinks, is one. God is never at war within God's self, and God never contradicts God's character or purposes. But, to really understand the impact of this vision, we need to clarify it a little bit more.

"Whole-iness", as much as perfection, can be seen as a personal quest that has nothing to do with anyone else. To think of God's "whole-iness" in this way, though, is to misunderstand it. As Matthew Fox points out, Luke's version of Jesus' command to "be perfect" is this: *"You must be compassionate, just as your Father is compassionate."*[116] God's "whole-iness" then, does not exist as a characteristic of a distant and isolated God, but includes and transforms all of God's creation in a circle of divine compassion. God's "whole-iness" is not only about being whole, but also about bringing wholeness.

Again, Jesus is our vision for what "whole-iness" looks like, and it is dramatically reflected in every word he spoke, every encounter he had with every person, and in every act he performed. Not only was Jesus whole, he brought wholeness wherever he went. Even as he was broken in death, he remained whole, and he continued to bring wholeness to those watching and those dying with him. This example of "whole-iness" lived and shared is surely the basis for John Wesley's statement that *"there is no holiness but social holiness."*[117] It is also why he defined holiness as *"perfect love"*.[118]

To expand the idea of compassion and wholeness even further, the creation-centred tradition of spirituality speaks of holiness as hospitality. As Matthew Fox writes:

> Hospitality is about a relationship – one cannot be hospitable without guests. God not only plays the host for us and becomes the banquet for us; God also has become guest for us.[119]

The idea of hospitality moves holiness out of the realm of the individual into the realm of relationships. It moves it out of the cold realm of personal achievement and into the warm realm of communal service, healing, nurturing and welcoming. Certainly the ministry of Jesus reflects this view of holiness throughout. Jesus did nothing if not welcome, heal and serve those with whom he interacted. He was the ultimate gracious host, and also the ultimate gracious guest, accepting the hospitality of all who offered it to him. In addition, the ultimate act that Jesus gave us to remember him by is a meal. Hospitality characterises the life of Christ that we are called to follow.

Finally, we find here a vision of holiness that can truly quicken our conscience. As our hearts and minds are filled with the ever-increasing awareness of God's wholeness, we find ourselves challenged to become the same. As we worship, God calls us to set ourselves apart for a life of wholeness, and a life – like that of Christ – of bringing wholeness to others. God's "whole-iness" challenges us to bring our thoughts, words, actions and being into alignment and to live from this place of integrity. And God's "whole-iness" creates in us a longing for wholeness in others and in our world, a longing to experience and share the hospitality of God.

Far more than obeying a set of laws, this vision of holiness inevitably wakes us up, and leads us to live differently. When your life is set apart for wholeness, it becomes impossible to deliberately do anything that hurts or breaks yourself or others. On the contrary, when "whole-iness" has taken hold of us, we cannot help but give ourselves in the quest to bring wholeness into every corner of our world, and to every person we encounter.

To take this conversation about holiness one step further, we must also consider God's justice. Our normal tendency is to think of God's holiness and justice as complementary parts of God's character. In this view, God's justice is enacted upon those who violate God's holiness by failing to live in holy way. In other words, God's justice and God's mercy are seen as opposites. However, as Marcus Borg points out, this is not how the Bible views justice.

> ...[S]eeing the opposite of justice as mercy distorts what the Bible means by justice. Most often in the Bible, the opposite of God's justice is not God's mercy, but human

injustice. The issue is the shape of our life together as societies, not whether the mercy of God will supersede the justice of God in the final judgement.[120]

When we view God's holiness as bringing wholeness, compassion and hospitality to the world, justice – the quest for all people to know a life of wholeness, compassion and hospitality – is inherent in it. It is not distinguished from God's mercy, but is the very expression of it. Justice, when we think of holiness as moral perfection or obedience to the law, must always be punitive and retributive. People who break the law and who fail to be perfect must be punished, and must pay. But, when we think of holiness in the way we have been describing, justice is always be restorative. People who are broken and who bring brokenness to others are invited into a compassionate, hospitable process of becoming whole. This sounds far more like the character of God that Jesus revealed.

Therapeutic Worship

William Temple suggests that it is in our worship that we are opened to this holiness of God. In this sense, worship can be thought of as being therapeutic – a wholeness-bringing activity. As William Willimon notes:

> My thesis... is not that we should use the liturgy as a new method of pastoral care, but that the liturgy itself and a congregation's experience of divine worship already functions, even if in a secondary way, as pastoral care. The pastoral care that occurs as we are meeting and being met by God in worship is a significant by-product that we have too often overlooked.[121]

An example of this therapeutic quality in worship can be seen when the shepherd boy, David, is called in to play the harp for King Saul who is tormented by an evil spirit. Since we know that David was a psalmist, and that many of his worship songs have found their way into the Bible, it is reasonable to assume that the music David played was an expression of his worship. And as David offered his devotion to God, including Saul in the experience, so the evil spirit would depart, and Saul would find peace.[122] Here we have a beautiful description of an encounter with God's compassion and whole-iness bringing wholeness to God's people.

This therapeutic nature of worship can be intentionally fostered in our service when we stop pretending that we're all alright and begin to be honest and open about our pain. When we make space for our grief and brokenness – and acknowledge our struggles – in prayers of confession, lament and intercession, we open ourselves to God's wholeness and compassion. When we ensure that our sanctuaries and worship services are welcoming for those who are visibly broken, like people in wheelchairs, or those who are hearing impaired, we create an environment in which we are all able to bring our brokenness to God.

A friend of mine, who is a Methodist Local preacher, is a paraplegic. She relates how on more than one occasion she has been asked to leave churches because her wheelchair was in the way of other people. I suspect little healing is able to happen in places where brokenness is not welcomed in.

Finally, we nurture therapeutic encounters with God's whole-iness when we create specific times of ministry. Whether through altar calls, healing services, or simple moments of prayer for healing and comfort, when we make opening to God's healing power an intentional part of our worship, we create the environment for transformation and healing to happen.

Craig Groeschel describes this therapeutic impact of worship:

> A vibrant and intimate relationship with God will empower you to heal from the hurts from your past, forgive what seems unforgivable, and change what seems unchangeable about yourself.[123]

In authentic worship, then, we are opened to a vision of God's compassionate holiness that calls us to a higher, more compassionate way of living, while simultaneously leading us into the wholeness that makes such living possible. Body, mind and soul are all embraced, cared for and healed by God's hospitality, leading us to be people who are more compassionate, nurturing, welcoming and serving.

Worship That Quickens The Conscience

Fortunately, we don't have to look far to find the practices that open our hearts to encounter our holy God. All that we do in worship is intended to lead us into an encounter with God. At the heart of this encounter is God's self-revelation, which means that everything we do in the sanctuary is potentially a communicator of God's holiness.

> ...[T]he liturgy, as a whole and in its constituent parts, shapes people for godly living in various different ways. Giving us strength and visions of holiness, allowing us to model responsible behaviour and to express contrition when we have failed to pattern our lives after that model: the corporate worship of the Church becomes the environment within which Christians discover what it means to be a moral being and how to live out of that understanding.[124]

The invitation, then, is simply for us to mindfully and intentionally engage in the act of worship, and allow the vision of God's holiness to take root in our souls. Within this context, though, there are some practices that are particularly useful in confronting us with the divine holiness that quickens our conscience.

When, in my late teenage years, I started my training to be a preacher, my mentor – a wise and gentle man who was around my father's age – guided me through the structure of worship in Methodist practice. He explained that **adoration** is traditionally the first movement in prayer, closely followed by **confession.** It is the vision of God and God's glory that praise offers that makes us aware of our own shortcomings and need of transformation.

In Isaiah's prophet-making vision, we see this principle at work as the adoration of the Seraphim proclaiming God's holiness confronts him with his own brokenness and that of his people. Paul hints at this same movement in Romans 3:23 when he states, *"For everyone has sinned; we all fall short of God's glorious standard."* The twin practices of adoration and confession are especially effective at revealing God's "whole-iness" and calling us to strive to become whole ourselves. And, of course, confession is always accompanied by the assurance of forgiveness, which inevitably challenges us to *"forgive those who sin against us"*,[125] to bring to others the wholeness we have received from God's grace toward us.

> To live a 'forgiven' life is not simply to live in a happy consciousness of having been absolved. Forgiveness is precisely the deep and abiding sense of what relation – with God or with other human beings – can and should be, and so it is itself a stimulus, and irritant, necessarily provoking protest at impoverished versions of social and personal relations.[126]

The next time you find yourself participating in moments of adoration and confession, intentionally ask yourself what vision of God is being communicated, and how this vision reflects God's "whole-iness". Think about the ways your life fails to reflect this same "whole-iness", and make this the heart of your confession. Then, reflect on how this vision of "whole-iness" challenges you to offer wholeness to others.

Intercession and **petition** (what I like to call "the prayers of request"), in which we pray for others and ourselves, when practiced with honesty and vulnerability, also offer us a vision of God's holiness. Essentially, all that we ask for relates, in some way, to a brokenness – a lack of wholeness – in us, in others, or in our world. As we bring these needs to God, we are asking that God's presence and activity would transform, restore, and heal us – that God's "whole-iness" would lead us to "whole-iness". It is impossible to authentically practice the prayers of request without growing more humble, more compassionate, and more concerned for justice in the world.

> In our intercessory prayer we not only ask God to intervene in the situations for which we pray, we commit ourselves to intervening in those situations ourselves.[127]

In the next week, whenever you pray for yourself or others, reflect on the lack of wholeness that is being manifest in the situations you pray for. Then ask yourself how God's "whole-iness" helps you to understand and pray for those circumstances. Finally, think about how you can be a bringer of wholeness to the ones for whom you pray.

Another effective practice for quickening the conscience is **Scripture reading.** This is why in many monastic traditions, large portions of the Bible are read at every daily worship gathering, and why the Revised Common Lectionary (the interdenominational guide of Bible readings for each Sunday of the year) lists four readings for every week – an Old Testament 'lesson', a Psalm, an Epistle reading, and a Gospel passage. Whether your worship follows the Lectionary or not, the Scriptures are still an important feature of Christian worship. James, in his letter, explains it this way:

> But don't just listen to God's word. You must do what it says. Otherwise, you are only fooling yourselves. For if you listen to the word and don't obey, it is like glancing at your face in a mirror. You see yourself, walk away, and forget what you look like. But if you look carefully into the perfect law that sets you free, and if you do what it says and don't forget what you heard, then God will bless you for doing it.[128]

According to James, the Scriptures can be compared to a mirror that shows us both our true selves and our blemishes, and that calls us to live up to the "whole-iness" that God created us for. When you read the Bible in the next few days, take a little more time. Read the words mindfully, allowing the Scriptures to be a mirror in which to see both God and yourself. Pray that God would show you how to live so that your 'reflection' more clearly reveals God's holiness.

Finally, when we mindfully reflect on the **symbols, sacraments, art and architecture** of our worship, we open ourselves to God's holiness. When I read the grand visions of God that the biblical writers share, I cannot help but be struck by the way they so often seem to struggle for words. This is why these visions are often so difficult to interpret, and must be treated so carefully. God's glory and holiness are beyond our ability to understand or describe, and so the prophets and psalmists often employ poetic descriptions, surprising metaphors and even disturbing images as they try to communicate what they have experienced.

Artists do the same work for us today. The power of art and architecture is that they are able to convey what words fail to communicate. When we reflect on the symbols, metaphors and images that are the vocabulary of every kind of artist we are touched and moved in the deepest parts of ourselves. When we share in the sacraments – particularly Holy Communion – we engage the Divine Presence with our whole selves. The limitations, justifications and objections of the mind are bypassed and our spirits are filled with a sense of God's glory, and a longing to reflect that glory through our fragile lives. As Susan White explains:

> For another contemporary exponent of the liturgical tradition, Lutheran Gordon Lathrop, the power of liturgical symbols lies in their ability to leave us longing for the fulfilment of God's reign. He speaks, for example, of the Lord's Supper as a 'hungry feast', 'where we receive only a sip of wine and a taste of bread, where we sing of the richness of God, but go away hungry; where we bind ourselves to the pain and hunger of the poor'.[129]

Next time you enter a place of worship, take time to look at the architecture, art and symbols around you. During the service pay attention to any artistic expressions of worship – the music, the poetry of the liturgy, the images that are projected or displayed, the liturgical colours. Allow yourself to meditate on these creative elements, and invite them to touch the deepest parts of yourself. After the service reflect on the experience, and how it can guide you in a life of "whole-iness", of compassion and of hospitality, especially to the "least".

Becoming Holy People

"To worship is to quicken the conscience by the holiness of God." In a world that suffers from a crisis of conscience, we need God's holiness to confront us. When we are faced with a vision of God, we cannot help but see our own deep brokenness and our own glorious potential to be holy. We are at once convicted and called, and the result is a transformation in which we seek to become whole and to bring wholeness wherever we are.

Authentic worship is to embrace this difficult but liberating discipline, to regularly and honestly expose ourselves to the light of God's "whole-iness" and to passionately and wholeheartedly embrace the quest to live that "whole-iness" out in our own lives – to become people who embody the compassion, integrity and hospitality of Christ. The question we must ask ourselves in the light of this reality is if we will choose to be courageous and mindful enough that the practises of adoration and confession, intercession and petition, Scripture reading, the sacraments and the arts will quicken our consciences and transform us by the glorious vision of our holy God that they offer.

Chapter Four

Becoming True

Jesus replied, "Believe Me, dear woman, the time is coming when it will no longer matter whether you worship the Father on this mountain or in Jerusalem. You Samaritans know very little about the One you worship, while we Jews know all about Him, for salvation comes through the Jews. But the time is coming—indeed it's here now—when true worshipers will worship the Father in spirit and in truth. The Father is looking for those who will worship Him that way. For God is Spirit, so those who worship Him must worship in spirit and in truth." (John 4:21-24)

I received an email a few months ago that left me deeply disturbed and more than a little angry. The heart of the message was a link to an emotive video that explained the "demographic problem" currently facing Europe and the United States. As a grave voice reported various statistics and research findings related to population growth and demographics in Western countries, a warning was issued, emphasised by the Arabic music playing noticeably in the background. The final call of the video was for us all to "wake up" to the "reality" that Muslim families are immigrating into America, England, France and Germany, producing more children than the resident populations, and taking over the world.

The tone of the video was alarmist and authoritative. The purpose was clearly to use the fear of radical Islamic terrorism to push a particular cultural and religious agenda, and it was achieved very effectively. This video has been referenced as "truth" many times on the internet, sometimes by journalists who should have known better, and has received millions of viewings on YouTube. What makes it so hard to fight this hate-mongering message is that, in one sense, some of what it says is true. But, the way this truth is presented makes it all totally and undeniably false. **It is possible for something to be both true and untrue at the same time.**

This is not the place to offer a detailed rebuttal of the Demographic Problem video, but suffice it to say that a significant amount of relevant research into the behaviour of immigrants and the history of Muslim people in Europe and the Americas was ignored. In addition, some 'facts' were expressed in such a way that, while no accusation of lying could be sustained, the inferences made, and the conclusions being subtly, but obviously, drawn were completely untrue.[130]

Truth and Untruth

As Malcolm Gladwell points out in his startling book, *Blink*, what we call 'truth' may not always be as true as we believe, and sometimes the results can be devastating. Take, for example, a test that was run by psychologists Claude Steele and Joshua Aronson, to determine the impact of racial stereotypes on college students:

> When the students were asked to identify their race on a pretest questionnaire, that simple act was sufficient to prime them with all the negative stereotypes associated with African Americans and academic achievement – and the number of items they got right were cut in half. As a society, we place enormous faith in tests because we think they are a reliable indicator of the test taker's ability and knowledge. But are they really? If a white student from a prestigious private high school gets a higher SAT score than a black student from an inner-city school, is it because she's truly a better student, or is it because to be

> white and to attend a prestigious high school is to be constantly primed with the idea of "smart"?[131]

Gladwell's point is clear and deeply challenging. The 'facts' may appear to say that black students under-perform on tests, but the 'truth' is far more complex than simply intelligence. Another example of the "truth problem" at work is related by Julie Clawson, author of *Everyday Justice*, on her blog.

> I am reminded of how my exasperated professor dealt with my rather obstinate historical research methods class in college. A few of the students had dismissed his attempts to teach them differing approaches to how people approach historical research as supportive of revisionist history (and therefore evil). They desperately wanted to cling to the notion that the "God Blessed America" version of history they believed was in fact the only true version of history – any attempts to tell the stories from the margins of women or minorities were simply revisionist corruptions. So the professor had us read a study that detailed the various ways the history of Williamsburg has been presented to tourists over time. **Depending on what was going on in the world at the time, the historical story as it was told by the reenactors varied tremendously over the years. Each version had an agenda and portrayed American colonialism in a way that shored up that agenda.** It was difficult for the students who were insisting that the very hero-centric pro-God version taught under the influence of 1950's anti-communism was the real history to continue to bang that drum when the evidence of how history is manipulated by the teller was laid out so blatantly before their eyes. (Emphasis mine)[132]

The point that is easy to miss in this story is that in every version of the history of Williamsburg that was presented, the essential facts – the "truth" of the history – remained the same, but the **meaning** of the facts – the "truth" of how we understand history – changed. The story was true, but it the way it was told varied in truth according to the period in which it was being communicated. So, in one sense, the history of Williamsburg **was simultaneously true and untrue.**

My own personal confrontation with the co-existence of truth and untruth happened when I was studying in the early eighties – a turbulent time in South Africa's history. One afternoon the Students' Christian Association of which I was a member held a gathering in which white students from Rhodes University were invited to meet black students from Fort Hare University in Alice, a small town some distance away. As we sat on the lawn of the Rhodes campus in small circles of about eight or ten students, we introduced ourselves and shared a few details of our lives.

I listened to many of my new friends tell their stories, and I was surprised to hear them use the term "middle class" to describe their circumstances. This disturbed me because I had planned to use the same label for myself, but their descriptions of "middle class" were surprisingly modest when compared to my own ideas. When my turn to speak came around, I confessed that our conversation had changed me deeply. For the first time in my life I had been confronted with a new truth about myself. Where, in my own, protected environment, it would have been true to call myself "middle class", I realised, in the face of this wider world I now found myself in, that it was no longer true. The basic facts of my life had not changed, but the truth of my life had changed significantly. I had now discovered that I was wealthy and privileged. In one sense, the label of "middle class", when applied to me, was simultaneously true and untrue.

The Power of Truth

The importance of how we think about truth cannot be over-stated when we realise how deeply we are influenced by what we believe to be true. In the realm of faith, the struggle for truth infiltrates every facet of our lives from how we read the Bible, to who is included or excluded; from how we deal with economic inequalities to how power is appropriately employed; from whether we believe that our planet is under threat to whether we should fear people from other religions or geographical regions. How we understand truth – and what we believe to be true – forms the foundation for every part of our being and our living. Our truth creates our world, and determines the way we act and interact in it. Pontius Pilate, in spite of his inability to deal with the answer, was right on the money when he asked, "What is truth?"[133]

The answer to Pilate's timeless question becomes even more significant when we turn our attention to worship and how it transforms us into Christ-following, contributing, abundantly alive human beings. The second statement in William Temple's definition of worship makes this claim:

To worship is to feed the mind with the truth of God.

Temple insists that worship gives us access to truth beyond ourselves and our limited human existence – God's truth. Jesus makes essentially the same claim in his words to the Samaritan woman: *"For God is Spirit, so those who worship Him must worship in spirit and in truth."*[134] Spirit and truth are not separate realities. As we encounter God intimately through the spiritual act of worship, we are drawn into God's truth. The central role of the mind in this intimate connection with God and God's purposes must not be underestimated, for when we open our minds to God's truth, it changes everything, and we are completely transformed. The apostle Paul expresses it this way:

> Therefore, I urge you, brothers, in view of God's mercy, to offer your bodies as living sacrifices, holy and pleasing to God—this is your spiritual act of worship. Do not conform any longer to the pattern of this world, but be transformed by the renewing of your mind. Then you will

be able to test and approve what God's will is—his good, pleasing and perfect will.[135]

In worship, our minds are renewed, with the result that we are utterly changed. The importance of the mind in spiritual development has been well recognised by Christian leaders, to the extent that some have described the journey to Christian maturity as a "battle for the mind".[136] The power of the mind in contributing to our psychological and physical well-being (or lack thereof) has also been widely described in both popular psychological and medical literature.[137] Because our minds hold such life-directing power, there can be few disciplines as urgent and important as constantly renewing our minds.

Meeting Our Minds

When we speak about the mind, it may be helpful to clarify what we mean. In Paul's reference to the renewed mind, he uses the Greek word *nous*, which probably derives from the base word *ginosko*, 'to know'.[138] Biblically, knowing has generally been understood as more than simply taking in information or harbouring abstract ideas. The Hebrew equivalent is used in Genesis 4:1 to refer to the sexual intimacy of Adam "knowing" Eve. To know is to engage, to experience, to relate to. The mind (*nous*), then, is the "knowing centre", the part of us that engages, experiences and relates to the world. In Greek thinking, the mind gives us the capacity to connect with God, and to perceive the true nature of things.

This perception of truth is not only about what we observe, though. To see things truthfully is not merely getting the right information about what we experience, **but also rightly interpreting what that data means.** That's why Paul strongly encourages believers to strive to possess *"the mind of Christ."*[139] If we can begin to perceive the world through God's "eyes", and understand the world as God does, even in some small measure, our ability to navigate that world, to live abundantly and to bring life to others is dramatically enhanced.

William Temple, taking his lead from Jesus, suggests that it is in our worship that we receive this "divine mind". In order to perceive and interpret truthfully, our minds need to be fed, and the nourishment we feed them greatly affects the influence our minds have on us – both consciously and sub-consciously. As in the case of the black college students who under-perform on tests when subtly 'fed' with racially profiled questions, our performance, our moods, our worldview, our well-being and our ability to navigate and contribute to the world, are all affected by what we feed our minds. When we see clearly, we are able to discern more accurately what is going on within us and around us – how power relationships are working and the impact they have on those involved; what the consequences of certain actions will be; what is really required in order to create a more just and equitable world. As the well-known old Cherokee legend suggests, who we are is largely determined by what we feed our minds.

> An old Cherokee is teaching his grandson about life. "A fight is going on inside me," he said to the boy. "It is a terrible fight and it is between two wolves. One is evil - he is anger, envy, sorrow, regret, greed, arrogance, self-pity, guilt, resentment, inferiority, lies, false pride, superiority, and ego." He continued, "The other is good - he is joy, peace, love, hope, serenity, humility, kindness, benevolence, empathy, generosity, truth, compassion, and faith. The same fight is going on inside you - and inside every other person, too."
>
> The grandson thought about it for a minute and then asked his grandfather, "Which wolf will win?"
>
> The old Cherokee simply replied, "The one you feed."[140]

The insight that William Temple offers is that worship teaches and enables us to feed the "good wolf" and to feed it with nourishing, strengthening food – God's truth. If Temple is right, and I believe he is, then we need to understand both what God's truth is, and how worship enables us to feed on this truth.

The Truth That Feeds The Mind

The most common mistake we make, when seeking God's truth, is to equate truth with facts. The variety of emails circulating in cyberspace that claim to "prove" the "truth" of the Bible bears witness to how easily we fall into this trap. From Joshua's missing day,[141] to the discovery of skeletons of the *Nephilim* giants of Genesis 6:4,[142] the misguided quest to find factual evidence of the biblical narrative persists. Unfortunately, when the poor research and factual misuse (or, in some cases, fabrication) is revealed, the credibility that is lost is far more devastating than the potential gain would ever have been.

Essentially, the idea that we need to prove the "facts" of the Bible misses the point entirely. The Bible's claim to be true is not based on how accurately it reports the 'facts'. Even if every 'fact' mentioned in the Bible was historically, scientifically and undoubtedly verifiable, we would gain no value from that proof. Facts, as we have seen, can be misleading. But, even if every biblical 'fact' were found to be historically false, the Scriptures would still be true. **What we have failed to realise is that fact and truth are not equal.**[143] This failure has stripped our encounter with God of life and power, while also keeping others from faith, because they believe they must sacrifice their intellectual integrity in order to believe.

> ...[T]he Bible has become a stumbling block for many. In the last half century, probably more Christians have left the church because of the Bible than for any other single reason. More precisely, they left because the earlier paradigm's way of seeing the Bible ceased to make sense to them. Contemporary biblical literalism – with its

emphasis on biblical infallibility, historical factuality, and moral and doctrinal absolutes – is an obstacle for millions of people.[144]

As one little girl was reported to have answered, when asked to define faith by her Sunday school teacher, *"faith is believing things when you know they are not true."* If we define God's truth only by 'the facts', we deny ourselves access to the real, transforming truth that God offers us. Facts, it turns out, are a poor substitute for truth.

One simple example can explain what I mean. When traumatic events overtake us, we may look at the facts and conclude that life is over, that we are finished, and that hope is gone. Believing that the resurrection is **a historical fact** can have no impact on our present suffering, however miraculous or unique such an event may have been. If, however, we believe that resurrection is **a deep and abiding truth** of our existence, then we will know – and experience – that, even in the midst of pain and death, life is at work to renew, restore and heal. The **truth** of resurrection opens us to God's work of resurrection – in our present lives and circumstances. The **fact** of resurrection is an interesting thing to know, but it lacks the power of resurrection **truth** to dry our tears.

If we can release our obsession with facts, we open ourselves to the surprising adventure of truth – which brings us back to Pilate's crucial question. When we search the Bible for an understanding of truth, the answer, it turns out, is rather surprising.

A Person And A Way

First and foremost, for the writers of Scripture, truth is not a thing, nor even an idea. Biblical truth is primarily a person. This is why Jesus boldly proclaims, *"I am the way, the truth, and the life. No one can come to the Father except through Me."*[145]

Brian McLaren beautifully paraphrases this claim in this way:

> As I read the passage, Jesus is saying, "Don't ask me to show you something apart from me. All you are looking for is found in me. I have spoken to you about the way to live. I have spoken to you of a truth to which many are blind. I have spoken to you of life, life of the ages, life to the full. Don't you realise it? The way is the truth, and the truth is the life, and the life is the truth, and the life is the way ... and all of these are found in me."[146]

What this means for us is that our primary access to God's truth is the person and work of Jesus. When we feed our minds with the stories, teachings, images and events of Jesus' life, we feed our minds with God's truth. When we enter into a relationship with, a "knowing" of, Jesus, we are nourished with God's truth. And, as Jesus explained, we connect with him through the Spirit of truth[147], who teaches us and leads us ever deeper into the truth he embodies.[148]

In order to see the world clearly, in order to interpret it rightly, in order to develop the *"mind of Christ"* we need to experience truth by constantly encountering the Risen Christ. Rob Bell, referring to John 1:1, explains what it means to find truth in Jesus.

> The word *Word* here in Greek is the word *logos*, which is where we get the English word *logic*.
>
> Logic, intelligence, design. The blueprint of creation...
>
> Jesus *is* the arrangement. Jesus *is* the design. Jesus *is* the intelligence. For a Christian, Jesus' moral teachings aren't to be followed because they are a nice way to live a moral life. They are to be followed because they are the best possible insight into how the world really works. They teach us how things are.[149]

Jesus, the person, is truth. And **the way** of Jesus – his teachings and example, his call to follow him – is truth. We speak about "being true" to our convictions, to our promises, to those we love and to standards of moral and ethical behaviour. In this sense, truth is all about how we choose to live. To choose biblical truth is to embrace **the way** of living that seeks to follow, and to imitate, the character and behaviours of Jesus the Way.

The call to live **this** truth is unashamedly repeated throughout the New Testament. Jesus proclaims that those who are faithful to his teachings will know the truth that sets them free.[150] Paul describes his ministry as teaching people to know the truth that leads them into godly living.[151] And, in an ever-repeated chorus, the Scriptures describe the way of truth in contrast to wickedness[152], trickery[153], deceit[154] and injustice[155].

You may be wondering – if truth is **a person** and **a way** – where the Bible fits in? Although the Scriptures usually reserve the name "Word of God" for Jesus, there is no question that in a few places this label is used for the Bible itself.[156] The crucial work, when it comes to finding truth through this Word of God, is to keep it in its proper place. On the one hand, the Scriptures give us access to the **person of truth** and enable us to know him and learn his way. On the other hand, the Bible demonstrates and explains what **the way** of truth looks like, and how to follow it. In neither case is the Bible an end in itself. Rather, it is the medium through which we are invited into relationship with Jesus and his way. This is why Jesus challenged the Pharisees on their use of Scripture:

> "You search the Scriptures because you think they give you eternal life. But the Scriptures point to Me![157]

As Marcus Borg so eloquently puts it:

> To call the Bible sacred scripture refers to both its status and its function. The two go together. Its sacred status for Christians means that it continues to be the most important collection of documents we know. As sacred scripture, it functions as:

- **Our foundation document:** the foundation upon which Christianity is built, without which the structure will fall into ruins.
- **Our identity document:** its stories and vision are to shape our sense of who we are and of what our life with God is about.
- **Our "wisdom tradition":** in its comprehensive sense, "wisdom" concerns the two most central questions of life: What is real? And how shall we live?

To be Christian means to be in a primary continuing conversation with the Bible as foundational for our identity and vision. If this conversation ceases or becomes haphazard, then we cease to be Christian, for the Bible is at the heart of Christianity.[158]

The quest for the truth that nourishes our mind – our ability to connect with God and to see the world and interpret it rightly – inevitably leads us to the person of Jesus, who embodies in himself the truth of God, and to the way of truth that Jesus taught and demonstrated. The search for truth is a constant and crucial ingredient for a life of joy, abundance, contribution and purpose, and it is in worship that this quest is best undertaken.

Didactic Worship

The moment we step into the sanctuary, we take the first step on a journey into God's truth. Everything we do in our worship is designed to captivate our minds, and to express and communicate the truth that feeds them. In this sense, then, worship can be thought of as *didactic* – teaching us to know, experience and live out God's truth as revealed in the person of Jesus and the way of Jesus.

Paul writes to the Colossian Church and instructs them to teach one another singing psalms hymns and spiritual songs, which indicates that in Paul's mind, worship had a significant role to play in teaching God's people the truths of their faith.[159]

This is one of the reasons I believe that it is important that worship is prepared **carefully, prayerfully and thematically.** When the preaching, the music, the prayers, the symbols and the liturgical actions all speak the same message, our faith is strengthened and we learn God's truth. Unfortunately, it is often the case that the "music" section of the service is prepared without thought for what will happen in the rest of the gathering. I have even been in services where the theology that is expressed through the lyrics of the songs has contradicted the message of the sermon!

In addition, it is important that we take note of how Jesus taught. He did not always wrap things up in easy steps or even clear structures and ideas. Jesus taught most often through parables, often without explanation, and invited people to exercise their minds as they listened.[160] It is surprising to note that in the Gospels Jesus frequently replies to questions not with answers, but with new questions.[161] In our worship and preaching, then, we may want to allow times for **symbols, rituals and stories** to speak without explanation, inviting us to exercise our minds, and do the work of learning God's truth.

One last consideration must be mentioned here. If worship is to be didactic, it is important that it be **"edu-taining"**. What I mean by this, is that it must take its educational role seriously, but offers teaching in entertaining ways. This is not to say that worship must be 'entertainment'. One of the primary meanings of the word "entertain" is to consider or hold on to a thought or idea. In this sense, to entertain someone, is to engage their mind, to hold their attention, to enable them to consider the ideas you are presenting. Essentially, if people are bored in our worship services, they will learn nothing. If, however, we can hold their attention while communicating our message, learning and growth occurs.

Worship That Feeds The Mind

A number of practices that are regular parts of our worship are particularly effective at facilitating our experience of truth. We have already explored the work of the Bible in connecting us to truth. In worship, this work is done intentionally through **Scripture reading.** Marcus Borg beautifully describes how the sacramental work of reading the Bible becomes a true feeding of the mind:

> The sacramental function of the Bible is also suggested by language of eating, feeding upon, and digesting it. In the Bible itself, Jeremiah, Ezekiel, and the author of Revelation all speak of "eating" God's words...The Bible becomes a nourishment, God's Word becomes daily bread. Like Jesus, the Bible is both the "Word of God" and the "bread of life".[162]

The discipline of Bible reading is for our minds like the eating of staple foods for our bodies – both necessary and nourishing. This is one of the reasons that I wrestle with the South African practice of providing "pew Bibles" for use in church. While I share the desire to have Bibles readily available for those who visit and may not have their own, I also long for people to use Bibles that they take home with them, so that the journey into truth continues during the week. You may want to consider taking your own Bible with you to worship, along with a pen to make notes as the Scriptures are read and spoken about. But, even if you choose not to do this, I would encourage you to engage more actively when the Bible is read in your church. Ask yourself what the words are saying, what they mean to you, and where you can find yourself in the passage being read. Then invite the Spirit of truth to feed your mind with the truth that is being offered to you.

In a similar way, the sacrament of **Holy Communion**, also invites us to be fed with God's truth. Through the bread and wine, God's truth is enacted and proclaimed, allowing us to

Chapter Four: Becoming True

use both the left- and right-brain to bring together the symbolism, the experience of the presence of God, and the message of truth. It is a true feeding, both literally and figuratively, that enables God's truth to reach into and transform the deepest parts of our beings. As I explained in my first book, *Food for the Road*:

> In taking the routine act of meal-sharing, and placing it in a context of worship, prayer and spiritual nourishment, we become aware of the connection between our inner and outer persons, and we learn to nourish both body and soul through one profound ritual. As we receive the bread and wine, we open ourselves to the truths of Jesus' Gospel, we welcome into our lives the divine presence, and we intentionally participate in the Spirit's activity in and through us.[163]

When next you share in this sacred meal, think of the bread and wine as "carriers of truth". As you take these ordinary elements into your body, think about what they mean to you, and what God might be saying to you through them. Then invite God's truth into your being along with the food of the sacrament.

One ancient worship practice that has been the source of much debate in liturgical circles lately is the reciting of **Creeds.** Part of the reason for this is that the purpose of these historical statements of faith is often unclear. If all we are doing is mouthing a few propositions in order to determine who is "in" and who is "out", then we are wasting our time. I believe that the creeds, rather than offering us ideas to agree with, describe truths by which we are called to live. When we proclaim that Jesus was born of a virgin, we acknowledge that God's purposes are brought into being through ordinary people, and we commit ourselves to be vessels that give birth to God's reign in our world. When we state that we believe in "one holy, catholic and apostolic church" we affirm our choice to belong to a universal (which is what catholic means) community of believers and to embrace all people of faith as brothers and sisters.

When you find yourself reciting a creed in worship, ask God to make one or two lines stand out for you. Reflect on what truth this faith statement seeks to communicate, and what your response to it should be. Then, invite this truth to take hold of you. Make a commitment to live out this truth in the week to come.

Closely linked with Communion, and the creeds that accompany it, are the "rites of entry" which every church practices. These include **baptism** or **dedication**, **confirmation** and **the welcoming of new members.** These rituals are more than simply bringing people into a church, a religion, or even a community. When we make our commitment to belong to a church, we are actually committing to the way of Jesus. We acknowledge that it is a way that needs the support and strength of companionship, and we promise to help each other to live the truth daily.

Although these rites of entry can often feel boring or irrelevant to those who are not directly involved, I find them to be significant opportunities for feeding on truth. As I watch and pray for those who are baptised or confirmed, I am reminded of what my commitment to Jesus means, and of **the way** that I seek to live. Then, I am able to renew my own vows and commitments, and give thanks for my companions who help me to stay true. I encourage you to do this act of renewal when next you worship in a service where rites of entry are performed.

Two other regular and simple practices that form part of almost every worship service are **confession** and the **offertory.** Both actions bring our lives under the scrutiny of God's truth. In confession we are reminded of what it means to live the way of Jesus, and of how Jesus lived, died and was raised in order to give us the example and the power to live this way. We acknowledge those places in our lives where truth is not our way, and we commit to truth again. In the offertory we bring our money – which really represents all that we are and all that we have – and we offer it for the work of God. The act of giving reminds us that we are not in control of our lives, and that we can only live abundantly when we place our trust in God and God's way of truth. This simple act dramatically loosens the hold of the values of materialism, consumerism and self-sufficiency, and invites us to trust the way of Jesus to which we offer ourselves.

When next you are in worship, take time to note the moments when your life is being challenged by God's truth. In confession ask God to reveal to you those places where you most need to be fed with the truth of God, and, as you make your offering, renew your commitment to live God's truth in every part of your life.

Becoming People of Truth

"To worship is to feed the mind with the truth of God." This, Jesus tells us, is the worship that God seeks – worship in Spirit and truth. Our mind – that part of us that knows, that experiences, that relates, that sees things clearly and consciously connects to God – can lead us into vibrant, abundant life, or can leave us lost, confused and desperate. The truth of God, embodied in the person of Jesus, and expressed in his way, is the food we need to transform our minds.

In the sanctuary we can always find this nourishing, wholesome food. If we mindfully and wholeheartedly embrace the acts of Scripture reading and Communion, if we renew our commitment to Jesus and his way through sharing in rites of entry, if we will constantly remember the truth that is communicated through our creeds, if we will confess our untruths, and if we will give ourselves to the way of Jesus through the offertory, we will find our minds growing strong and alive. And when our minds are strong, so are our bodies, our relationships, our communities and the contribution we make to the world.

Chapter Five

Becoming Beautiful

And now, dear brothers and sisters, one final thing. Fix your thoughts on what is true, and honourable, and right, and pure, and lovely, and admirable. Think about things that are excellent and worthy of praise. Keep putting into practice all you learned and received from me – everything you heard from me and saw me doing. Then the God of peace will be with you.
(Philippians 4:8-9)

There have been many moments that have changed me, but one that stands out was an extraordinary experience in an ordinary place. As part of our weekly Sabbath, my wife, Debbie, and I had decided to visit a prominent Johannesburg art gallery. We made our way through the halls and rooms, drifting alone and together, stopping whenever something drew us into more focussed attention. As I moved into one of the main chambers, my eyes scanned the pieces displayed along the walls. Within a few seconds I was drawn to a small, subdued canvass that managed to stand out in spite of its quiet simplicity. I moved to within a few feet, searching the image for its message, and then I became transfixed, as my awareness of all else faded away. I have no idea how long I stood there, but as I stared at this tiny masterpiece, the picture, and its meaning, were burned into my mind.

The colours were dark – greys, greens and browns – and the lighting was muted and soft. There was very little background detail as the presence of one, striking person filled the frame and, it seemed, the room. She was a warrior, dignified and strong. She was not beautiful in the popular sense, but attractive because of some inner, indefinable quality. She was kneeling, face turned toward the heavens, weapons forgotten on the ground beside her, and in a bowl in front of her lay what must have been all her worldly treasures. Her prayerfulness and devotion were unmistakable, and her nakedness gave her a vulnerability that was a surprising contrast to her strength. I recognised in her a passionate devotion to her God, and a desire to be wholly given over in worship. I hardly needed to read the title card to know that this painting was *The Offering*.

Here, on a normal day, in an unexpected place, a work of art became for me a burning bush. I found myself on holy ground faced with the presence of God, and I could do nothing but offer myself in worship. That moment regularly returns to still me in the sanctuary, to awaken my awareness of God in the created world and to remind me to submit myself to God's grace and purpose. There is now no question in my mind that beauty changes us.

The Power of Beauty

Art and beauty are sometimes viewed as luxuries – the privilege of the wealthy – or as frivolous – the distractions of those peculiar "creative types". But, even a cursory examination reveals that beauty has a profound impact on the well-being and growth of individuals and communities. Physically, psychologically, emotionally and relationally, beautiful objects and environments strengthen us, inspire us, challenge us, confront us, heal us and awaken us. Without beauty, our souls shrivel and our lives grow cold and small, but when we are able to find or create beauty, we are given access to our best selves. In his book, *Creativity: Where the Divine and the Human Meet*, Matthew Fox relates a moving story of one teacher's experience of what creating beauty can do.

A few years ago a woman from Ohio approached me at a lecture I was giving and told me this story. A judge in her city had begged her to invent a high school where he could send tough teen-age kids, who were dropping out of the public school and getting in trouble – "an alternative to jail" was his request. She told me she was reading my books at that time, and she launched a school based *entirely on creativity.* From nine in the morning to four in the afternoon the students engaged in painting, music, poetry, rap, video, theatre, dance, storytelling. What happened? First, the students showed up everyday. They often stayed after hours and begged the instructors to do the same. Second, they found a language for their anger and their hurt and their dreams. Third, after a while, they started asking questions about history, geography, Shakespeare, algebra.[164]

Beauty, and the act of creating beauty, is a deeply transforming gift. Perhaps this is why the message of the prophets was so often expressed through drama, mime, music, poetry, visions and tableau.[165] The prophets were artists, and, in many historical movements, artists have been the prophets.[166] For example, in Sophiatown, outside of Johannesburg, a bohemian, multi-racial community of artists, lawyers and political activists existed during the apartheid years. The ideological threat of this place and its prophetic voice was too much for the Nationalist government to ignore, and so, starting in 1955 and continuing for the next eight years, 65,000 residents were forcibly removed, many to Meadowlands in the township of Soweto. A number of prominent artists were forced into exile – notably Hugh Masekela and Miriam Makeba. Almost all of the homes were bulldozed, and a new suburb, optimistically named Triomf (Triumph) was created in its place. Ultimately, though, this did little to silence the prophets, as history has shown, and in 2006 Triomf was re-christened as Sophiatown once again.[167]

It should come as no surprise, then, that William Temple notes the power of beauty to change us, and the significance of beauty in our worship life. In the third statement in his definition of worship, he states:

> *To worship is to purge the imagination by the beauty of God.*

The Dangerous Imagination

The creation and enjoyment of beauty is an act of imagination. The human capacity to 're-vision' past experiences, envision possible futures, re-imagine present realities, and picture what does not exist is one of our most powerful – and dangerous – abilities. An overwhelming proportion of the material and tools that make up our world began as an idea in some creative person's imagination. Equally, our worst inhumanities and our greatest instruments of destruction grew from seeds within the human imagination. Our imagination holds within it the promise of a better world, and the curse of total annihilation – this is not overstating the case. Perhaps this is why the Church has tended to be rather suspicious of the imagination.

A quick overview of the use of the word 'imagination' (sometimes also used in the plural form 'imaginations') in the Bible is rather depressing. Pretty much every use of the word is associated with rebellion against God and the worst of human depravity. Two representative passages, one from the Old Testament and one from the New, are enough to illustrate. Genesis 6, noting the wickedness of humanity, states that God saw *"that every imagination of the thoughts of his heart was only evil continually"*[168] and Paul, describing the spiritual warfare in which followers of Christ are engaged, instructs us to 'cast down' *"imaginations, and every high thing that exalteth itself against the knowledge of God"*[169]. In the face of this biblical testimony it is not surprising that some Christians have come to believe that

"*Satan lives in the imagination.*"[170] And there is considerable historical support for this fear as well. Our Christian ancestors, from Augustine to Luther to Calvin and others, all expressed caution with regard to human creativity, and tended to be wary of the emotions that great art and music could stir up.[171]

If that's not enough, the evidence for the destructive power of the imagination continues to pile up in our time. An awful lot of human depravity – from weapons of mass destruction, to the terrorist's plot to fly planes into skyscrapers, from instruments of torture and humiliation to new innovations in cybercrime – flows from imaginative human thinking.

Must we, then, imprison our imaginations, or reject them altogether for fear of being led into evil? Is the imagination nothing more than a frightening and depraved human characteristic that has no hope for redemption? Or, is it possible that the imagination can be a powerful and creative force for goodness and godliness? Before we offer a simple "the Bible says" response, there are, perhaps, a couple of truths to consider.

To begin with, we must acknowledge that human beings are created by God, and so the capacity to imagine, which is part of that creation, is therefore a God-given gift. Further, the Scriptures make it clear that God's creation of us was *"very good"*[172] and that we are created in God's image.[173] Arguably the first characteristic of God that every human being encounters is God's creativity, and even the Bible uses God's creative activity as its starting point.[174] This means that, at least in part, the divine image within us is manifested through our creative ability. And, it hardly needs to be stated that creativity does not exist without imagination.

Further, without imagination, it would be impossible for us to move beyond the realities that surround us in order to realise the new reality of God's reign. No prophetic vision and no apocalyptic warning could ever have been communicated without stirring the listeners to visualise the events and images that were being described. When Jesus chose the creative technique of parable as his primary teaching method, he was relying on the imaginations of his hearers to get the message across.

But, how do we reconcile these insights with the Bible's apparently negative view of the imagination? A closer look at the passages that refer to human imagination shows that it is not the **capacity** for imagination that the Bible is concerned about, but rather the **content** with which it is filled. The Bible does not criticise the fact **that** human beings imagined things, but it does oppose **what** they imagined – depravity, evil, destruction and rebellion against God.

There can be no question, though, that the opposite potential resides within the human imagination as well. Beauty, goodness, truth, healing, altruism, compassion, and medical and scientific progress all find their roots in creative human minds. As we wrestle with the big issues of global injustice, economic inequality, limited water supplies, climate change, our dependence on fossil fuels, terrorism and war, our only hope comes from our ability to imagine alternative futures and to allow these visions to lead us. Matthew Fox is right when he states *"creativity can redeem and save our species."*[175]

Our conversation thus far has led us, then, to two inescapable conclusions. Firstly, the imagination is a powerful force that can generate both great evil and great goodness. Secondly, in order to direct the imagination away from death and toward life, it needs to be purged, refined, made pure. William Temple suggests that the best way to inspire the imagination to nobility and godliness is to fill it with God's beauty.

Purging the Imagination

The quest for God's beauty inevitably leads us down some surprising paths. Since it is not possible to apprehend God through the senses, we can only search for signs of God's beauty in the things God has made. Like the work of any artist, God's creation reveals its Creator, and so it is there – in the material, created world, and in God's action in that world – that we must seek and find God's beauty.

One of the ancient temptations of faith communities has been to separate the world into 'sacred' and 'secular' spheres. The Bible knows no such division, however, and points, rather, to this simple truth – all things, be they spiritual or material, are one.[176] Once we recognise this, the world and all of its creatures, formations and inhabitants are alive with reflections of God's beauty, and we find ourselves echoing the song of the Psalmist, *"The heavens proclaim the glory of God. The skies display his craftsmanship"*[177] and agreeing with Paul's affirmation that *"...the basic reality of God is plain enough. Open your eyes and there it is! By taking a long and thoughtful look at what God has created, people have always been able to see what their eyes as such can't see: eternal power, for instance, and the mystery of his divine being."*[178] Truly, as Matthew Fox affirms, *"the primary sacrament is creation itself – which includes every person and being who lives."*[179] Every moment, every place and every person we encounter is filled with the beauty of God, as are the works of beauty created by human beings who carry the divine image. We need only to learn to open our eyes and see it.

There is a word of caution needed here. As we have already noted, the world of human affairs is filled with a lot that is not beautiful. To say that God's beauty can be encountered through creation leaves us wondering how we are to distinguish between what is really beautiful and what is not. As the old saying goes, "all that glitters is not gold" – and all that appears beautiful is not necessarily as it seems. Even the Scriptures warn us that evil sometimes clothes itself as an *"angel of light"*.[180] If our imaginations are to be purged by God's beauty, we need the discernment to distinguish between the seemingly beautiful and the truly beautiful.

The ancient Greeks were guided in this discernment by the suggestion of Plato that there were three transcendent qualities in the world that were interrelated and that could lead us to God – beauty, truth and goodness. Each transcendent needs to be evaluated in terms of the other two. So, what is true is known because it is both good and beautiful. What is good is revealed by its nature as both beautiful and true. And what is beautiful is defined by truth and goodness.[181]

This offers us a way, then, to test the true beauty of someone or something. You may want to imagine comparing two photographs. The first is a surgically enhanced, airbrushed centrefold of a young model, and the second is a candid shot of a wrinkled and overweight elderly woman who has loved, and been loved, deeply. Which would you consider to be more beautiful? Which holds more truth and goodness?

How we think about and experience beauty is a life-directing consideration. When we reduce beauty simply to the 'pretty' or call things that are untrue or lacking in goodness beautiful, our souls grow dry and brittle and our lives manifest a spiritual poverty. When we lose our capacity to discern authentic beauty, we inevitably try to fill our longing with poor, artificial substitutes that demand nothing of us, and that fail to satisfy.

It is both disturbing, and an indictment on our inadequate sense of beauty, that a growing trend among wealthy American families is to give breast augmentation surgery as a gift to daughters graduating high school.[182] Similarly, the increasing problem of pornography addiction bears testimony to our retarded capacity for true beauty.[183] Even within the community of faith, we have struggled to embrace authentic beauty, resisting any art that challenges, questions or disturbs, and preferring instead what is 'pretty', 'cute' and 'safe'.[184]

Yet, true, authentic beauty is at the heart of the Gospel, and is both a remarkable means of grace and a powerful agent of transformation. This is why Paul encourages us as followers of Christ to immerse ourselves in beauty – in whatever is true, honourable, right, pure, lovely, admirable, excellent and worthy of praise.[185] As we embrace what is really beautiful and good and true, we are nurtured and inspired in every part of our beings and we encounter, in Paul's words, the "God of peace" and know this God to be with us.

The struggle we face as we search for beauty, though, is that biblical beauty is seldom 'pretty'. It is often deeply disturbing, ruthlessly honest and searching in its questions. The Cross is perhaps the best example of this. Hymn writers and artists through the centuries have celebrated the "wonder" and the "beauty" and the "glory" of the Cross, and rightly so – it is truly a thing of deep and transforming beauty. But, it is the furthest thing from 'pretty'. It is brutal, bloody, shocking, agonising, diabolical and dehumanising, and yet, within all of this 'ugliness' it is ultimately good and absolutely true.

It is beauty of this kind that truly purges and refines our imaginations and turns us all into God-reflecting artists that, through beautiful lives, change our world in deep and healing ways. As John De Gruchy explains:

> We are, in a profound sense, redeemed by...beauty, for art does not simply mirror reality but challenges its destructive and alienating tendencies, making up what is lacking and anticipating future possibilities.[186]

I suspect that this is not far from what Paul meant when he said we should *"fix our thoughts"* on what is truly beautiful.

The power of beauty is in its ability to move us beyond words into a deeper, whole-souled knowing. When we encounter the truly beautiful, we know it because it changes us, because we do not merely observe it at distance, because it stirs within us the desire to reach for our best selves, and to invite others into the encounter. When we encounter the truly beautiful we begin to imagine that we, and our world, can be different from what we currently are.

As George Bernard Shaw is reported to have said: *"Some [people] see things as they are and say, "Why?" I dream of things that never were and say, "Why not?"*[187] This is why the world – and the Church – needs more beauty, not less. James Smith, in his important book *Desiring the Kingdom*, eloquently explains how a vision of beauty, or a beautiful life, captures us and drives us to live out that life.

> It's not so much that we're intellectually convinced and then must muster the willpower to pursue what we ought; rather, at a precognitive level, we are attracted to a vision of the good life that has been painted for us in stories and myths, images and icons. It is not primarily our minds that are captivated but rather our *imaginations* that are captured, and when our imagination is hooked, *we're* hooked (and sometimes our imaginations can be hooked by very different visions than what we're feeding into our minds)...Thus we become certain types of people; we begin to emulate, mimic, and mirror the particular vision that we desire. Attracted by it and moved toward it, we begin to live into this vision of the good life and start to look like citizens who inhabit the world that we picture as the good life. We become little microcosms of that envisioned world as we try to embody it in the here and now.[188]

What Smith describes here is one of the most powerful and important functions of our worship. As we gather, our imaginations are hooked with a vision of the good life from God's perspective (what Jesus called the Kingdom of God, or the Kingdom of Heaven, or Eternal Life, depending on which Gospel you're reading). In our worship our desire for this good life is fed so that we begin to live it out in our daily activities and environments. There is, then, a strong connection between our aesthetics and our ethics, or between the beauty we behold and the way we choose to live our lives.[189]

Apocalyptic Worship

In this sense, then, worship is *apocalyptic*. The Greek word *apocalypsis* is often thought to mean hellfire and destruction

– the end of the world accompanied by the most dramatic special effects Hollywood can muster. In fact, though, this word means simply **revelation,** and is the Greek title for the last book of the Bible.[190] To reveal something is to bring it into the light, to allow it to be seen, to make it known. Worship, then, is apocalyptic in that it makes God's beauty and glory 'visible' to us, enabling us to experience and 'know' God's beauty in ways that touch and change us.

There are a number of considerations we can bring to our gatherings in order to foster this apocalyptic character of worship. When we engage our **whole bodies** in worship, and not just our minds, we open ourselves to encountering God's beauty in ways that touch us deep inside. Movement, processions, different postures and even dancing, allow our bodies to become part of our devotion. Using all the senses – by filling the sanctuary with beautiful sights (images, art), smells (incense, flowers, fragrant candles), tastes (communion, bread, honey, milk), sounds (music, or sound effects like wind, fire or rain) and textures to touch (like nails, thorns or seeds) – can open us to God's beauty in profound ways.

In addition, when we use **stories, symbols** and **metaphors** to communicate our message – not always feeling the need to explain or dictate a particular meaning for what we're doing – we invite people to think more deeply, to use their imaginations and to open to God's beauty. What follows are some specific and practical suggestions for engaging with beauty in worship.

Worship and Beauty

The worship service, as it is intended to be, is a place of radical and diverse beauty. Through the ages, the worship life of the church has called out the best skills and talents of artists of every kind – so much so that almost everything we know about art in the Western World has grown out of worship. From polyphony and notation in music to the visual art of frescos, icons and sculptures, to the drama of the mass and mystery plays, to the poetry of the liturgy and the dances of pilgrimage and labyrinth walks, the arts have always ensured that God's worshipping people receive a vision of beauty that reflects the beauty and glory of the God they worship.

In this great tradition, the worship that purges our imagination is worship that is filled with both God's creativity and the creativity of God's people. By God's creativity, I mean that the beauty of the God-created world can be brought into the sanctuary. This is a simple and good theological reason for the practice of **decorating the sanctuary** with flowers, banners and icons, and for bringing produce into the sanctuary at celebrations like **Harvest Festivals.** In some cases, this theological approach has even impacted the architecture of some churches, leading to whole walls being made of glass in order to allow the beauty of the world outside to be seen from inside the sanctuary.

Next time you enter a place of worship, take time to look around you. Take in the architecture, the décor and the symbolism and reflect on what they represent for you, what they say to you. Find a beautiful image or object and focus your attention on it for a few moments, allowing it to open your awareness to God's presence, and prepare for the encounter with God that the worship service will bring.

God's beauty is also seen through the creativity of God's people. **Music** is the most common way that human creativity is expressed in worship, which puts a lot of responsibility on the hymn writers of the Church. Unfortunately, while the worship music industry has ensured that a constant supply of new worship music is available to churches, the content and quality of that music is often driven by market considerations rather than theological ones. This means that we have found ourselves, particularly in the contemporary worship realm, with an abundance of songs about Christ's forgiveness, and

God's power as Creator, but a dearth of good music for the festivals of the liturgical calendar, or for any themes outside of the standard evangelical message. Nevertheless, as worshippers have experienced through the millennia, music remains a powerful medium for connection with God.

Music is also not the only way that beauty is expressed in worship. **Visual art** expressed through banners, paintings and photography, ritual actions and liturgical dance, the use of symbols and stories for meditation and other elements of décor can all help to create an environment on which we are drawn into an encounter with the beauty of God.

A few weeks ago I visited a friend of mine who is a pastor of a vibrant and creative church community in Johannesburg. As he showed me around their sanctuary, I was excited by the array of creative and beautiful artistic expressions that filled the worship space – walls painted with Bible verses in beautiful calligraphy, works of art done by members of the community hanging on the walls, carefully painted walls using different colours, textures, and even written poetry, to give the sanctuary a sense of beauty and creativity. Some of the art and décor had been created during worship gatherings and the entire space could easily have held me in contemplative reflection for a long time. One banner in particular stood out for me.

It was filled with footprints in different shades of greens and blues, beneath which the remains of black writing could still be seen. The text had been taken from Isaiah 58 – the famous call of the prophet for God's people to practice a "true fast" and bring justice to their community – and the banner had been produced as part of a congregational journey to *"stomp on injustice"*.

Another challenging and hope-inspiring example of the transforming power of beauty in worship comes from New Providence Community Church in the Bahamas, where pastor Clint Kemp and his congregation transformed a dump site into a place of beauty, creativity and worship. They carried away the junk, and cleaned up the beach. They nurtured the surrounding bushes and plants, landscaping areas where it was appropriate, and they invited a sculptor from the community to carve some of the dead trees into beautiful works of art. This place is now called *Sacred Space* and has become well known as a place of great beauty and spirituality.[191] What is remarkable here is that this place of beauty often draws people into spontaneous expressions of worship, and that the very creation of beauty from such a place of neglect and ugliness flowed from the worship life of the church – a life in which, clearly, the importance and power of beauty was recognised and valued.

As you share in worship in this coming week, take time to notice the varied artistic expressions that play a role in your encounter with God. Take note of the beauty of the music, the banners and any works of art, carpentry or decoration that you can see. Give thanks to the artists for their contribution, and open yourself to any new understanding or experience of God that these acts of creativity may offer. You may also consider any way that you could make your own creativity an offering of worship in some way.

The beauty of God, and the beauty of God's people, is not just seen in acts or 'products' of creativity, however. A deeply transforming facet of Christian worship is that it is always communal. As bearers of the image of God, **all people** are to be seen as reflections of God's beauty. When our worship enables us to see beyond the marks of wear and tear that life leaves on our bodies and faces, we begin to recognise, and draw out, the beauty of God from each other. This mutual celebration of beauty is a profoundly healing process, and it opens us to the vision of who we can become through Christ. Perhaps this recognition of God's beauty in one another is most heightened, and most easily accessible, through the children within our communities.

All **children** are inherently beautiful, and in their playfulness, they call the adults around them into the creativity and beauty of play. Doing actions for children's songs, listening to the stories of a children's address, watching the children participate in short plays or activities, all open us to the playfulness of God[192], and ignite our God-purged imaginations. As Matthew Fox describes: *"Children are still capable of living in a world of wonder. To reconnect to wonder is to awaken the child inside, and to do that is to tap into all kinds of Creative Spirits and muses."*[193] This is one of the reasons why I so enjoy all-age worship.

When next you spend time in a worship gathering, take a moment to look at the faces of the people around you. Search for God's beauty within them, and give thanks for the community that embodies and reflects God's glory. If there are children present, open yourself to be led by their playfulness, and ask God to remind you of your own inner child and your own God-given beauty.

In addition to these general encounters with beauty in worship, there are many practices that we commonly adopt that lead us into encounters with our beautiful God. **Praise** is foremost among these, as it opens us up to recognise God's beauty and presence around us. Again, Matthew Fox offers an insightful explanation:

> With praise, the human is doing what we were birthed by the universe to do: to tell the truth of the wonders and the goodness of what is. Learning to praise is the opposite of taking for granted. It is *taking notice*.[194]

Not far removed from praise is the practice of **thanksgiving,** which similarly lends itself to a creative noticing and celebration of what God has done. As these two practices occur in your worship this week, allow the prayers to ignite your imagination and open you to a new vision of God's beauty. Think of the images that the words evoke, and allow your imagination to turn the words into pictures that can reveal God's glory.

The **liturgical calendar** also offers innumerable opportunities for creativity and the expression of beauty in our worship. The festivals of Advent, Christmas, Epiphany,

Lent, Holy Week and Easter all ask for our most creative energies and offer a variety of resources – from Scripture readings and specific rituals to particular colours and symbols – which can all be woven together in beautiful and transforming ways. Likewise the important **rites of passage** that we celebrate – baptisms, confirmations, weddings and funerals – open us to new experiences of our beautiful God.

All it takes is for us to enter these moments mindfully, allowing the specific details of the time of year, or the event at the heart of our worship, to speak into our imaginations. As we worship we can hold images in our mind of the world outside – the sun and warmth of summer, the coloured leaves of autumn, the stark beauty of winter – or of the people we remember or celebrate, allowing our imaginations to connect us with our world, with our companions in life, and with the God who creates them all.

Becoming People of Beauty

If we are to envision the world as God desires it, as Jesus pictured it in his teachings of the Kingdom, we need imagination. If we are to embrace the hope that Christ offers us, and live out the faith to which we have been called, we need imagination. But, if we are to use our imaginations as effective instruments of transformation, we need them to be purged – refined and made pure – through encounters with God's beauty.

William Temple rightly points to our worship as the place in which this purging can happen. For our worship to be a place of life-changing beauty, though, it needs the best creative energies we can muster, and the willingness to recognise and celebrate the beauty in each worshipper. If we will have the courage to embark on this quest, I have no doubt that worship will not only stop being boring, but will lead us back out into the rest of our lives to spread beauty wherever we may go. What a wonderfully different world that would be.

Chapter Six

Becoming Loving

Dear friends, let us continue to love one another, for love comes from God. Anyone who loves is a child of God and knows God. But anyone who does not love does not know God, for God is love. (1 John 4:7-8)

"Why do you want to be married in Church?"

It was a question I asked every couple who came to me to be married, but with these two people I was particularly concerned for what the answer would be.

It was late on Thursday afternoon, and I was catching up on some work while waiting for an evening meeting, when my secretary informed me that a couple had arrived asking to see a minister about a wedding. As they walked into my office, I noticed that they were both in their late forties or early fifties. There was a strange tension about them, although they seemed to be very much in love. Then the bride-to-be informed me that they wanted the wedding to happen as soon as possible, but definitely no later than Saturday. As I questioned them about the urgency, they explained that they had both been married before, but that now they had found the love they had always been looking for. I gently encouraged them to consider slowing the process down and joining one of our pre-marriage courses in order to build a solid foundation for their life together, but they were insistent that this was unnecessary, and that the wedding had to go ahead as quickly as possible. It was then that I asked them why they wanted a church wedding.

"If we are married in church," the bride replied, "then God will bless our marriage, and we won't have the problems we had with our first marriages." As I tried to explain the discomfort I felt at this response, and that there was no guarantee of success that came with a church wedding, the bride grew increasingly upset. Finally, as she got up to leave, she blurted out, "You don't understand a love like ours! You just see love as work!"

She was right, of course. I do believe that love takes work – hard work, and lots of it. After nearly twenty-four years of what I consider to be the happiest and most fulfilling of marriages, I know that the joy that Debbie and I share has not been easily won. After raising two sons into early adulthood, I know that a deep and sustained connection with my children does not come without constant effort and attention. And, after years of working with communities of faith, I have no doubt in my mind that the love that Jesus taught is the hardest and most difficult task we could ever take on. As Scott Peck explains:

> When we love someone our love becomes demonstrable or real only through our exertion – through the fact that for that someone (or for ourselves) we take an extra step or walk an extra mile. Love is not effortless. To the contrary, love is effortful.[195]

If I were to think about living my life in the easiest possible way, putting the least amount of work into each day, I would not choose to be a person of love. It is far easier to close my heart than to open it. It is far easier to consider only my own needs, my own safety and my own self-protection than to seek the good of others. The work of opening the heart to love takes continuous, conscious and strenuous work. But, it is worth every ounce of sweat, every painful wound and every humiliating recognition of my own brokenness. It is easier to close my heart and protect myself from love, but that is not where life is found.

The Law of Love

In the Gospels of Matthew and Mark, when Jesus is questioned about the greatest commandment, his answer is decisive and simple: *"'...you must love the LORD your God with all your heart, all your soul, all your mind, and all your strength.' [And] 'Love your neighbour as yourself.' No other commandment is greater than these."*[196] If we take a moment to understand what was happening when Jesus said these words, the impact of his message is even more startling.

Both of these Gospels place this conversation directly after Jesus' triumphal entry into Jerusalem. Some scholars have indicated that there may well have been two processions riding into town that day.[197] The first, arriving from the west in pomp and ceremony, with the central figure on a white warhorse surrounded by a demonstration of the military might of Rome, was that of Pontius Pilate, the Governor. Passover was always a volatile time in Israel because of the reminders of the ancient liberation of God's people from Egypt, and so the procession was intended to remind the Jews of Rome's power, and warn them to behave lest that power be used against them.

The second procession, arriving from the east, was that of Jesus. The picture here was completely different. The warhorse was replaced by a donkey's foal. The Roman military display was replaced by a ragtag group of ordinary people singing and celebrating. The subversive, peace-making, empire-defying message was clear, and it ultimately got Jesus killed. After this procession, Jesus went into the Temple and overturned the tables of the money changers and animal sellers. This act of defiance against the corruption of the sacrificial system – in which people were forced to purchase animals from the Temple sellers using only Temple currency obtained from the Temple money changers, for which the priests received a significant cut[198] – caught the attention of the religious leaders. As a result a debate ensued which covered the three most significant issues in human experience – power,[199] money,[200] and sexuality.[201]

It is in the context of these two processions, the cleansing of the Temple and the debate with the religious leaders over life's big issues that the question of the greatest commandment was raised. Jesus' response, then, must be taken as a guide for how all of life is to be approached. In the face of oppression and political or military dominance, in the face of power struggles and abuses, in the face of economic struggles and disparities, in the face of our sexuality and the question of gender roles and equality, we are called to one task – to love God and our neighbours and ourselves. This one commandment, Jesus taught, summarises the entire Bible.[202] For Matthew and Mark, Jesus is portrayed as a new Moses, bringing a new law – or rather, re-establishing the lost heart of the ancient law – to those who would seek God and God's life.

The other two Gospels follow different routes to the same goal. In Luke's Gospel the question is framed by a lawyer who seeks to test Jesus by asking how he can inherit eternal life. Jesus asks him how he understands the law, and the lawyer responds by quoting the great commandment exactly as Jesus does in Matthew and Mark. Jesus' reply is emphatic: *"Do this and you will live."*[203] Then, in response to the ongoing challenge of the lawyer, Jesus tells the parable of the Good Samaritan. Again, the connection is clear – life is inescapably bound up in the law of love.

In the fourth and final Gospel, John doesn't ever quote the great commandment as the other three do. However, he does something just as powerful and significant. John also seeks to make the connection between Jesus and Moses, and does so in many ways in his Gospel.[204] The pivotal moment comes at the feast of the Passover in the famous words from John 13:34: *"So now I am giving you **a new commandment:** Love each other. Just as I have loved you, you should love each other."* (Emphasis mine).

There can be no question, then, that for Jesus the doorway to life is love. The only commandment that followers of Jesus have been given is the command to love. The way to inherit eternal life is through love. The essential guiding principle as we face all of life's big questions is love. To love the way Jesus did – the way he calls us to love – takes both work and a wide open heart.

Living with an Open Heart

According to William Temple, it is worship that challenges us to experience, to embrace and to embody this love. As he states in the fourth part of his definition:

To worship is to open the heart to the love of God.

In worship, God's love reaches out to us, coaxing us to release our self-protectiveness and closed-heartedness, and to gently open our hearts. In worship we hear the whisper of God's Spirit telling us over and over that we are deeply, passionately, loved, that nothing we have done or could do could stop us from being loved. And in this reassurance lies an unavoidable challenge. When we know we are truly and deeply loved, we are required to respond, to make a choice – to decide whether we will open our hearts to this love or retreat into ourselves, close our hearts, and send love on its way. This decision to open the heart is, as Henri Nouwen suggests, what conversion is really all about.

> Maybe we remember the few occasions in our life in which we were able to show someone we love our real self: not only our good intentions but also our bitter motives, not only our radiant face but also our dark shadow. It takes a lot of courage, but it might just open a new horizon, a new way of living. It is this breaking through the closed circle, often described as a conversion experience, which may come suddenly and unexpectedly or slowly and gradually. People might call us a crazy idealist, an unrealistic

dreamer, a first class romanticist, but it does not touch us very deeply because we know with a new form of certainty which we had never experienced before that peace, forgiveness, justice, and inner freedom are more than mere words. **Conversion is the discovery of the possibility of love.** (Emphasis mine)[205]

As Marcus Borg points out, the word "heart" in the Scriptures speaks of our entire inner self, the deepest part of us, the spiritual centre.[206] One of the most attractive and potent realities of the Christian faith is that, in Jesus, we have an embodied, human example of what the open heart looks like. In Christ we see not only what God's love looks like, and how God's love acts toward us as it seeks us and woos us, but also what it looks like to open the heart to this love. In Christ we are offered a vision of a heart that is so softened by God's love, that it opens widely and recklessly to all, and we are invited to follow Christ into this way of the open heart. The apostle John patiently explains this in his first letter:

> "Dear friends, I am not writing a new commandment for you; rather it is an old one you have had from the very beginning. This old commandment – to love one another – is the same message you heard before. Yet it is also new. **Jesus lived the truth of this commandment, and you also are living it.** For the darkness is disappearing, and the true light is already shining."[207]

For Jesus, every moment, every decision and every interaction is an opportunity to open the heart, and to welcome the other in. Jesus did not only teach love, he lived it, with all of its unpredictable challenges.

A good example of this is the surprising interaction between Jesus and a Canaanite woman who comes pleading with him for the life of her daughter.[208] After ignoring her pleas for him to free the child from the demon that was tormenting her, and being encouraged by the disciples to turn her away, he finally relents and gives her his attention – but

Chapter Six: Becoming Loving

only to discourage her with a rather exclusive mission statement: he has come to serve the Jews.

This woman is not to be put off so easily, though, and persists in her pleading. Finally, Jesus responds, but his words have challenged commentators for a very long time: *"First I should feed the children – My own family, the Jews. It isn't right to take food from the children and throw it to the dogs."* Is this an attempt to offend her enough that she will leave him alone? Is he just hungry or tired, and so unable to muster his usual grace? Is he frustrated by her persistence? One commentator even suggests that if this were the only story of Jesus that he knew about, he would be *"turned off"*.[209]

The woman, however, is still undeterred. In a display of shocking bravado and defiance of cultural norms, she challenges him: *"That's true, Lord, but even dogs are allowed to eat the scraps that fall beneath their masters' table."* This response brings about one of the most surprising and inspiring moments in Jesus' ministry. **He changes his mind and his attitude toward her,** and he relents. This Gentile woman wins the argument, and her daughter is healed.[210] In his capacity to be confronted by others, in his willingness to be forced to listen, and in his openness to change his mind and actions in order to live his mission of love more effectively, Jesus offers us a unique and profound picture of what it means to live with an open heart.

But, of course, this is not the only 'open-hearted' moment that Jesus showed. In his dealings with Zacchaeus,[211] the woman caught in adultery[212] and the gracious way he responded, in spite of his own pain and humiliation, to the crucified thief who begged him to remember him,[213] we learn what an open heart really looks like. When faced with Jesus as the example of the open heart, the call to love can be seen as the primary task of following Jesus,[214] the heart of the Gospel message, and the definitive mark of the Christian life.[215] John even goes so far as to suggest that our capacity for love and our knowledge of God are inextricably intertwined

– as demonstrated in the passage quoted at the start of this chapter. The challenge grows even more emphatic, though, when we recognise that this love is to be extended not just to fellow believers[216] or family members,[217] but to neighbours[218] and even enemies.[219] It's like the "one another" that Jesus commands us to love is an expanding circle that must ultimately embrace every person that we may ever encounter.[220]

The Love of God

Opening our hearts to the love of God, then, is not just about learning that we are wholly beloved, but also about becoming passionate and indiscriminate lovers of all. In worship God's love comes to us, welcomes us and teaches us that we are loved, which begins the process of opening our hearts. Then, as our hearts grow more and more open, we discover our own love for God and others increasing, which then opens our hearts still further. The question that automatically arises from this truth is this: what is God's love, really?

To seek to answer this question is to seek to plumb the very nature of God since, as John proclaimed, God **is** love.[221] In some sense, then, God's very being is defined and expressed in love. As C.S. Lewis very careful explains, this does not mean that the opposite is also true – love is not God, since God cannot be defined by, or reduced to, any single idea, and to set love up as a god is to create out of love a destructive and dangerous demon.[222] Nevertheless, in so far as we are able to grasp, in our finite minds, what God is like, we must begin by understanding what it means for God to be love.

At this point it is common to note that, where English has only one word for love, the original Greek of the New Testament has four different words: *Storge* (affection – as in a parent for a child), *Philia* (friendship), *Eros* (often translated as "sexual love", although, as C.S. Lewis points out, the sex act may or may not be part of *Eros*. In the light of this, it may be more accurate to think of *Eros* as the desire to be wholly and intimately united with another), and *Agape* (which Lewis translates as 'charity', and others have called the "God kind of love").

The temptation here is to refer to the first three loves as "human" loves, and the fourth (*agape*) as "divine" love. There are some good reasons why we would be wise to avoid this distinction. Firstly, if only God can express *agape*, then it would be impossible for us to obey Christ's command to love, since all of the Gospels use the word *agape* here. Secondly, if the other loves are not found in God – if God's love is only *agape* and not also *storge, philia* and *eros*, then we fall into a dangerous dualism in which our *agape* love for God and neighbour is somehow dispassionate, unemotional and 'removed' from the embodied realities of human love. Any attempt to love like this would not look like love at all. It would be aloof, cold and inhuman – rather like the disturbingly disengaged and ultimately destructive "love" shown by the women in the movie *The Stepford Wives*. In some way, all loves – including parental affection, companionable friendship and passionate desire for intimacy – must flow from God, or they are not really love at all. And all of these God-given loves, including *agape*, must be embodied in our human existence, or we end up being neither loving nor truly human. As Rob Bell writes:

> When we deny the spiritual dimension to our existence, we end up living like animals. And when we deny the physical, sexual dimension to our existence, we end up living like angels. And both ways are destructive, because God made us human.[223]

Where the Greek words help us is in understanding the differences between what C.S. Lewis calls "need-love" and "gift-love". He explains that God's love for us is not based in any need within God that we can fulfil. God does not love us in order to get something from us. God's love is wholly and purely a gift given for our benefit. Our love for God, on the other hand, arises from our need for God. We run to God, like children to a compassionate and protective parent, because we need God's care, nurture and provision in order to survive.

Affection, friendship and intimacy are all loves that arise largely from our need of the other. We love because we fulfil a need within ourselves to be parents or lovers, or because the other inspires, motivates or excites us, or because we are drawn to something in the other person that we find attractive. These loves are all "need-loves". *Agape*, by definition, is love that is given freely, unconditionally, and without any desire for personal gain – it is "gift-love". This may be why *agape* is considered to be the love most appropriately ascribed to God. The challenge that lies in our quest to understand God's love is to recognise that the essential quality of *agape* – its selfless, unconditional self-giving – must be expressed in all loves.

And so we find God coming to us with the *storge* love of a parent,[224] but without the typical need of human parents for their goodness to be validated or their life to be fulfilled through their child. We find God coming to us with the *philia* love of a friend and counsellor,[225] but without the typical human need for reciprocation. We find God coming to us with the *eros* love of an intimate partner,[226] but without the typical human need to possess or use the beloved. It is really only this "no-strings-attached" love, which comes to us in these different ways, that creates a safe enough space for us to risk opening our hearts. Then as our hearts open to this selfless love of God, we find our own ability to love is changed, and we begin to shift away from being primarily "need-lovers" to becoming "gift-lovers".

It was this selfless, self-giving love that Jesus demonstrated in John 13 as he washed the feet of his disciples – including the one who would betray him. Describing this act, John comments that Jesus had loved his disciples throughout his ministry and that now he loved them *"to the very end"*. The New International Version translates it this way: *"he now showed them the full extent of his love"*. In his commitment to serve his disciples in the face of their coming betrayal, denial and desertion, Jesus demonstrates a love that is the ultimate unconditional gift. But, Jesus doesn't stop there. After expressing his love for his disciples, he invites them into this love, encouraging them to follow his example, and love one another as he has loved them. This is not a call to love in some superhuman, "otherworldly" way, but simply to allow this generous, self-giving *agape* quality to flood into and transform all of their loves. In one sense, then, God's love is not so much a *thing* as it is a *quality*.

In a similar way, when teaching about the love that followers of Christ are called to embody, Paul describes the quality of this love in extravagantly sacrificial and self-giving terms:

> Love is patient and kind. Love is not jealous or boastful or proud or rude. It does not demand its own way. It is not irritable, and it keeps no record of being wronged. It does not rejoice about injustice but rejoices whenever the truth wins out. Love never gives up, never loses faith, is always hopeful, and endures through every circumstance. Prophecy and speaking in unknown languages and special knowledge will become useless. But love will last forever![227]

It is significant that this call to love comes in the middle of Paul's teaching about the Church's worship gatherings. Starting in chapter 11 and running all the way through to the end of chapter 14, Paul's words focus on prayer, the Lord's Supper and spiritual gifts as they are employed in corporate times of worship. Chapter 13 nestles into the middle of this discourse, and affirms, as William Temple does, that it is in worship, as we gather together, that we are challenged and taught to love.

As we open our hearts, we find that love is not something we do so much as something we become. And as love becomes our central nature, we find that our behaviour, our relationships and our ethics are all transformed. Love becomes our only law, and it is one that is followed as a natural outworking of our being. As Peter Rollins explains:

> Love is the law that tells us when to subvert the law, when to obey the law and when to break with laws, yet love is a lawless law that cannot be argued for...Here the binary between faith and works is devastated, as the work of love is faith by another word. The love that Christ spoke of is born of God, and when we see it at work, we know that the person has been born of God. If the works being carried out are for other reasons (such as the desire for salvation), then it is not love that we are witnessing. This love is not the narcissistic love that we see all around us and within us; this love is more radical than we can ever imagine.[228]

Koinoniac Worship

It is the power of worship to lead us into this love and to transform us into lovers that makes it *koinoniac*. The Greek word *koinonia* is used in the New Testament to refer to the shared life, the fellowship, the deep community of the early believers. Perhaps the best-known occurrence of the word is in the description of the newly birthed church in Acts:

> All the believers devoted themselves to the apostles' teaching, and to fellowship, and to sharing in meals (including the Lord's Supper), and to prayer. A deep sense of awe came over them all, and the apostles performed many miraculous signs and wonders. And all the believers met together in one place and shared everything they had. They sold their property and possessions and shared the money with those in need. They worshiped together at the Temple each day, met in homes for the Lord's Supper, and shared their meals with great joy and generosity – all the while praising God and enjoying the goodwill of all the

people. And each day the Lord added to their fellowship those who were being saved.[229]

It is important to note the central role that worship – both in homes and in the Temple, including both Word and Sacrament – played in the development and growth of this community of love. It is also important to recognise that the love that is expressed here is primarily described in "gift" terms. While there were clearly those who had needs that were addressed, the emphasis is placed on the way the believers learned to give and share. Finally, it is startling to recognise the way in which this community easily expanded and drew 'outsiders' into the sharing of love and life. Worship that opens our hearts to God's love will always reflect this sharing of life, this *koinoniac* character. It is challenging to note the way the Bible speaks about the shared life of God's people. In one of his psalms, David celebrates the life that we receive when we *"live together in harmony"*.[230] In a stark contrast though, Paul indicates that life is lost when we fail to *"honour the body of Christ"* and allow divisions to separate us.[231]

A number of simple characteristics can be developed in our gatherings in order to create this *koinoniac* experience. Primarily, if we are to know God's *koinonia*, we need to be churches where all people are **welcomed**, and given a space – which includes being given a voice. If people are in any way silenced or marginalised, then they are not truly a part of the *koinonia*, and we all suffer from a reduced experience of God's love.

A few years ago I ran a workshop in a church where they were grieving the lack of children in their community. The church was ageing, and the congregation really wanted to become more child-friendly. However, as we spoke, I was informed that there was an eleven year-old girl among them who was a talented flautist. She had not been allowed to play as part of the worship team, though, because she was considered too young. By not giving her a voice, they had inadvertently sent the message that children were not welcome, and they had all suffered as a result.

Of course, this means that we need to learn to **serve** and **include** one another in our worship. *Koinonia* does not mean that we all like the same things, or that we always agree. However, as we make space in our services for different theological views, musical preferences, and dress codes, we send the message to one another, and to the world, that we are learning to be a people who love indiscriminately. Simply by embracing a worship 'style' that I do not enjoy in order to welcome someone who is different from me is an act of deep love and service that opens the whole community to God's love.

Worship That Opens The Heart

Once again, when seeking to understand the particular practices in worship that enable this heart-opening love journey to happen for us, we quickly discover that the entire activity of worship is designed to facilitate this process. In the **liturgical calendar** we encounter the story of God's self-giving love in Christ. In the **sacraments** we enact God's unconditional welcome and proclaim God's gift of love made available in Jesus. In our **prayers** we take God's gift of God's presence seriously and dare to believe that we can enter a real relationship with God. In our **reading and preaching of the Scriptures** we hear again and again the love song of God for the humanity that is created in God's image. The challenge for us as worshippers is to mindfully participate in these practices and to turn the ears and eyes of our hearts to hear and see the divine overtures of love.

As we participate in worship we discover that the practices we use are also the model for the life we are called to live. Even as we are drawn into a vision of Christ's character and life, we are taught to imitate this life. And while a loving life is the natural outflow of a heart that has become open, learning the practices of love can also be a way to allow the opening of our hearts to happen.

There are two particular ways that the worship service calls us into open-hearted, love-embodying living. The **words** that we regularly use in worship – **praise, confession, thanksgiving, intercession, dedication** – are the same kinds of words that, when spoken to another, bring grace, healing, comfort and connection. In the sanctuary we address these words to God, but as we live our daily lives, allowing these words to teach us how to speak to one another, our worship continues because whatever we have done to the least, we have done to Christ.[232]

As we allow our speech to be transformed by our worship, we discover that we become people who readily and easily affirm (praise) others, who quickly and genuinely apologise when we offend or hurt another (confession), who gladly ask for, and offer, assistance when help is needed (intercession), who constantly give thanks for the good that we enjoy (thanksgiving) and who vulnerably express our affection for, and commitment to, others (dedication).

A helpful devotional practice can be to reflect daily on the way our speech employs the same kinds of words that we use in worship. As we examine ourselves we can remember our conversations from the last few days, and measure the extent to which we have been affirming as opposed to critical, thankful as opposed to grumbling, humble and quick to apologise as opposed to self-justifying and defensive. Then, when we gather for worship, we can use our words mindfully, allowing our liturgical language to be more than just an expression of worship, but to settle into our hearts and become part of us.

In a similar way, the actions we perform in worship teach us to act in Christ-like, loving ways. In worship we regularly **serve** one another (whether making tea or playing an instrument or welcoming those coming into the church), we **give** (through the offering) sharing the abundance that we enjoy, we **weep** with those who grieve and **celebrate** with those who are joyful (especially at funerals, weddings and baptisms), we **eat together** (especially in Holy Communion).

All of these actions teach us what embodied love looks like. We have only to continue to live this love in our homes, places of work and communities.

Again, as with our words, we can use times of personal reflection to measure our actions against the standards of love that our worship teaches. And, as we gather for worship, we can allow the rituals and actions of the liturgy to express our love for God, and to change us into people who instinctively act and interact in these loving ways in whatever situation we find ourselves.

Within this general work of "training in love" that worship offers, there are a few particular worship practices that are especially good at opening our hearts. The practice of **Christian greeting** or **"Passing the Peace"** is a simple but profound ritual that calls us to acknowledge and recognise the others who are part of our community. In taking the time to welcome each other and declare our peace with each other, we are rescued from our natural tendency to individualistic, self-gratifying spirituality, and we are reminded once again that faith, and life, is a shared journey in which we are all connected and in which our very survival depends on our capacity to love one another. You may find it helpful to intentionally seek to greet as many people as you can – especially those you have not met before – as you arrive at church for worship, asking God to fill you with love and gratitude for those who share their lives with you in your community.

Perhaps one of the most central acts of Christian worship, and one that has already been explored in other chapters, is the prayer of **intercession.** In our quest to love and be loved, there can be few acts as powerful as praying for others – especially those with whom we disagree or with whom we are in conflict. Genuine prayer does not seek for our desires to be imposed on the other, but seeks to see the other through God's eyes, and participate with God's loving purposes for the other. This implies that prayers are not just something we say, but that the act of praying is in itself a call for us to become the loving answers to our own prayers. The apostle Paul dramatically illustrates the power of a love-filled prayer life when he proclaims that he would willingly allow God to curse him, if it meant that his Jewish brothers and sisters would be saved as a result.[233] In contemporary terms, Paul is saying that if God asked him to agree to be the only person to go to hell in return for every one of Paul's countrymen and women receiving a guaranteed place in heaven, he would sign up for that deal in a heartbeat!

As you enter into times of intercession in your worship this week, take a moment to think of those who have hurt you, with whom you struggle or disagree. Make sure that you include these people in your prayers, and notice how your attitude toward them shifts into a kinder, more loving place.

Finally, the practice of gathering around the Lord's Table in **Holy Communion** is profoundly effective at opening our hearts. In the first place, we come to the Table deeply aware of God's undeserved, unconditional love, which alone makes it possible for us to be there. Then, the humility and gratitude that naturally arise can only lead us to welcome other "unworthy" ones to find their place alongside us, acknowledging our common need and our common humanity. Finally, as we are captured by God's love for us, we naturally begin to long for all people to know this welcome, and so we leave the Table changed, with hearts open to every opportunity to love that may arise in our daily living.

Take time to notice the people around you when next you share in Holy Communion. Recognise the humanity that you share, and your common hopes, dreams, fears and hurts. As you share together in the bread and wine, feel your connectedness with these other guests at the meal, give thanks for them, and offer a prayer for them as an act of love.

Becoming People of Love

As the old song lamented, *"What the world needs now is love, sweet love. That's the only thing that there's just too little of."*[234] In every corner of our world, in every relationship, in every place and time, Jesus proclaimed love as the necessary ingredient for wholeness, peace and well-being. This love is neither easy nor comfortable, but requires the work, attention and sacrifice of living with open hearts.

As William Temple declares, it is in our worship, as we are embraced by God's unconditional love, that we find the safety we need to risk this open-heartedness. If we are willing to allow worship to change us, if we desire love enough, we will discover in ourselves the capacity to become self-giving lovers of God, of our neighbours and of ourselves. We will know, with absolute clarity, that love requires sustained and difficult work, but we will eagerly roll up our sleeves and get started. Because we will also know that life – for us and for our world – can be found in no other way.

Chapter Seven

Becoming Purposeful

"The Spirit of the LORD is upon Me, for He has anointed Me to bring Good News to the poor. He has sent Me to proclaim that captives will be released, that the blind will see, that the oppressed will be set free, and that the time of the LORD's favour has come." (Luke 4:18,19)

Everything I had hoped for, I had achieved. I had fulfilled my calling as completely as I could ever have wished for. I had come as far as I had ever imagined I would. From that point on it could only be, at best, marking time or, at worst, a slow downhill slide.

For years I had worked and dreamed, imagining my life and ministry as I believed they should be, as I hoped they could be. There had been many unexpected turns along the way, and the final reality was quite different from the original picture I had held in my mind, but there was no mistaking it – I had reached every one of my goals.

There was a moment of celebration, a brief glow of pride and thankfulness at what my life had become, and then a surprising shift occurred. As I contemplated the journey I had travelled, I found myself, almost reluctantly, turning to look at the future that stretched out ahead of me. With a sudden tightness in my chest, I realised that there was nowhere left to go. There were no more dreams, no unattained goals, no open doorways hinting at miraculous possibilities beyond. There was only the slow descent from this place of fulfilment into the netherworld of remembering the good times.

I was thirty-seven years old.

It may have been the next morning, or it may have been weeks later that I recognised the signs of the gentle depression that had settled around me like a shroud. It was not debilitating – I continued my work and remained engaged with my family – but there was no denying the shadow that fell over my mind and heart, draining the joy and energy from every thought, every relationship, every activity. Each day became a study in commitment as I forced myself to go through the motions. Any sense of meaning or direction was lost – drowned in the growing fear that I had squandered the best years of my life, and that all that was left to me was the inexorable dreariness of decline.

The Power of Purpose

When life loses its sense of purpose, it ceases to be life at all. Human beings, as James Smith correctly observes are "intentional beings" – beings who are designed to be always moving toward some objective, always seeking to fulfil a purpose, always striving to find, create and share meaning.

He writes:

> Rather than thinking about human persons as static containers for ideas or beliefs, this way of thinking about humans as intentional emphasises that our being-in-the-world is always characterised by a dynamic "ek-static" orientation that "intends" the world or "aims at" the world as an object of consciousness…So the human person is not the sort of creature that can be diagrammed with a dot or an "X marks the spot"; rather, because of this dynamic, intentional nature of our being, the first move is to sketch the human person as an arrow that intends the world or aims at the world.[235]

This simply means that the primary way that we live as human beings is with intention – with purpose. When we feel that our lives are given over to a purpose that is noble, that is important and that engages our best capabilities and characteristics, then our lives have meaning and a sense of fulfilment, even though our circumstances may not always be optimal. On the other hand, when we feel that our lives have no direction or purpose, that our gifts and abilities are being wasted or used inadequately or badly, and that we are simply marking time, with no contribution being made, and no hope for change in the future, then we grow depressed, despondent and despairing, no matter how outwardly good our circumstances may appear.

It is now a rather clichéd and well-worn quote from George Bernard Shaw, but these words still ring true for the human condition:

> This is the true joy in life, the being used for a purpose recognised by yourself as a mighty one; the being thoroughly worn out before you are thrown on the scrap heap; the being a force of Nature instead of a feverish selfish little clod of ailments and grievances complaining that the world will not devote itself to making you happy.[236]

Benjamin Zander notes the difference that a sense of contribution and purpose makes to even small details in a person's life through his observations of orchestral musicians and the 'disease' he calls "second fiddle-itis". String players, particularly second violinists, often feel insignificant in the orchestra, both because there are so many of them, and because their parts are often duplicated by other instruments. As a result they tend to develop a laxness in both their practice schedules and their performances. In contrast, first oboists are unlikely to stop making reeds or to miss rehearsals because their contribution is very noticeable. Zander observes:

> In all my years of conducting, I do not believe I have ever known a first oboe to be late for a rehearsal. Is it because

the oboe has to be there at the beginning to tune everyone to the A?[237]

The Bible agrees with the view that human beings are intentional, that our best lives are found when we know a sense of "call" and when our energies and focus are aimed at a significant purpose. The judges, kings and prophets of Israel all possessed a strong sense of calling, and this was often enacted publicly through an anointing ceremony.[238] One of the most dramatic human encounters with God's purpose is described in the account of the prophetic call of Jeremiah:

> The LORD gave me this message: "I knew you before I formed you in your mother's womb. Before you were born I set you apart and appointed you as My prophet to the nations." "O Sovereign LORD," I said, "I can't speak for You! I'm too young!" The LORD replied, "Don't say, 'I'm too young,' for you must go wherever I send you and say whatever I tell you. And don't be afraid of the people, for I will be with you and will protect you. I, the LORD, have spoken!"[239]

While there is some debate among scholars whether Jeremiah's experience can be taken as typical for all human servants of God throughout all times, there is no question that the word to Jeremiah indicates that he passionately believed that **he** was **born** for a particular, unique purpose. When I read the story of Jeremiah's life, I can't help but wonder if it was this sense of divine call that sustained him through what was a very long, difficult, unpopular and sacrificial ministry.

It does seem to be the testimony of the Scriptures, though, that all human beings, at least to some extent, have an inherent, God-given purpose. In a song that beautifully echoes Jeremiah's experience, David offers this vision:

> Thank You for making me so wonderfully complex! Your workmanship is marvellous – how well I know it. You

watched me as I was being formed in utter seclusion, as I was woven together in the dark of the womb. You saw me before I was born. Every day of my life was recorded in Your book. Every moment was laid out before a single day had passed.[240]

Since the psalms were sung corporately in the worship of Israel, it can be assumed that, for David at least, this statement was meant to apply to all of God's people. In the New Testament, Paul expresses this same sense of being called from before his birth.[241] In his teachings on spiritual gifts he indicates that it is the task of every follower of Christ to discern their place within the shared life and mission of Christ's body, the Church.[242]

The Downside of Purpose

There is, however, some danger inherent in the human need for purpose. There are times when our sense of purpose, and our commitment to fulfilling it, can lead us into destructive attitudes and behaviours, rather than creative, contributing ones. If we begin to believe that our purpose is somehow uniquely divine, and that God appoints us to some superior, "messianic" task, then we can find ourselves claiming divine right and usurping divine authority.

Some years ago a young woman approached me after a worship service. She was obviously frightened by something, and as we spoke it became very clear what it was. She told me that a young Christian man had approached her with the insistence that God had told him she was to be his wife. She had never met the man before, and was, quite understandably, completely opposed to his suggestion. The young man refused to relent, however, and had been continually stalking her and accusing her of resisting God's will. After praying with her, I agreed to meet with the young man. When he came to see me, he was cold, aggressive and completely convinced that he had discerned God's purpose for both his life and that of the young woman he believed God had 'given' him. Nothing I could say would sway him or get him to admit even the slightest doubt, and he quoted verse after verse from the Bible to 'prove' his story, with complete disregard for background or context. In the end, the young woman had no other alternative but to get a restraining order against this man.

In a similar way, some high profile religious and political leaders have claimed both the anointing and the guidance of God in their appointment to their positions. As a result of this distorted sense of purpose, and the power they wield over their followers and supporters, they have, at times, said and done things that have been both irresponsible and even dangerous.[243] Clearly, while human beings need a sense of purpose for the sake of our well-being, the nature of that purpose is a significant factor in the impact we have on our world. This is true not just for public figures, but for every person as we seek to live meaningful lives, while sharing the world that is our home.

The Purpose of God

In the final phrase of his definition of worship, William Temple addresses the issue of purpose:

To worship is to devote the will to the purpose of God.

For Temple, worship is a purposeful activity that confronts us with God's purpose for our lives. While this may appear to contain all of the dangers of purpose that we have just been discussing, it is the way we understand the words "of God" that make all the difference. If we are to be people of purpose whose sense of calling leads us to creativity and not destruction, to contribution and compassion and not to coldness and judgment, then we need to be very clear on what the purpose of God for our lives really is. Since our calling as Christians is to follow Christ, a good starting point from which to begin our exploration of purpose would be to try and grasp

Chapter Seven: Becoming Purposeful

how Jesus understood his own purpose. Many of us have grown up to believe that the reason Jesus was born and lived on earth was so that our sins could be forgiven and we could go to heaven when we die. As important as forgiveness is, and as much as we need the hope of life after death, the reality is that the Gospels make far less of these two purposes than we might imagine. Rather, as Brian McLaren notes, the Bible indicates that Jesus came **to bring heaven to earth.** Using the Lord's Prayer as an example, McLaren notes that our "evacuation theology" would actually require a different prayer from the one that Jesus gave us. If forgiveness and going to heaven were Jesus' purposes, then the prayer should perhaps have been worded something like this: *"Our Father who art in heaven, hallowed be Thy Name. May we go to heaven after we die. May we leave here and go to your kingdom in heaven, which is unlike earth because there your will is done."* But, of course this is not the prayer that Jesus taught us. Rather, Jesus gave us a prayer which says, *"your kingdom come, your will be done **on earth** as it is heaven."*[244] (Emphasis mine).[245] The purpose of Jesus, then, as described in the prayer that he gave us, is for us to know and share the reality of God's reign among us now.

This purpose is made even clearer when we reflect on how Jesus spoke about his ministry. In the fourth chapter of Luke's Gospel, we read the account of the beginning of Jesus' work. After his baptism he had been led by God's Spirit into the desert where he fasted for forty days, and was tempted.[246] Immediately after this Luke tells the story of his visit to a synagogue in his home town of Nazareth. Perhaps because of the reputation he had already begun to develop as a preacher, Jesus is invited to read the Scriptures, and is given the scroll of Isaiah's prophecy. He turns to these words from Isaiah 61:1-2:

> "The Spirit of the LORD is upon Me, for He has anointed Me to bring Good News to the poor. He has sent Me to proclaim that captives will be released, that the blind will

see, that the oppressed will be set free, and that the time of the LORD's favour has come."[247]

Then as he sits down – a sign that he was about to deliver a sermon based on the words he had just read[248] – he makes a startling claim. *"The Scripture you've just heard has been fulfilled this very day!"*[249] This would indicate that for Jesus, these words summed up his ministry – he had come to be the fulfilment of this promise. The picture that Jesus paints here may well have been a reference to the Jubilee year of the Old Testament[250] – the feast to be celebrated every fifty years in which land and wealth were to be redistributed, slaves set free, and no work to be done, in order to allow the land to lie fallow after years of intense farming.[251] Jesus indicates that his ministry was all about bringing the Jubilee – which, as far as historical evidence shows, was never actually celebrated in Israel – into being now. As Brian McLaren notes:

> But, for Jesus, the dream of Isaiah and the other prophets – of a time when good news would come to the poor, the prisoners, the blind, the oppressed, and the indebted – was not five hundred or a thousand years in the future: the dream was being fulfilled today.[252]

This, then, is how Jesus understood his purpose – as proclaiming and demonstrating the Kingdom or reign of God, and calling others into a kingdom way of being.[253] What is important here is that this was clearly, in Jesus' mind, and in the mind of the Gospel writers who wrote about him later, a purpose that was God-given. But, it was not self-aggrandising, it was not self-enriching, it was not exclusive and it was not about domination, coercion or exploitation in any form. It was, as Brian McLaren notes, a proclamation of God's reign – or *"God's new benevolent society"*[254] – which was already available, among the people, and at work.

If the Scriptures are to be taken seriously, this is the acid test of a God-given purpose. Whenever we claim that God has given us a purpose, it must be tested against this benevolent purpose of Christ. If it contains the same characteristics, then we can continue to explore the truth and the implementation of this call. If however, it contradicts the purpose that Jesus proclaimed and demonstrated, then we need to reject that purpose as not being genuinely from God.

In his book *Everything Must Change*, Brian McLaren points out the practical implications of measuring our purpose against Christ's life and preaching in the various facets of human existence. One striking example is his reflection on how our eschatology – our theology of the end times and Christ's second coming – informs our sense of purpose and our actions today:

> If we believe that Jesus came in peace the first time, but that wasn't his "real" and decisive coming – it was just a kind of warm-up for the real thing – then we leave the door open to envision a second coming that will be characterised by violence, killing, domination, and eternal torture. This vision reflects a deconversion, a return to trust in the power of Pilate, not the unarmed truth that stood before Pilate, refusing to fight. This eschatological understanding of a violent second coming leads us to believe…that in the end, even God finds it impossible to fix the world apart from violence and coercion; no one should be surprised when those shaped by this theology behave accordingly.[255]

And so the purpose of God must be understood in the light of how Jesus lived and preached, and our own sense of purpose must be seen as following Christ in fulfilling this life-bringing mission. Whatever our jobs may be, whatever gifts and abilities we may have, whatever environment or circumstance we find ourselves in, the purpose of God for our lives is to follow Christ's way of Jubilee, and to reflect Christ's purpose and character in our daily lives. The apostle Paul, quoting what was almost certainly a first century hymn of the Church, explains it this way:

You must have the same attitude that Christ Jesus had. Though He was God, He did not think of equality with God as something to cling to. Instead, He gave up His divine privileges; He took the humble position of a slave and was born as a human being. When He appeared in human form, He humbled Himself in obedience to God and died a criminal's death on a cross. Therefore, God elevated Him to the place of highest honour and gave Him the name above all other names, that at the name of Jesus every knee should bow, in heaven and on earth and under the earth, and every tongue confess that Jesus Christ is Lord, to the glory of God the Father.[256]

Devoting the Will to God's Purpose

Once we have noted what God's purpose is generally, and how God's purpose is to be expressed or worked out in **our** lives specifically, we can then go about seeking to live in accordance with this purpose. Living like this is quite simply a choice – a decision that is made by the will. This is why William Temple indicates that an essential aspect of our worship is to devote our will to the purpose of God. Our worship, then, must on the one hand, continually draw us into a detailed and practical vision of God's purpose, and on the other hand, strengthen our will and our devotion so that we embrace this vision not just as an idea, but as the centre of gravity for every facet of our lives.

We tend to have rather ambivalent feelings about the will, though. This most basic of human characteristics is really nothing more or less than our capacity to make and implement decisions and choices, and yet we all know the crises of "willpower" that often accompany our attempts to develop a consistent exercise regime or stick to a weight loss program. Somehow we know that if we want to live 'better' lives, our will has to play a significant role, but we also know that our will is often just not up to the job.

Even Paul recognised this in his famous confession in Romans 7:15 – *"I don't really understand myself, for I want to*

Chapter Seven: Becoming Purposeful

do what is right, but I don't do it. Instead, I do what I hate." After exploring in detail the frustrating and painful problem of "willpower failure", though, Paul turns to the hope that is found in God's Spirit and the purpose God calls us into: *"So now there is no condemnation for those who belong to Christ Jesus. And because you belong to Him, the power of the life-giving Spirit has freed you from the power of sin that leads to death."*[257] He then continues to explore the vibrancy and contribution that are experienced by those who are led by God's Spirit into God's purpose:

> For all who are led by the Spirit of God are children of God... And since we are His children, we are His heirs. In fact, together with Christ we are heirs of God's glory. But if we are to share His glory, we must also share His suffering... For all creation is waiting eagerly for that future day when God will reveal who His children really are... And we know that God causes everything to work together for the good of those who love God and are called according to His purpose for them. For God knew His people in advance, and He chose them to become like His Son, so that His Son would be the firstborn among many brothers and sisters. And having chosen them, He called them to come to Him. And having called them, He gave them right standing with Himself. And having given them right standing, He gave them His glory.[258]

Essentially what Paul demonstrates here is that our will, which on its own can tend to be fickle and unreliable, finds it strength and transforming power when it is captured by God's purpose and inspired by God's Spirit. A clear and inspiring vision of God's purpose creates in us the desire to live with meaning and intention, and develops within us the strength to act on this vision and become part of implementing God's Kingdom way of being in the world. As Paul writes in the section immediately following his hymn about Christ's obedience, *"For God is working in you, giving you the desire and the power to do what pleases Him."*[259]

As followers of Christ, then, we are to be people whose wills are surrendered and devoted to the purpose of God as it is manifested in Christ, and whose lives are given to living out this purpose in every moment and every situation. This was a clear and central priority in Jesus' ministry, and in the ongoing of work God in Christian individuals and communities through the Holy Spirit. As Dallard Willard movingly explains:

> The assumption of Jesus' programme for his people on earth was that they would live their lives as his students and co-labourers. They would find him so admirable in every respect – wise, beautiful, powerful and good – and that they would constantly seek to be in his presence and be guided, instructed and helped by him in every aspect of their lives. For he is indeed the living head of the community of prayerful love across all time and space.
>
> The effect of such continuous study under Jesus would naturally be that we learn how to do everything we do 'in the name of the Lord Jesus' (Col.3:17); that is, on his behalf or in his place; that is, once again, as if he himself were doing it. And of course that means we would learn 'to conform to everything I have commanded you' (Matt. 28:20). **In his presence our inner life will be transformed, and we will become the kind of people for whom his course of action is the natural (and supernatural) course of action.** (Emphasis mine)[260]

Kerygmatic Worship

In the face of God's purpose, and the need for our wills to be devoted to it in order for us to live lives that are, on the one hand, fulfilled and meaningful and, on the other hand, contributing and creative, we cannot avoid the crucial role of worship. As William temple suggests, it is our worship that impresses upon us the vision and implications of God's Kingdom purpose. It is in worship that we are called to participate in this purpose. It is in worship that we surrender our wills such that we become devoted not just to the God of heaven, but also to bringing God's heaven to earth. It is worship that opens us up to the Spirit of God that strengthens and inspires our will such that it can be consistently and completely devoted to God's purpose.

In this sense our worship can be thought of as *kerygmatic*. The Greek word *kerygma* (and the associated word *kerusso* used of preachers) is used in the New Testament to refer to the preaching of the Good News of God's Kingdom in word and action. It is used to refer to John the Baptist announcing Jesus' arrival.[261] Jesus uses it in the statement of purpose in Luke 4 that we have already explored. Paul uses it in speaking of the need for preachers in order for people to hear and believe.[262] In worship the *kerygma*[263] – the Gospel message of God's reign among us – is proclaimed through music, prayer, silence, sacrament, Scripture, preaching and symbol, and we, the worshippers, are captivated by God's call to proclaim the Good News through word and action in the routines and relationships of our daily lives.[264]

Although we often separate the proclamation of the Gospel from worship, the Bible does not do this. In some "seeker-sensitive" churches it is common to say that believers and seekers cannot worship together, because the former want intimate connection with God, while the latter need the proclamation of God's message. In truth, both groups need both, and the Scriptures, surprisingly indicate that our worship needs to take the presence of visitors into account. In Paul's letter to the Corinthians, he encourages them to be careful when speaking in tongues (giving messages in a language that is not naturally understood) in case a visitor comes in and thinks they are all insane. Instead, he suggests that they embrace prophecy (giving messages in a language that is naturally understood) in order to include the visitors in the worship, and make space for God to convict them.[265]

Part of this proclamation is to ensure that we always keep Jesus and the work of God's reign central in our gatherings. It can be tempting to 'worship' mothers on Mothers' Day, gifts on Christmas Day, and people in weddings and funerals, but in all of our worship services, unless we keep Christ at the centre, our actions cease to be worship. It is also important that we proclaim, in word and action both the **invitation** of the Gospel – to find life and salvation in Jesus – and the **confrontation** of the Gospel – challenging injustice and accepting God's call to a higher standard. This means that in our worship gatherings, it is important that we ensure that we do not tolerate injustice in any form. This is one of the reasons that I advocate strongly for the use of gender inclusive language in our hymns and liturgies. In a world where women are still under threat, this small, but significant, action can be a powerful proclamation of God's justice.

Worship that Captivates the Will

As we gather, then, we are invited to engage in regular practices of worship that call us to devote our will to God's purposes. In one sense, worship offers us the opportunity to 'practice' devoting our will to God's purpose through the simple decision to commit to a life of worship. A common phrase used by the psalmists in the songs of Israel is "I will". The hymns of God's people, then, encourage worshippers to constantly affirm that they "will" praise, give thanks, rejoice and sing.[266] This small act of the will is a training exercise for the larger, life-encompassing act of devoting our wills to live out God's purpose in every facet of our being. Susan J. White describes how this happens in and through the weekly act of worship:

> The common worship of the Church teaches us who we are by allowing us to be who we are; the liturgy teaches us our calling by inviting us to exercise that calling in the liturgical assembly.[267]

In addition to this general exercise of the will that happens in worship, there are a number of worship practices that we repeat each week which are particularly effective at captivating our wills and leading us into devotion to God's purpose. At the start and end of every worship service are the often-overlooked (or missed, due to late arrival or early departure) elements of the **call to worship** and the **benediction** and **dismissal.**

As we gather for worship, we all too often allow the start of our services to become little more than a time of chaotic greeting and quick information sharing through what is often called the 'notices'. While these announcements do have an important role to play in calling us into God's purpose (which I will discuss shortly), it is important that the start of the service is not drained of power and impact through "getting things out of the way". Rather, when a call to worship is allowed to do its work, we are immediately given a sense of God's presence and activity among us, we are reminded that the time we spend in the sanctuary is not an **escape** from life, but a **re-orientation** of our lives to God's purpose.

We are invited into a deep and transforming journey into God's calling for us as individuals and as the faith community. Done thoughtfully, and with careful consideration for the circumstances and events that have impacted the community over the last week, the call to worship sets the tone for the rest of the act of worship, and can, in the first few minutes, mean the difference between a heartfelt act of worship or a heartless observance of religious habit.

When next you participate in a worship service, try to enter the sanctuary with less haste, and more intention. Take a moment to recognise the purpose of the gathering, and prepare your heart for what is to come. As the service starts, immediately call yourself to attention, and choose to engage and participate wholeheartedly. Notice the difference this makes to your experience of the rest of the service. Richard Foster takes the preparation of the heart for worship even further, suggesting that we begin the night before, examining ourselves, reading through the Scriptures and hymns (if we know what they are), and getting to bed early.[268] There is no question that the better we prepare, the more we will be impacted by the *kerygma* of the service and be drawn into God's purpose for our lives.

In a similar way, the manner in which a service is ended can determine whether we connect our worship with the realities of our lives, or enter the rest of the week unchanged. A benediction – literally, a spoken blessing – can be little more than an announcement of the end of the service, or it can be a meaningful challenge to live out the transformation that worship has initiated in us. It can be make a huge difference to the week to know that as we leave the service we go as people who are **sent** as God's messengers to proclaim the Good News in lives of compassion, service, forgiveness, inclusivity and peace-making. As Richard Foster expresses it:

> Just as worship begins in holy expectancy, it ends in holy obedience. If worship does not propel us into greater obedience, it has not been worship... Worship enables us to hear the call to service clearly so that we respond, 'Here am I! Send me' (Isa.6:8).[269]

When your next time of worship comes to an end, you may want to resist the urge to rush out of the sanctuary. Rather, slow yourself down, and take a moment to reflect consciously on how the worship service has spoken to your life. Ask yourself what you can take with you into the coming week, and make a commitment to at least one specific action or discipline that you are going to try and implement in the coming days.

In between these two moments in our worship, there is a lot that happens that draws us into a will-captivating encounter with God's purpose. Two practices that are often viewed with much ambivalence, but which have a profound impact on worshippers are the **notices** or **announcements** and the **offering.**

When we take the time to inform people of the activities and interests of our particular community, this is a *kerygmatic* – a proclamatory act. I often like to refer to the bulletin that most churches hand out to worshippers as the appendix to the Bible. While the Bible tells us of God's work for all of humanity through all time, the bulletin, and the announcements that highlight important features of it, tells us of God's work in a specific community in a particular time. If we want to know what God is doing in a church, we must listen carefully to the announcements. And as we listen, we are called to participate in this work of God and find our unique place of purpose within it.

When Debbie and I first arrived at our new home – Sea Point Methodist Church in Cape Town – one of the leaders showed Debbie a collection of pulpit notices that had been kept through almost the entire history of our church. As she read through the various announcements that had been made over the years, she had a unique window into the life and ministry of this church that she had now been called to lead. We saw how, from its earliest days, Sea Point Methodist had been involved in the struggle for justice and equality for oppressed black South Africans, and how it had always been a diverse and creative community in worship and service in this place. How tragic it would have been if these records had not been valued, and if the announcements in those years had just been "got out of the way"!

Perhaps, this week, you can bring the bulletin home with you from your church. Place it in a place where you will be sure to see it and use it during the week. Each day take time to read through it and pray for the events and people listed there. Ask God if there is any ministry that you should be getting involved in, or if there is anything that you are already doing that the church might want to know about and pray for or support.

The offering is another part of most worship services that is treated with some embarrassment and awkwardness. The importance of this act is often obscured by its other common name – which I do not like at all – the 'collection'. However, in the work of responding to God's call and purpose for us as individuals and communities, there can hardly be a more important act of worship. In our consumerist, materialist world, where success is measured by the number of zeros in the bank account, giving is an act of prophetic foolishness and defiance. As the offering is received, we do not give only the bit of money we place in the bag. Rather, we use the symbol of money – the means by which we feed, clothe and house ourselves – to represent **everything** we have and **everything** we are. The act of giving, then, places our entire lives into God's hand, and devotes our entire being to God's purposes. It is a radical act of obedience, and a dangerous prayer of commitment. Perhaps this is why we so often reduce its importance and prominence in our worship.

You may find it helpful to spend some time in prayer before you decide what to give in your next worship gathering. Allow God's Spirit to remind you of God's provision and grace, and ask God to give you the courage to give sacrificially. As you make your decision, think about what it might mean for you to commit your whole life to God's use.

It is almost superfluous to say that **preaching** is a practice that orients us to God's purpose, but in a world in which it has come under intense, and often, negative scrutiny, the power of preaching needs to be re-affirmed. While I am the first to admit that sermons that are thoughtless, filled with clichés and platitudes, and that are delivered in predictable, prosaic ways are both unhelpful and lacking in transforming power, this does not mean that preaching itself is dead. The spoken word remains a powerful and effective way to communicate, and, as the motivational speaking industry demonstrates, can be an attractive and meaningful part of any gathering. The key here is for preachers to use every tool they can – technology, story-telling, props, images, video – in creative and surprising ways, and for listeners to do the work of engaging with the word thoughtfully, critically and prayerfully. Ultimately, in my opinion, the best sermons are not a monologue, but a dialogue – even if no one but the preacher actually speaks in church. When we feel listened to and understood by a preacher, we are drawn into the Gospel message, and when we listen with a desire to be touched and changed by God, a sermon can be a life-changing event. As Frederick Buechner so poetically describes it:

> At the level of words, what do they say, these prophet-preachers? ...They put words to both the wonder and the horror of the world, ...but because these words are poetry, are image and symbol as well as meaning, are sound and rhythm, maybe above all are passion, they set echoes going the way a choir in a great cathedral does, only it is we who become the cathedral and in us that the words echo (Emphasis mine).[270]

Take some time to reflect on your feelings about sermons. Do you have negative associations, or have you found the preaching part of the service helpful? In what ways do you 'dialogue' with the preacher as the sermon is being delivered? How can you do this more? It may be helpful for you to buy a small notebook and to develop the habit of taking notes during the sermon, or setting aside some time to journal your experience of worship when you get home. As you listen to the word, ask yourself how the Scriptures and proclamations relate to your own daily routines and relationships, and commit to applying at least one truth in the coming week.

Finally, one more worship practice must be highlighted – the sacrament of **baptism**. At its heart, baptism is an affirmation of our identity and our vocation as children of God and messengers of the Gospel. Baptism never 'happens' only to the one baptised (whether infant or adult). It is always a communal event: a welcoming of people into the community, and a reminder, for all of us, of what the identity and purpose of the community are. In the Methodist Worship Book, whenever a baptism is performed, the congregation is asked to make a vow: *"Will you so maintain the life of worship and service that [these brothers and sisters who have been baptised] may grow in grace and in the knowledge and love of God and of his Son Jesus Christ our Lord?"*[271] In this promise, we recognise that our communal task is to be a people who know, live and share God's grace and love. And it is out of this shared identity – proclaimed every time we practice baptism – that we each find our own unique sense of identity and calling, as William Willimon explains: *"To the question, Who am I? baptism responds that I am the one who is called, washed, named, promised, and commissioned."*[272]

Next time a baptism is celebrated in your church, pay attention to the vows and words that are spoken. Remember, if you can, your own baptism, or that of a friend or child, and take hold of God's promises again. Allow the ritual to remind you that God has chosen and called you, and consider how you can live your baptism out more meaningfully and intentionally in your daily life.

Becoming People of Purpose

Through these, and other, regular practices of worship, we are given a vision of God's purpose for us and our world, we are called to experience the benefits of this purpose for ourselves, and to commit ourselves to participate in bringing this Kingdom vision into being in our world. Then, knowing that our commitments often reflect a desire of our hearts that our wills are unable to fulfil, we open ourselves to God's Spirit who captures us and strengthens us so that we become wholly devoted to this purpose of God in every facet of our lives.

God's invitation to a purpose-filled life is offered every time we gather for worship. The resources we need to live this life of purpose are, likewise, available to us every time we worship. All that is required is for us to offer ourselves back to God, and allow our worship to remind us that we are **people with purpose,** and that our purpose is connected – intimately and completely – with God's saving, restoring activity in the world. As this reality begins to take hold of us we cannot deny the truth that our worship, truly and amazingly, holds the key to our healing and transformation, and that of every person and circumstance we encounter.

Conclusion

Living the Change

But thank God! He has made us His captives and continues to lead us along in Christ's triumphal procession. Now He uses us to spread the knowledge of Christ everywhere, like a sweet perfume. Our lives are a Christ-like fragrance rising up to God.
(2 Corinthians 2:14-15a)

A thousand years of worship. My eyes filled with tears as I realised that I had just become part of this long liturgical procession. I was joining history, but more than that, I felt the presence of eternity as never before. It was Evensong, and Debbie and I had arrived just in time to join the other worshippers in Westminster Abbey. After a whirlwind day of sight seeing around London, time fell away as the choir sang, and the rhythms of the liturgy drew me in. After the service, as we made our way to Heathrow to catch our flight home, we reflected on how moved we had both been to be part of a community that had offered worship on that site every day for a millennium. It was a fitting end to a significant week.

We were in London to catch a connecting flight home to South Africa, after flying in from Chicago where we had been delegates to the Willow Creek Arts Conference. Here we had experienced almost a week of intense creativity, excitement and passion, gathering with thousands of other worshippers from around the world. It had been an exhausting time of learning, dialogue and reflection, and I had come away with lots to think about and implement. My heart, though, had been strangely unmoved.

As I settled into the plane to head home, I realised that my soul had been fed more by an hour in the ancient rhythms of the Abbey, than by days in the energetic stimulation of the mega church. This, of course, says a lot more about me than it does about either of these two worship settings, but it did bring home to me the gentle power of worship as a repeated discipline. This does not mean that creativity and energy are bad for worship. On the contrary, they are often inspiring and transforming. Nor do I mean to imply that tradition and structure are always good for worship. In truth, they can often become constrictive and dry. But, whatever our preference for style or form, the need for a regular, committed discipline of worship cannot be denied. It is when we return to the sanctuary mindfully and whole-heartedly, again and again, that the encounter with God gently and consistently changes us. There was something about being in a place where devoted followers of Christ had expressed their worship for centuries that effected this change in me at least a little – even though I only shared in this historical community once. And it is this constant, gentle transformation of God's Spirit that we all need.

But, it gets bigger than only us. We live in a world that faces some huge challenges, and the systems that we have created are breaking under the strain. It is not sustainable that a small percentage of the world lives in extravagant wealth while the rest struggle to feed their families and keep a roof over their heads. It is not possible that our addiction to power and violence as a means to address our conflicts and protect our interests can lead us to peace and co-existence. We cannot expect the world to be a place of joy and abundant life as long as health care is denied to people who legitimately need it simply because they live in the wrong country, or they cannot afford the spiralling costs. We cannot find rest in a world where we live in fear of those who believe, or look, or love differently from us. And we cannot expect to be healthy while our greed and short-sighted consumption makes our planet sick.

We need to be woken up, as human inhabitants of a radically connected planet, and recognise that we have a part to play in our own healing and that of our world. We need a radical re-organisation of how we relate to one another and the earth. We need to take responsibility for our own contribution to the world's sickness or healing. It is not naïve to believe that worship has a significant role to play in bringing about these changes. Unfortunately, it has too often been part of the problem. Martin Luther King Jr. alluded to this in an interview in 1963 at Western Michigan University when he said:

> We must face the fact that in America, the church is still the most segregated major institution in America. At 11:00 on Sunday morning when we stand and sing and Christ has no east or west, we stand at the most segregated hour in this nation. This is tragic.[273]

In a similar vein, Wendell Berry points to the role of the Church in contributing to the world's pain:

> If it comes to a choice between the extermination of the fowls of the air and the lilies of the field and the extermination of the building fund, the organised church will elect – indeed, has already elected – to save the building fund... [T]he fowls of the air and the lilies of the field can be preserved only by true religion, by the practice of a proper love and respect for them as creatures of God. No wonder so many sermons are devoted exclusively to "spiritual" subjects. If one is living by the tithes of history's most destructive economy, then the disembodiment of the soul becomes the chief of worldly conveniences.[274]

But, worship can be different. It can be more than a weekly emotional fix to carry us through our days. It can be more than cheap entertainment. It can be more than a spiritual waiting room where we indulge in a pleasing vision of the life that waits for us after death. It can be more than dry ritual and religious duty. The act of worship, properly understood and whole-heartedly practiced, can change everything. It can give us a new vision of ourselves and our world. Worship can lead us out of our ethic of expediency to becoming reflections of God's whole-iness. It can shift us beyond factual debates into the glorious truth of following Jesus and his way. Worship can lift us from our despair and pessimism into the creativity and inspiration of God-beautified imaginations. It can move us from our fear-based tribalism into an open-hearted love for all, and it can challenge us to go beyond a meaningless, "come-what-may" existence to a life that is energised and given purpose by a vision of God's reign.

If we will refuse to settle for anything less, if we will commit ourselves to worship that truly confronts us with God's presence and activity, we will find ourselves becoming very different people. And, it is when we commit to being changed ourselves that we are most likely to be an agent for positive change in the world. As Mark Labberton eloquently argues:

> Everything. That's what's at stake in worship. The urgent, indeed troubling, message of Scripture is that everything that matters is at stake in worship.
>
> Worship names what matters most: the way human beings are created to reflect God's glory by embodying God's character in lives that seek righteousness and do justice. Such comprehensive worship redefines all we call ordinary. Worship turns out to be the dangerous act of waking up to God and to the purposes of God in the world, and then living lives that actually show it.[275]

It's been almost thirty years since I was first asked, as a teenager, to lead the singing in the youth group at my church. Since that time I have facilitated worship gatherings in churches and conferences, in hospitals and homes for the

Conclusion: Living the Change

mentally disabled, in prisons, schools and universities, in cell groups and homes for the aged, in townships and suburbs. I have been involved with teams that have led worship for multiple generations, languages, races and cultures, in homes, huts and recently even in a stadium. I have used liturgy, choir and organ, and I have played guitar with rock bands, following almost no structure at all. And in every one of these situations I have recognised one consistent reality. We long for God, and God is available to us.

Sometimes we think our longing is for dramatic, miraculous, world-shaking events like those we read about in the Bible. Sometimes we believe that if only God would send the plagues or divide the waters, multiply the loaves or raise the dead everything would be all right. And sometimes we allow these thoughts to control our worship. But, in the deep places within us, where we know truths that we have not yet thought, and where we hold our deepest desires and hopes, we recognise that **we** are the miracle. That everything the world needs is already ours – held in trust in our own bodies and minds, our own relationships and networks. We know that God is not just with us, but within us, and that together we really can make a difference for future generations, and turn the world around.

More than that, we know that God believes in us, that God has placed God's work in our hands. And so, we know that all we really need to do is make our connection with God as real and strong and transforming as we can. It is when we enter the sanctuary with this knowledge, and with the readiness for what we know to become how we live, that worship becomes the hour that really does change everything.

I pray that this journey has been exciting and challenging, comforting and disturbing. But, most of all, I pray that your journey into worship, and into a life that flows from worship, does not stop the moment you put this book back on the shelf. My prayer is that what you have experienced over the last fifty days will continue to influence and change you for the next fifty years, and that those who cross your path will know that they have met a true worshipper, because their lives will be more whole, more true, more beautiful, more loving and more purposeful as a result.

Appendix A

Guides for Daily Devotions

This book is not simply about its content. It is meant to be a manual – a journey into a deeper worship life. To facilitate this, I encourage you to set aside a few minutes each day to reflect on the material in each chapter.

The idea is that you take a week to read each chapter slowly and prayerfully, and, while you're doing that, work with the content through Scripture reading, personal reflection and prayer. The following devotional guides are intended to help you do this work.

The readings, reflections and prayers offered here are not meant to be part of the 'teaching' work of the book, but are intended as spiritual exercises. For this reason I have taken a more contemplative approach, coming at the material indirectly, and inviting you to do this work from the heart, more than from the head. You will also notice that some of the prayers use plural language (us, we and our, as opposed to I, me and my). This is to help you remember your connection to the community of faith, even though you may be alone as you do these devotions.

I pray that you will enter into this journey with courage and commitment, and that you will find your heart and soul nourished and challenged as you encounter God each day.

Week One: An Invitation to Intimacy

Day One:

Read: Psalm 42

Reflect:

The cry of the psalmist is the cry of every person who has ever lived. Whether we acknowledge it or not, whether we use the name 'God' or not, we all long for intimacy with God, with Spirit, with the transcendent reality that sustains the universe. Like the psalmist we can all remember times when had a glimpse of this reality, when, in an unexpected moment, we became gloriously aware of God's presence and love. In this psalm, the writer uses his memory of such a time to inspire and encourage him to hope for the future. Because he once knew intimacy with God, he is able to believe that God is still present even though he may not feel it, and he is able to commit to the quest for intimacy again.

How does the psalmist's longing resonate with you? When have you experienced times of close connection with God? To what extent do you feel that worship draws you into intimacy with God in your life now? How can you commit to the quest for intimacy in a more purposeful, intentional way over the next seven weeks?

Pray:

I am one who seeks after love,
    I long for its touch, I yearn for the warm softness of its kiss
In this place I wait
    and open my heart
I am one who remembers my Lover,
    The God who seeks, the God who calls my name;
    The God that I love because God loved me first;
    The God who invites me into joyful intimacy;
    The Lover whose offer I will not neglect.
This is my time to respond and to worship.
Alleluia.
Amen.

Day Two:

Read: Song of Solomon 1:1-4

Reflect:
The Song of Solomon is an ancient love poem, thought to have been written by King Solomon. The language is passionate and, in places, quite explicit. It is clear that the Scriptures are very comfortable with sexual language.

Throughout the centuries this song has been seen as an allegory of God's love for God's people. It resonates with the sexual language that is used in the Bible to describe our intimacy with God, and invites us to become passionate in our worship of our Divine Lover. There are some reasons why we sometimes get uncomfortable with entering worship in this way, though. For some of us we have separated the spiritual and the physical aspects of our lives so much that it seems wrong to think of worship in this way. For others, particularly men, we have become so used to masculine language – or other-worldly language – for God that we find it uncomfortable to think of God as a 'Lover' like this. But, perhaps, if we can open ourselves to this idea, and invite God to show us what it might mean for us to experience God intimately and passionately, we can find a new joy and energy in our faith and our worship. Are you willing to try it?

Read the passage again, slowly. How does this language feel to you? In what way could you begin to explore the metaphor of 'Lover' in your relationship with God? How do you think it might change your faith and your worship to begin to embrace true intimacy with God? What might be standing in your way and keeping you from this journey?

Pray:
O Divine Lover,
How relentless You are
   in drawing our attention to Your devotion to us:
You embody Yourself in planets and worlds,

in creatures and beauty
   and You fill our lives with colour and with joy.

You decant Your desire for us
   into the hearts of our friends and families
   and touch us through their comfort and their compassion.

Yours is a subversive, uncontainable love, O Beloved.
   It finds us even when we try to hide;
   It reaches us, though all the world
      would seek to build walls against it.
And it has invaded our hearts,
   softening them and igniting love for You in us.

We praise You for this love.
   And we bring the love-token of our worship in return.

Amen.

Day Three:

Read: John 17:21-23

Reflect:

This prayer is often called "The High Priestly Prayer of Jesus". Here Jesus comes to God and prays on behalf of his followers – those who were with him back then, and those of us who have chosen to follow him throughout the ages since. One word summarises the content of this prayer – 'unity'. Jesus prays that all his followers would be one; inviting us into the unity Jesus enjoyed with God the Father and the Holy Spirit. The intimate union of the Godhead is available for us to share! And it is in knowing God – in moving into deep connection and union with God – that we find eternal life, abundant life, life to the full (John17:3). What grace and generosity we find in God. What a wonderful opportunity God gives us to live lives that are filled with God's presence.

What do the words "one with God' mean for you? In what ways do you already experience being one with God? How do you think worship can help you to connect with God even more? Why not try and spend today in a constant sense of union with God, and see what kind of difference that makes?

Pray:
You never really get tired of knocking, do you, Jesus?
Your gentle persistence as you seek a welcome
   is both amazing and disturbing;

There are times when I wish you would just leave me alone,
    times when I don't want to have to deal with you;
  Your constant seeking of attention
    for the hidden and voiceless ones,
  your gentle call to live always from the best of me,
  your persistent presence making itself known
    in all I do and say and think.

But, most of the time, I am grateful that you seek to be welcomed;
  I am glad that you give me the choice to invite you in
    and that you welcome me so freely;

It seems strange that, as God, you don't just demand entrance
    but wait for me to open the door;
  that you don't just radiate your glory
    and make your knocking unmistakeable,
  instead of hiding in the faces of children and creatures,
    earth and sky, broken and wounded ones.

But, for all its mystery, your coming, your knocking,
  your gentle asking for access
    is a gift beyond measure;
  A gift that I receive, when I remember who you are,
    with humble thanks and open submission.

Amen.

Day Four:

Read: Isaiah 6:1-9a

Reflect:
In a nation that was in turbulence after the death of good king Uzziah, Isaiah finds his way to the Temple. Here he is confronted with a glorious, disturbing, transforming vision of God. Notice how, although Isaiah is fearful, expecting God's judgement, God is kind, inviting and gracious. It is clear here that although God is glorious and way beyond Isaiah's – or our – attempts to understand God, the Divine Lover seeks relationship with human beings. And as Isaiah accepts God's invitation, he is able to hear God's call, and become a partner with God.

In what ways do you find encountering God frightening? Are there times when you expect nothing but judgement from God? When have you been surprised by God's grace? Think about what it means that God is God – the majestic, eternal Creator of all – and yet, that God seeks relationship with you. How do you feel about this? In what ways can you offer yourself to be God's partner today?

Pray:
We would never have expected it,
   but you chose us.
We would never have believed it,
   but you have called us to follow you.
We would never have known it could happen,
   but you have given us a place
      in your liberating work of salvation.

We are people of unclean lips,
   sinful men and women,
      weak and unworthy to be called by your name;
   and yet, against all expectations,
      not because we deserve it,
      but because you are gracious and loving,
we are chosen.

Thank you.
Amen.

Day Five:

Read: Philippians 2:6-11

Reflect:
This ancient hymn of the Church tells the story of Jesus in a concise and poetic way. This demonstrates both how God's story formed the foundation for the faith of the early Christians, and also how this story was told and retold in their worship. The call of this worship is for followers of Christ to embrace this story-telling not just as mindless repetition, but as an opportunity to open to God's Spirit again, and move into intimacy with God.

In what ways does the hymn of Philippians 2 speak to you of God's story? Read it again slowly, as an act of prayer and worship. As you do, become aware of God's Spirit reaching out to you through the words. Reflect on how this experience feels for you, and ask yourself how you can develop a regular discipline, both in church and on your own, of listening to God's story.

Pray:
Lord Jesus, in You we recognise what life can be:
    Recklessly loving, abundantly forgiving,
        and limitlessly free.
Thank You for offering this life to us again, now.
Thank You for removing the barriers
    that would keep us from this life,
    and for making us new again.
We praise You for the way You lived – opening doors of pain
    and guilt,
    and releasing captives.
We praise You for the way You died – forgiving sinners,
    and denying revenge.

We praise You for the way You returned from death –
   opening graves,
   and re-awakening hopes and dreams.
And, we praise You for the way You come to us now –
   stirring love in our hearts, and passion in our lives.

Amen.

Day Six:

Read: Hebrews 11:23-40

Reflect:
The Bible is filled with the names of people. The stories of those who lived out their faith in God are an inspiration for us, which is why they are listed in this amazing passage in Hebrews, but they also indicate a very important truth: our stories are important to God. As we gather for worship, we are invited to bring our shared struggles, and our personal concerns, and we know that God listens and welcomes us. As we cry out or celebrate, dream or wrestle in God's presence, our spirits reach for a connection with God, and God's Spirit is there to receive us. As we bring our stories into the sanctuary, and open our lives to God's grace and love, we find the intimacy with God that we seek.

Take a moment to think about the story of your life as if you were going to tell it to a friend. Go back a few weeks or a month, and think about the high points and the low times, the joys and griefs, the things you were proud of or pleased with and the things you regret. Now, in a simple prayer, offer this story to God. As you do, invite God's Spirit to fill you, and wait for a sense of God's peace or presence to come to you. Now spend a few minutes praying over any specific concerns or longings that you hold in your heart.

Pray:
This is my story, Jesus;
   It's very ordinary, very normal;

There are the usual small victories,
    small celebrations and signs of new life;
And there are the common small struggles,
    small failures and tears of grief.

I offer you my story, Jesus;
    Not just as an interesting bunch of facts about me,
        but as the pulse of my heart, the rhythm of my life,
    As a way of opening myself to your grace and love,
        so that we can become one,
        and so that my story may reflect your story
            a little more clearly.

Amen.

Day Seven:

Read: Hebrews 10:21-25

Reflect:

We may wish that life and faith were easy, that we could enjoy the best of both with minimal work and commitment, but we know this is not the case. All good things cost us in sweat and sometimes in tears. That's why the Bible often encourages us to "hold fast" or "hold on tightly" to our faith, to our hope, to our love, to God's promises, to God's Spirit. A big part of "holding on tightly" is to find encouragement in our gathering together, and in the regular, sustained disciplines of faith. It is as we continue, day after day, week after week, to pray, read the Scriptures, sing, share in Communion and meet in gatherings of worship that we build a history with God that takes our intimacy with God ever deeper. That's why we are encouraged not to give up meeting together.

How do you feel when it's time to go to church? Are you excited and expectant, or do you find it hard to motivate yourself to go? How do you feel about the idea that faith takes work, discipline, and sustained repetition of the act of worship? Have you fallen into 'consumer Christianity' where you go to church for the 'high' and to be entertained – for what you can "get out of it"? Or have you made a commitment to show up each week not for the goose bumps, not for the people, not for the spectacle, but for the long-term nourishment of your soul? Can you make – or renew – such a commitment today, and embrace your church as the place that helps you to build a history of intimacy with God?

Pray:
Sometimes it's hard, Jesus,
    to work on my soul;
When each day is filled with bills to pay,
    and the demands of people,
When I feel so often like I just need a break,
    a time to rest without the need for discipline.

But, I do know, although I forget sometimes,
    that my soul needs regular care,
        regular feeding and nurture,
        just like my body.
And so I pray that you would help me
    to see past the things that I don't like
        in some of my fellow worshippers;
    to let go of my need
        to be entertained or hyped up;
    to stop focusing on short-term thrills,
        or easy quick-fix spirituality.

Help me to find my place among your people,
    to find the glory in a community of faith,
    and to find the nourishment my soul needs,
        in the discipline of building a history
        of constant intimacy with you.

Amen.

Week Two: Welcome to a New World

Day Eight:

Read: 2 Corinthians 3:13-18

Reflect:

After forty days on the mountain with God, Moses rejoined the people, but they were afraid to look at him because his face was radiant with God's glory. In those days they believed that if they looked on God's glory they would die because sinful people cannot bear the holiness of God. But, now, for us everything has changed. Jesus has made it possible for us to enjoy intimacy with God, and has also made it possible for us to reflect God's grace and mercy through our lives and relationships. We need no veil. We don't need to hide from God's presence, and we don't need to hide the character of God that is beginning to be revealed through us. As we worship, we are invited to become people who encounter God, who 'see' God face to face, and to be people who carry the radiance of God with us into the world.

Who have you known that has reflected God's glory and grace to you? What was it about them that touched you? How have you experienced being changed by worship to be a little more like Jesus? Has this change been noticed by anyone else? What can you do this week to allow God's presence to be seen through you?

Pray:

You are God and I am me;
   and yet you welcome me into your presence,
      into your heart;

You are God and I am me;
   and yet you fill me with your Spirit,
      with your glory;

O Glorious God,
May my worship keep drawing me closer to you,

And may my worship change me,
> so that everyone I meet in whatever time or place,
may know your awesome goodness,
> through the ordinary person that I am.

Day Nine:

Read: Romans 12:1-3

Reflect:

Sacrifice is an unpopular word today, but in the Old Testament it was a normal part of life. In order to ensure that personal concerns, failures or desires did not break relationship with God, the people of Israel got used to a system of sacrifices – of giving to God out of the very best of their possessions. These sacrifices helped God's people to remember to whom they belonged, and who was caring for them, forgiving them and providing for them. While sacrifices are always difficult, the cost is worth the reward of intimacy with God. In Romans, Paul reminds the church of all this and invites them into a new sacrificial system – one in which they offer themselves to God completely and whole-heartedly. Through their offering of themselves to God in worship they would become people who were different from the people around them – free from the competitiveness, selfishness, aggression and disregard for one another that so often characterises human behaviour. Rather, they would become people who would reflect Christ's grace, humility and goodness.

How do you feel about the idea of offering yourself as a sacrifice to God? Do you have any hesitations or fears? Can you shift your thinking away from the negative – the cost – of the sacrifice, and toward the positive – the benefit – of greater intimacy with God? Have you experienced how offering yourself to Christ leads you into a more peaceful, humble, loving and fulfilling way of life? If yes, give thanks for this. If no, pray that God would lead you into this 'living-sacrifice' kind of living.

Pray:
I'm a little nervous of the word, Jesus;
   'sacrifice' sounds so negative, so painful,
   so little like the abundant life you promise.

So it takes faith to approach the altar, and lay myself down,
   to trust that what dies in me as I worship,
      is only what keeps me from life, from you,
   and that what is resurrected on the other side
      is what opens me to true goodness and grace and life.

Give me the courage and the love for you
   to offer myself as a living sacrifice
   to die every day, so that every day I can truly live.
Amen.

Day Ten:

Read: James 1:22-27

Reflect:
One of the main criticisms of Christians in today's world is that we are hypocrites. People get frustrated that they hear Christians professing to believe one thing, but then acting in a completely different way. It seems that James was frustrated by the same thing in his day. True religion – true worship of, and relationship with, God – must be expressed not just in word, but in action. As we encounter God in our worship gatherings, we cannot help but be impacted by God's grace and self-giving, God's love and service of us. But, if all we do is give thanks that we are now 'saved', if we fail to let God's character take hold of us and change us into true Christ-likeness, we have missed the point. And James makes it clear: Christ-likeness is shown by how we treat the "least" – the most vulnerable and weak among us.

Are there any areas of your life where what you say and what you do are different? Are there parts of your life that you are protecting from your worship, refusing to allow them to be changed by God? How do you think this is affecting your own well-being, and your relationship with God? In what ways are you prepared to invite God's Spirit to challenge you and change you? Who are the "least" in your world that could use some kindness, some "true religion" from you? How can you allow worship to show you how to serve them?

Pray:
Your words are important to me, Jesus,
> they inspire and comfort me,
>> they teach me and guide me,
> thank you for your words.

But sometimes your words are hard, Jesus,
> sometimes they ask me to **do** them,
>> to live them out in actions and words,
> and sometimes I wish I could ignore them.
Give me the courage to receive your words
>> not just into my heart,
> but into my life, my body and my mouth,
>> into my actions and attitudes and interactions,
> and let the truth of what I sing and pray in my worship,
>> be seen in how I live.

Amen.

Day Eleven:

Read: 1 Peter 2:5-10

Reflect:
Think for a moment about the 'world' you live in. What is the physical environment in which you live out your days?

Who are the people that you rub shoulders with every day? How do you believe this world 'works'? What are the values, ideas and attitudes that you carry with you through your life? Peter speaks about the way Jesus moves us out of a broken human context for living (darkness) into a whole, God-filled life (light). Which best describes your life at the moment – darkness or light?

The choice of what context we will live in is one that we must make each day. As we seek to live in the light, recognising the world as filled with God, and allowing our awareness of God's presence to be our guide, we become those who reveal God's goodness to others. Our worship is intended to teach us to recognise God's presence and light in every moment, every place and every person. This changes the way we see the world, and the way we live in it – it effectively changes our world, and makes it a different place for us. Are you willing for your worship to change your world? In what way can you allow your worship to help you make today a day lived in the light?

Pray:
The bits and pieces of this physical world are so real, Jesus,
    that it can be difficult to recognise your presence
        within it all;
But, in spite of the darkness that threatens to overwhelm us,
    the darkness of despair and cynicism
        of greed and exploitation,
        of violence and conflict,
We choose to believe in the light,
    and we ask you to open our eyes to your presence
        and grace
    so that we can live each moment as those
        whose lives are filled with light,
        and who bring light to everyone we encounter.
Amen.

Day Twelve:

Read: Exodus 3:1-6

Reflect:
Moses, after killing an Egyptian, had fled into the wilderness, as far from his people, and as far from God as he could go. But, years later, on an ordinary day, God captured his attention through the burning bush, and told him that he was standing on holy ground. What a surprise this must have been for Moses, that God had sought him out, that God had chosen to take an ordinary piece of real estate and turn it into a place of significance, of purpose. I suspect Moses walked more lightly on the earth after this encounter!

Think for a moment about the spaces that you live in – the buildings, the town or city, the architecture. Think about the building in which your community worships. Do any of these remind you of God's presence? Do any of the spaces of your world ever feel like holy ground? How can you allow your worship to make you more mindful of the spaces you inhabit, and open you to a sense of the sacred in every place? How can you change some of the spaces where you live in order to make them more helpful for living a God-aware life?

Pray:
I wish I could see a burning bush, God;
    I wish your presence would just "show up" in dramatic
        and arresting ways,
    making it impossible for me to miss you;
Yet, when I remember, I find burning bushes all around me,
    I discover that your presence is everywhere,
        and all the world is alive with God;
Forgive me when I miss you,
    when I go through my world oblivious to your glory,
        when I stumble blindly through the spaces of my life,
        unaware of their sacredness, and your Spirit.
Open my eyes to what worship is trying to teach me,
    and make me a person who respects the earth,

and the different kinds of spaces in it,
    as burning bushes all.
Amen.

Day Thirteen:

Read: Mark 1:14-18

Reflect:
    What is your relationship with time like? Are you always late and in a rush, or do you rarely consider time, focussing instead on other concerns? As Jesus began his ministry he proclaimed that God's *kairos* – appointed time – had come. This was a significant moment, a time when God's promised salvation had arrived and was available. Then, he began to call disciples to follow him. The *kairos* always seeks a response from us, and we can choose whether we will continue to be driven by the clock, or, while still living within normal time – we cannot escape it – we will open ourselves to God's activity and grace.
    As you think about the days ahead, what will you do if you suddenly become aware of a *kairos* moment? Can you use your worship, and your personal times of prayer and devotions, to prepare your heart to move to God's rhythms? In what ways are you able to practice the work-rest rhythms of Sabbath? Could you be more intentional about this?

Pray:
In the race against time, we often like we're losing, Jesus;
    it seems that there is never enough time,
        and that we have to ration our selves,
        our relationships, our energy.
How easily we forget that we are creatures of eternity!

Teach us how to recognise
    the *kairos* moments in our lives, Jesus;
    show us how to slow down,

how to open our eyes and our hearts,
and to dance to the rhythms
   of your grace.

Amen.

Day Fourteen:

Read: Matthew 18:19-22

Reflect:

There can be no question that for Jesus life – and faith – is worked out in relationships. There is no such thing as purely individual faith in the Bible. While we do need to work out our own relationship with God, we also need the companionship, the challenge and the sharing that comes from belonging to a group. If we are to become more Christ-like we need friends who love us enough to point out the areas of our lives where we fall short of God's standard of grace and love, and they need us for the same reason. This is why, when we pray together there is a special power – prayer mobilises as us a community. It is also why gathering together for worship gives us a special sense of God's presence – we discover new facets of God's character and work as we share with other spiritual seekers and learn from them and their stories.

To what extent do you try to keep your faith to yourself and make it purely personal? How connected are you to the community where you worship? How connected do you want to be? How do you feel about the idea of other people correcting you and reflecting back the broken parts of your life? Can you allow your worship, and your relationship with God, to make you more open to the gentle challenges and criticisms of others? In what way does the community help you to encounter God more profoundly in your worship?

Pray:
We long to find a place to relax, O God,
   to lean into the welcome and the love of real friends

>   who stay true no matter who we are or what we've done.
> We want to be known – not just our names, but our selves,
>   our dreams and longings, our fears and failings
>   and be warmly, unrestrainedly welcomed.
> We yearn to know the joy of opening our arms to others
>   and seeing them melt and grow soft in the safety
>   of our acceptance.
> And you have created a place like this for us
>   a place of people, with failings and disagreements
>   who still look out for one another;
>   a place of difference and struggle
>   where we can all belong;
>   a place of faith and deep doubt,
>   a place of awkward stumbling toward Christlikeness;
>   a place of worship, of mystery and of rest.
>
> And though we can't always see it,
>   although sometimes it doesn't feel like it;
>   the Church is the place.
> Not the buildings and the furniture – no, the people
>   who gather each week in your name
>   and try so hard to remember each other's;
> And so for the place of belonging we find in Church,
>   and for your being with us,
>   We give our heartfelt gratitude and devotion.
>
> Amen.

Week Three: Becoming Holy

Day Fifteen:

Read: 1 Peter 1:15-25

Reflect:

How do you feel about the word 'holiness'? Peter suggests to his readers that we are to be holy as God is holy – a daunting thought! But as we have seen in this week's chapter, holiness is not about obeying laws. It is about wholeness, compassion and hospitality. Once we have tasted God's hospitality, compassion and the gift of wholeness that God offers, we embrace holiness with joy, finding it to be the path to freedom and abundant life, not a life-limiting legalism. And, as Peter explains, the only reason we can even imagine becoming people of wholeness, compassion and hospitality is because of the sacrificial work of Christ. What a wonderful gift Jesus has given us!

Where, in your life, do you feel less than whole? In what ways do you struggle to bring your thoughts, your words, your beliefs and your actions together? To whom do you most struggle to show compassion? In what ways are you already offering hospitality to others, and where do you find it difficult to do this? Spend some time in silence reflecting on God's whole-iness, and asking God to make you a little more holy each day. Think about how your discipline of worship can help you in this quest.

Pray:
Sometimes it feels like it doesn't really matter, God,
   if we ignore the needs of our spouse,
   or shout at the kids unnecessarily,
   or elaborate on the truth just a little, so we look better,
   or waste the resources our world so generously gives;
Sometimes it just feels silly
    to worry about making things beautiful,
   to keep reaching for the best of the good,
     and not just the easy,
   to stay true to what is true.
What difference does it really make,
    in the big scheme of things,
   if we just take the easy way,
    the not-bad-but-could-be-better way?

And then we go to worship, and we remember.
You do not change to accommodate our good-enoughness,
 our that'll-do-ness;
You do not darken the sun just a little,
 so we won't feel so dull,
 or switch off some of the stars
 to keep us from feeling small.

You are holy – whole-y – one and complete and God;
 You are Light and Life and Love and Fullness –
 you can be no other;
 You are Beauty and Goodness and Truth –
 brilliant and dazzling;
And it is we who must change, we who gather to worship,
 It is we who must choose
 to gaze on your holiness & beauty,
 and be changed into glory.

And, so here we are, God. Please, show us yourself.
Amen.

Day Sixteen:

Read: 2 Corinthians 5:14-21

Reflect:

To experience God's holiness is to become a new creation. It is a radical change from what we knew before, who we were before, to seeing ourselves and others differently, to living with different values, motivations and attitudes. Two words that describe this new-creation living: love and reconciliation. We are controlled by Christ's love, and, having been reconciled to God, we are now called to be reconcilers. How better could we answer the call to become holy – whole, compassionate and hospitable?

How has your faith changed you? What does it mean for you to see yourself through God's eyes? How easily do you view others through the lens of God's love? Where in your life do you need to experience and share God's love more? Where do you need to embrace the ministry of reconciliation?

Pray:
A new creation – that's what you call me;
    a new person, with new attitudes and ideas,
        new ways of being, new ways of relating,
    thank you for this incredible gift.

But, to be honest, I don't always feel new;
    all too often the old person manages to creep back in,
        take over the reigns,
        and entrap me in my own brokenness.
Thank you, Jesus, for all that you did to make me new,
    and for all you keep doing to help me stay that way;
Thank you, Jesus, that in you I can see myself
        and others differently,
    and discover the freedom and joy of being
        both reconciled and reconciler.

Amen.

Day Seventeen:

Read: Matthew 5:33-37

Reflect:
Words have a frightening power, but it is often not what we say, but what we do that makes the biggest impact. When our words and actions align, when people see us and know us as people of integrity, we find wholeness and bring wholeness to others. But, when our words and actions are out of sync, when what we say cannot be trusted, when what we do contradicts what we stand for, the result is confusion and brokenness for us and for those with whom we rub shoulders every day.

To what extent is your life one of this kind of whole-iness? How do your words and actions align? Do you think people experience you as a person of integrity? Where are the places in your life that you know are not yet wholly like this? Are you willing to offer them to God as you worship this week, and allow God to make you more whole? How can you allow God's holiness to be your guide as you speak and act today?

Pray:
The simplest word,
   easy to say and quickly forgotten,
can leave a legacy of pain,
   or a long-lingering joy.
Yet we fill the air with our words,
   oblivious, or simply dismissive,
     of their impact,
   of the lives changed, for better or worse,
     by our careless chatter.
Forgive us, gracious and creative Word of God.

Teach us the wisdom of careful speech, and actions to match,
   the power of blessing,
     the healing of forgiving,
       the gift of truth-telling;
And give us the courage to speak out, to act out,
   to do our part in filling the world
     with life.

Amen.

Day Eighteen:

Read: Matthew 6:22-23

Reflect:
Light is a common metaphor for holiness. Light makes things visible, able to be seen and understood. Light guides us

and ensures that we do not get lost or hurt by stumbling over hidden objects. Light offers protection and comfort. God's holiness is like a light that leads us into safe and welcoming paths. And as our lives are flooded with God's light, we become light to those around us, pointing to the wholeness and hospitality that God offers. That's why we need eyes that are filled with God's light – that see things through the lens of God's wholeness and compassion.

What does light mean for you? List all of the ways you depend on light for your well-being, and give thanks for the gift of light. What does it mean for your eyes to be filled with light? In what ways do you think your eyes may still be filled with darkness? How can your worship help you to dispel this darkness in your life, and invite God's light in still more? Will you commit to one light-bringing act today?

Pray:
How we long to understand, O God,
    the simple logic of Light;

The power of a single glow to dispel darkness;
    the capacity of a single spark to create warmth;
    the immense energy in a single drop of sunlight.
 It's a simple logic, this message you speak:
    the light shines in the darkness,
        and the darkness cannot overcome it;

We praise you for the light,
    and for it's simple resistance to darkness;
We praise you for the radiance
    that never ceases to stream into us and our world,

And we praise you for the tinder
      that you have placed within us
    that waits patiently and quietly

for us to allow a single ember into our hearts
so that we might be set ablaze with You.

Amen.

Day Nineteen:

Read: Galatians 5:13-23

Reflect:
Paul offers a challenging contrast in his letter to the Galatians. On the one hand he speaks about a 'lawless' life – a life of following destructive desires – and a 'lawful' life – a life of following the Law of Moses, which brings no freedom or joy. On the other hand he speaks about love as the fulfilment of the law, and of the fruit of the Spirit that is produced in the lives of those who truly follow Christ. There is no law needed for this kind of life. If we ever needed to know that holiness is not about following rules, we know it now. But, this life of love can be a much harder way to live than following the law. It calls us to be compassionate even to our enemies. It challenges us to offer hospitality even to those we would rather not associate with. It confronts us with our own brokenness and the way it hurts others, while offering us wholeness, leaving us no excuse for not becoming 'wholeness-bringing' people. Can there be a more whole way of living than the fruit of the Spirit? And if it is so readily available to us, what stops us from receiving it?

In what ways are you still trying to achieve holiness by following laws? In what ways have you missed the freedom, and the glorious captivity, of living in love? Which of the fruit of the Spirit do you think are most evident in your life? Which are the least evident? In what ways can your worship help you to grow this spiritual fruit more abundantly in your life? Can you make a commitment now to open yourself to God's Spirit to do this work in you as you worship this week?

Pray:
It's so easy to live by the law, God;
>   just tick the commandments off on a list,
>>   and silence the whisper of conscience
>>>   with a legal score card;
>   no mess, no fuss,
>>   no people, no relationships, no confusing circumstances
>>   to consider.

But, that's not what you call me to, is it?
>   you ask of me a much simpler, more complicated thing,
>>   the nurturing of fruit that brings life and love,
>   the freedom - and the constraints - of character-building,
>>   of people blessing, of holiness finding.

As I grow closer to you, Jesus,
>   may I also become more like you,
>   may the fruit of your Spirit begin to grow in me,
>   and may I know, and share, the abundant life it brings.

Amen.

Day Twenty:

Read: 1 Thessalonians 5:14-28

Reflect:

It is tempting to fall into a kind of spiritual fatalism, leaving everything up to God – our needs, our purpose and our growth as Christ-followers. Equally it can be tempting to make spirituality another achievement – something we work hard at, excel at, and then show off to others once we have 'made it'. For Paul, though holiness is both God's work and ours. We watch Jesus carefully, learn from his ways and, through daily effort, we put into practice what we observe.

But, then we also wait, pray, rest, receive, and allow God's Spirit to work in us, to keep us, to challenge us, to inspire us, to strengthen us and to change us.

In what ways are you working to become holy? In what ways can you see evidence of God's Spirit working to make you holy? In worship this combination of God's work and our work comes together beautifully as we sing, pray, listen to the Scriptures and participate in the actions of giving and communion, while also opening ourselves to God's presence and transforming power. How can you be more open to the Spirit's work in you as you worship this week? And how can you be more intentionally engaged in worship – choosing to participate more in the 'work' of worship?

Pray:
I long to be holy as you are holy,
    to be whole and aligned
        in thought word and deed,
    to be compassionate
        to myself and my neighbours,
    to know the comfort and safety
        of giving and receiving true hospitality,
    and so I commit myself to this work today, Jesus.

But, you also long for me to be holy,
    to reflect your wholeness
        to the world,
    to be the instrument that shares your compassion
        with the weak, the poor, the excluded, the broken,
    to welcome all people into the home of my heart
        in your name;
    and so I open myself to your holy-making Spirit.

Thank you that we are in this together,
    that it doesn't all depend on me,

>   but that I have the dignity of being your partner
>   in my own becoming.

Amen.

Day Twenty-One:

Read: Philippians 1:3-11

Reflect:
Paul knew the value of a life of holiness, and so he often mentions praying for the churches he ministered to that they grow in their life of faith. He is very comfortable expressing his love for his companions in Christ, and reminding them of God's love for, and work in, them. In all of this prayer and encouragement is a simple message – holiness is a worthwhile goal to aim for, a worthwhile project to engage our lives in. And once again the essence of holiness is clearly explained: love and a fruit-producing life that reflects Christ's character.

To what extent have you seen holiness (whole-iness) as a goal to aim for in your life? How would you feel to have Christian friends praying for you to grow in holiness? Why not set up a small prayer group with some friends and commit to praying daily for each other to grow in holiness for the next few weeks? What small, daily discipline could you establish to keep you focussed on your journey to holiness, and how can you allow your worship to help you to stay on track?

Pray:
> God, whose word spoke life and creativity
>   into a formless universe,
>   and order to a nation of escaped slaves,
>   whose strong and compassionate voice
>   challenged injustice through frail prophets,
>   we praise you.

Jesus, whose touch smoothed the broken skin of lepers,
    and brought a bleeding woman back to health and belonging,
  whose hand raised dead girls,
    and refused to throw stones at prostitutes,
  we praise you.

Spirit, whose breath restores souls and bodies,
    and whose presence comforts the grieving,
  whose fire ignites compassion within us
    for the healing of the nations,
  we praise you.

God of wholeness,
  we celebrate the healing you bring to us and our world,
  and we celebrate the promised wholeness
    that awaits all of creation
    in your eternal reign.

Amen.

Week Four: Becoming True

Day Twenty-Two:

Read: John 18:33-40

Reflect:

How would you respond to Pilate's question, "What is truth?" How have you usually understood truth? What role does truth play in your life? Jesus tells Pilate that he has come into the world to "testify to the truth". This statement is the reason for Pilate's question, which is never answered, according to John's account. Perhaps Pilate was not really asking. Perhaps he was throwing his hands up and showing his scepticism of truth through a rhetorical question. There a similar 'suspicion' of truth in our world today, but perhaps that is because we have failed to take the question seriously. From Jesus' perspective, though, truth is real, available and important.

As you meditate on truth, ask yourself what the word 'truth' means to you. In what ways is your life built on truth? In what areas of your life do you think you're failing to be true? What it does it mean for you that Jesus "testifies to truth"? In what ways does your worship help you to find truth and live truthfully? How can you be more open to God's truth?

Pray:
We speak about truth all the time, God,
    defending it as if it was fragile and weak,
        as if we were its guardians,
        as if we could possibly hold its weight in our hands;

But, truth does not need us to protect it,
    nothing we could do can stop it being true,
        nothing we could do can make it more true;

But, when we think that our weak grasp of it,
    our small understanding of it,
        is the whole picture,
    we rob ourselves of the wonder, the mystery,
        the life-long journey
        that the quest for truth can be.

Help us to learn that the power of truth lies not in owning it,
    but in always searching,
        always questioning,
        always discovering;
    and help us to learn that truth can surprise us
        at any time,
        through any one.
Amen.

Appendix A: Guidelines for Daily Devotions

Day Twenty-Three:

Read: John 14:1-9

Reflect:

The startling declaration of Jesus – I am the way and the truth and the life – has been the cause of much pain both inside the Church and in those the Church has sought to reach. It has become a club with which to beat people of other beliefs and religions over the head. I wonder if this is really what Jesus wants us to do with these words. Perhaps, all he was trying to do was move our view of truth away from ideas, dogmas, doctrines, and toward relationship. Perhaps, Jesus wanted us to see truth not as a 'thing' but as a person – a person who shows us what God is really like.

How would it change the way you think of truth to see it like this? What would it mean for you to search for truth by searching for Jesus? And what does Jesus reveal to you about God? What if finding truth is less about getting the ideas right, and more about being connected with God, other people, yourself and the earth? How can you begin to make this quest for truth a bigger part of your life? How can worship help you to search for the truth that is a person?

Pray:

I need to look at you more, Jesus;
   I mean really look at you:
      what you spoke and the way you listened,
      how you treated people, how you prayed,
      the stories you told, and the love in your eyes;
I need to get to know you more, Jesus;
   I mean not just information, but connection:
      your presence, closer than breathing,
      your whisper guiding my ways,
      your example calling me to follow,
      your world, and everything in it, filled with you;

I need you, Jesus, because you are the truth,
   and the way to truth and life,

and the life that shows the way,
and the truth about the way of true life,
I need you;
and so I thank you
that you are here right now.

Day Twenty-Four:

Read: John 16:7-16

Reflect:
What an amazing privilege we have! What an awesome gift God's Spirit is! How wonderful to know that we do not walk this road alone, that following Christ is not just up to us, that we do not have only our own resources to draw on! The promise of God is the Holy Spirit who is available to each of us at all times, and who leads, teaches and empowers us. Now we know that truth is not something static, something fixed that Jesus spoke once and for all, but is a quest, a way, a journey. Now we know that we have a guide who will continue to lead us into truth. Notice that we enter truth. It does not come into us as if we own it or can contain it. It is far too big for us. We can only enter it, swim around in it, immerse ourselves in it, recognising that as much as we discover, there is always an eternity of truth still to be explored. This is why we need the constant whisper of God's Spirit calling us deeper.

What does it mean for you to be led into truth? How have you experienced the Holy Spirit doing this for you? How has God's Spirit helped you to view truth humbly, as something far bigger than yourself, something to be discovered for all eternity? How does worship offer you the gift of this humility, and the openness to God's Spirit of truth?

Pray:
God of infinite, eternal truth,
forgive me when I make truth small,

> when I feel that I can capture it,
> contain it,
> hold it,
> deal with it on my own terms;
> forgive me when I feel that I've got it sorted,
> that I no longer need a teacher,
> a guide,
> a counsellor;

Holy Spirit of Truth,
I humbly invite you to teach me,
to guide me, step by tiny step,
for all eternity,
into the truth that is far bigger than me.
Thank you for being so willing
to work with slow learners like me.

Amen.

Day Twenty-Five:

Read: 1 Corinthians 2:10-16

Reflect:

The mind of Christ. What an incredible thought! Does this mean that we know everything that God knows? Clearly not – our knowledge of the world is still so limited, and there are parts of the universe we have never even seen. Does it mean we never make mistakes, or we always have exactly the right assessment of what's going on? Again, experience shows us that this is not the case. So, what could it mean that, by God's Spirit, we have the mind of Christ? It must be related to the fact that Jesus is the truth, which means that as we follow Christ, and allow the Spirit to teach us to live out the Gospel of God's reign, we get God's perspective on the world. We think of justice and mercy, neighbours and enemies, the earth and its wealth from a Gospel viewpoint. We no longer think of truth as a set of ideas, and we no longer follow truth according to 'popular' opinion. Rather, we recognise truth as a way, and we embrace that way as Jesus did, understanding the world, and relating to it, as Jesus did. And this is the 'mind of Christ' that offers us truth.

When have you experienced seeing the world, or a specific situation, from a new, God-oriented perspective? How has following Jesus helped you to understand the world better, to relate to other people better, and to live in a more meaningful way? How does it feel to think of this as the 'mind of Christ' that is developing in you? In what ways has worshipped helped you to receive this Christ-perspective? How can you be more intentional in allowing God's Spirit to teach you through worship?

Pray:
It's your world, Jesus,
   and I can't understand it,
      I can't find my way in it,
      I can't act, or interact effectively,
   without you.
I need your mind, Jesus,
   your perspective,
      your example,
      your Spirit,
   if I am to find abundant life,
      and share it with others.
Amen.

Day Twenty-Six:

Read: John 17:10-19

Reflect:

God's Word is often the source of much controversy. On the one hand there are those who ignore it and believe that it is only a human book that is no longer relevant. On the other hand are those who idolise it and exalt it to a book of magic, and almost a fourth person of the Trinity. But, for Jesus the word is both important and subservient. It is a signpost that points to Jesus, a sacrament through which God's presence comes to us, a guide that shows us how to become holy and Christ-like. Without Jesus, the Bible is just words on paper. Without the Bible we would have no real access to the life and teaching of Jesus. In the sense that the Bible leads us to Jesus, and leads us in the way of Jesus, it is truth. But, if it begins to become an end in itself, it ceases to be truth and becomes the worst kind of deception. That's why Jesus prayed that we be made holy by God's truth – and in the role it plays in this process, the Bible is both God's word and God's truth.

What is your relationship with the Bible like? In what ways has it been truth for you? How has it pointed you to Jesus, and helped you to follow his way? Have you found the use of Scripture in worship to be helpful? How does worship help you to receive God's word, and be changed by it?

Pray:
Thank you for your word, Jesus,
    for the record of your life and work,
        for the wisdom it offers,
        and the truth it contains;
    Thank you that you meet me in its pages,
        that your Spirit speaks to me in its words,
        that your presence comes to me as I read it.

Thank you for giving me this signpost,
    this holy-maker,
        this search light,
    that examines my heart and life,
        and leads me in your ways.

As I follow you Jesus, I give thanks for your word,
    even as I remember that it points me to you.

Day Twenty-Seven:

Read: 1 Timothy 3:14-16

Reflect:
The Church is the community of faith in Jesus that preserves his teaching and seeks to follow his way. In this sense we are the pillar and foundation of truth – because we are the "Body of Christ". This means that the world should be able to see the truth of Jesus and his way in us. We should be a doorway to the truth that is Jesus. Unfortunately all too often the Church has been the exact opposite. We have kept truth from others, and have lived in ways that represent Jesus badly. Rather than lead people to truth, we have often turned them off it! Have you experienced this in Church?

But, sometimes we get it right, and the community of Christ followers really does reveal the truth of Jesus to the world. When have you experienced the Church as a doorway to truth? In what ways has the worship life of the Body of Christ helped you to encounter Jesus as truth? In what ways has the worship of the Church helped you to be a person who leads others to truth, and who reveals Jesus to your world? In your worship this week, seek to open yourself to a new experience of truth, and a new vision of Jesus and his way.

Pray:
We are the Church, Jesus,
   but sometimes we fail to believe it,
      and so we focus more on what divides us
         than on your call and the unconditional welcome
           that joins us.
   May your Spirit flow through us
      to bind and connect us in ways that not our diversity
         nor our self-righteousness, nor our sin can separate.

We are your Body, Jesus
   but sometimes we fail to act like it,

and so we grow more concerned with ourselves
    than the others you call us to serve
May your grace and compassion flow through us
    to heal and embrace all who are broken and wounded

We are your Messengers, Jesus,
    but sometimes it's easier to carry bad news, or no news
        than to challenge the powers that be, or to oppose injustice
    with the message of the Gospel.
May your prophetic voice be proclaimed in us
    in ways that encourage the despairing,
        liberate the oppressed
        and hold the powerful accountable.

Forgive us when we fail to be who we are –
    who you have called us to be
and teach us to live and to love
    as your presence in this world.

For Christ's Sake.
Amen.

Day Twenty-Eight:

Read: John 4:19-26

Reflect:
    Spirit and truth – two words that Jesus used to describe our worship. These two elements are not separate from each other. Our worship needs to be focussed on relationship – on intimate encounter with the one who is both Spirit and truth. The key here is the humility and openness that such worship requires. The Samaritan woman wants to talk about the "right" place to worship, the "right" way to do things. Jesus cuts across this and points to the sanctuary of the heart

which is where worship really happens. True worship is when we encounter God by the Spirit and find union with God. Worship in the Spirit is when we let go of our own preconceptions and idolatrous ideas about God, and allow the One who is Truth to meet us and change us. There is no "right" way to worship in this statement of Jesus. There is only the freedom to be lovers of God, and to allow our whole lives to be caught up in this wonderful union that changes everything.

How would you interpret the phrase "in spirit and in truth"? In what ways are they connected for you? How do you experience worship as being "in spirit and in truth"? Do you ever find yourself worrying over the "right" way to do things in Church? How does this affect your intimacy with God? What would it mean for you to abandon yourself to a "spirit-and-truth love affair" with God? Try it next time you worship.

Pray:
You are the pre-dawn glow
    that promises yet another new beginning;
You are the still dusk
    that brings rest to a weary world;

You are the prophecy
    of God's life-giving Word inscribed on our hearts;
You are the law
    that finds its fulfilment in love;
You are the mountain
    where the presence of God blazes and burns;
You are the valley
    where the face of God peeks out from suffering eyes;

You are the glory that we long for,
    the whispered rumour of a different order,
    the Shining One who transfigures all things.

You are the One we worship,
    in spirit and in truth,

in freedom and with abandon.
You are the One.

Amen.

Week Five: Becoming Beautiful

Day Twenty-Nine:

Read: Psalm 27:1-7

Reflect:
In a world that can be threatening and painful, a refuge that provides comfort, safety and strength is a valuable gift. The psalmist seeks such a refuge in the presence of God where he can gaze on God's beauty and learn from God. Beauty – especially the beauty of God – can be a healing and empowering refuge in times of crisis. Oppressed communities often use art to express their pain and to sustain their life and strength – think of the protest songs of the apartheid era, or the spirituals of the American slaves. In worship God offers this refuge, this place of safety where we can be inspired and empowered by God and God's beauty.

Where in your life do you feel threatened or at risk at the moment? Where do you feel in need of strength and a refuge? Can you enter worship as a place of safety? In what ways does worship help you to experience God's beauty, and how does this strengthen and inspire you? Why not allow God's beauty to heal you this week?

Pray:
It seems frivolous to speak of beauty,
   when the world is in pain,
      and we feel so threatened and unsafe;
But as we gaze on your beauty, O God,
   we find a surprising thing begins to happen:
      we see the world differently,

we are opened to possibilities we had missed,
we are filled with hope and faith,
and our strength and conviction rises again.

Thank you for giving us a sanctuary, a place of worship
   where we can find refuge in you,
   and be restored by the simple, mysterious act
      of gazing on your beauty.

Amen.

Day Thirty:

Read: Ecclesiastes 3:1-11

Reflect:
Life follows its own rhythms – there is a time for everything, and we all experience seasons of great joy and seasons of deep grief. Yet, if we will look, if we will open ourselves to the eternity that God has placed in our hearts, we will discover that in every moment, whether sad or happy, whether good or bad, there is beauty waiting to be discovered. God has made all things beautiful in its time, and if we will just open our eyes and hearts to this ever-present beauty, we find healing and strength and joy, even in the midst of the deepest pain. And God has given us the gift of worship to teach us to recognise and embrace life's many beauties.

When have you found beauty and joy in the midst of suffering and grief? What has enabled you to see it? How does worship help you to be more aware of God's beauty in the world and in your life? Won't you make a commitment today to seek for the beauty that is hidden all around you, and allow God to heal you a little more through his ever-present beauty?

Pray:
The Master has crammed His canvas with all that is beautiful
   filling it beyond capacity with hues and fragrances,

textures, tastes and musics to awaken the soul.
How glorious to live in this universe, O God!
    how our hearts vibrate with the artistry of Your love;
how our senses and spirits are enlivened
    by the beauty of Your glory
    revealed within and around us!
Our praise is too small to express our appreciation,
    our joy and our love
    that You have blessed us so.

How it must grieve You, O God, when we run from beauty,
    terrified of the passions it might awaken in us
        fearful that it may not last, that it might deceive us.
How your tears must flow when we choose
    what is ugly,
    utilitarian,
    functional alone.

Forgive us, Beautiful God, when we fail to embrace,
    and enjoy and be
    the beauty that You have desired and created;
And when we have robbed us others of beauty.

Renew in us the capacity for beauty which was in Jesus,
    and may we both reflect and celebrate Your glory
        because of it.

Amen.

Day Thirty-One:

Read: Matthew 6:25-34

Reflect:
    It is all too easy to get lost in the stress of worrying about our daily needs. Life is hard, and ensuring that we provide for

our families emotionally and materially, that we do what is required for our work, and also do what it takes to keep ourselves healthy, can all feel like too much to carry. But, if we can lift our eyes, just for a moment, to look around at the natural world, we may find our faith growing. Jesus certainly believed that the beauty of the birds and the flowers is able to teach us and strengthen our trust in God's grace and provision. What a difference it makes to life when we take the time to get in touch with nature. What wonderful lessons, and what amazing grace, we find among the creatures and plants that God has made.

How often do you get out into nature just to enjoy its beauty? How does your relationship with the created world (or lack of) affect your soul, do you think? When you see a beautiful sunset or flower, an amazing animal or a breathtaking vista, does this grow your faith? Why do you think that happens? In worship God teaches us to appreciate beauty and find wholeness and inspiration in it. How can you open yourself to worship and to its lessons of beauty-appreciation this week?

Pray:
When life gets difficult, God,
   it's tempting to just put my head down
      and work even harder to survive;
   it's tough not to feel like anything beautiful,
     natural,
        unproductive
   is a waste of time and energy.

But, you call me to lift my eyes, to open my soul,
   to allow the world to teach me,
      to soothe my stressed-out mind;
   and in the visions of beauty I see,
      the birds and the flowers,
      the trees and the hills,
   I discover your grace again,

and I am able to trust you
a little more.

Day Thirty-Two:

Read: Acts 10:1-16

Reflect:

It took great imagination to get Peter, the faithful Jewish follower of Christ, to understand that God wanted to bring Gentiles into the community of faith. It took great imagination for Cornelius, the God-fearing Gentile soldier, to believe that he could invite a faithful Jew into his home. No theological discussions or ordinary reading of the Scriptures could have done this. But, God believed in the power of the human imagination, and so God sends a vision – a gift of imagination – to Cornelius, which inspires him to send a messenger to Peter. And God sends a vision to Peter to prepare him to accept Cornelius' invitation. And as a result of these imaginative moments the Church, and the world, are forever changed.

How do you feel about the imagination as a gift of God? How comfortable are you using your imagination as a way to communicate with God or to hear from God? How open are you to offering your imagination to God, and allowing God to purge it and make it useful for God's purposes? Can you start by allowing worship to engage your imagination this week?

Pray:
It's like a children's game, this imagination of mine;
   it can be fun perhaps,
      maybe even creative in a frivolous kind of way,
   but, an instrument of God's reign?
      I'm not so sure...
But, then I read of visions and dreams,
   of people's whole worlds being changed
      as a result of imaginative moments,

and I have to acknowledge,
>   you gave us our imaginations, God,
>   and you want to use our imaginations for your purpose!

Teach me to make friends with my imagination,
>   to offer it to you as a gift of worship,
>   to listen to it as a translator of your voice,
>   and give me the courage to follow
>   where my Spirit-led imagination might lead.

Amen.

Day Thirty-Three:

Read: Psalm 96:1-13
Reflect:

The beauty and creativity of God are seen in all that God has made, and in this psalm the celebration is loud, vibrant and creative in return. Singing, rejoicing, bowing, bringing offerings – The Message translation even includes dancing – all are creative ways to express worship, and the context is "the beauty of holiness" or "God's holy splendour" (vs.9). In worship we are invited to recognise the beauty of God that surrounds us – both in the physical world we inhabit, and in the spiritual reality that flows through and around the physical. Wherever God is, there is beauty, and wherever beauty is, there is worship. All we need to do is join the celebration, and allow the beauty of God's holiness to draw us into deeper intimacy with God.

In what ways have you become more aware of God's presence through the created world? How have you become more aware of God's presence through "spiritual" activities like prayer, Scripture reading and worship? How have these activities helped you to be more aware of God's presence everywhere and in every moment? When you become aware of

God's presence, how do you usually respond? Can you open yourself to worship and let it teach you to become a more celebratory person, joining the worship of creation whenever you can?

Pray:
What an amazing thought!
> What a glorious reality!
Celebration is going on all the time!
> animals and angels,
> people and plants,
> all caught up in a majestic symphony of praise!

And I'm no gatecrasher – I'm invited, the door is open;
> all I need to do is join in,
>> to see the beauty all around me,
>> and give thanks
>> in whatever way I can.

Thank you, God, for your ever-present beauty,
> and for the eternal celebration
>> that reminds me of your grace and love
>> in every moment.

Amen.

Day Thirty-Four:

Read: Philippians 4:4-9

Reflect:
We are people with choices, and one of the most profound choices we can make, is with what we will fill our lives. The decision we make in this regard will change us, for better or worse. We can focus on loss and bitterness, on all that is wrong and how hard things are for us, and we will find

ourselves growing dark and despairing, and our lives becoming dry and brittle. Or we can choose to rejoice and give thanks, to focus on what is good and beautiful, to act and think in ways that are positive and contributory. If we will make this our choice, we will find our lives growing lighter and more beautiful, peaceful and fulfilling. And those around us will enjoy the benefit of our beautiful way of life. This doesn't require lots of money or special talents. Nor is it a 'Pollyanna-ish' ignorance of the world's pain and injustice. It is simply the recognition that the best way to extinguish the darkness is to light a candle.

Where are you tempted to focus on the negative, the broken, in your life and world? What impact does this have on you and those around you? When have you chosen to allow beauty and goodness to transform you? What has the impact of this choice been? How can you allow your worship to lead you into a life that dwells on goodness and beauty? Start practicing this kind of worship today!

Pray:
If our world needs anything, God, it's a new vision of beauty
    When we hate and make war on each other,
        we need to recognise the beauty in those
            who are different from us;
    When we exploit and rape the earth that sustains us;
        and the creatures that call it home,
        we need to recognise the beauty of creation;
    When we fear and hide and run from life's dangers,
        we need to recognise the beauty in living;
    When we suffer and grieve and die,
        we need to remember the beauty
            that remains even in darkness.

Teach us to know and love all that is beautiful, O God;
    Lead us into beautiful lives that open the senses of others
        to glory and wonder
    And through us, let the beauty of Your kingdom take root,

just a little more, in our midst.
For the sake of Jesus and His loving, saving purpose, we pray.

Amen.

Day Thirty-Five:

Read: Psalm 150:1-6

Reflect:
When it comes to worship, the best creative energies of human beings have always been employed. In this, and other psalms, loud music, dancing, and the beauty of nature and human creativity are invited to join the celebration of God's glory. Throughout the history of God's people, music, art, sculpture, dancing, poetry, stories, drama and architecture have all been offered to God in praise of God's majesty. What a tragedy that we have grown so suspicious of the arts in the Church! What a tragedy when those who serve the Creator of all should shut down their creativity out of fear or religious legalism. In a world that faces unprecedented challenges, we need creative people more than ever. And each of us – created in God's creative image – is one of the creatives that our world needs.

How do you feel about creativity in worship? When have you struggled with the creativity of other people and wanted to shut it down? When have you been afraid to express your own creativity? How does it feel for you to realise that you are made in God's creative image? In what ways can you offer your creativity to God as an act of worship? How can you let the worship gatherings of your church help you to do this?

Pray:
Creativity can be scary, Jesus;
    it questions the way things are,
        and offers new ways of thinking, of acting, of being;
    it expresses our deepest thoughts and feelings,

and leaves us vulnerable and open.
But it can also be inspiring and healing, Jesus;
   it leads us out of stagnant and destructive habits,
      and creates new possibilities;
   it shows us what we can do, and be and contribute,
      and makes us stronger and more hopeful.
Forgive me when I have been tempted to pretend
      that I have no creative ability,
   or when I have disparaged the creativity
      of my brothers and sisters;
Give me the courage to accept the invitation,
      to join the celebration,
   and to live my life as one
      who is made in your creative image.

Amen.

Week Six: Becoming Loving

Day Thirty-Six:

Read: Matthew 22:34-40

Reflect:

Love, it seems, can be a frightening thing. We don't really trust it, if we're honest. We think of love as something soft and fickle, something wishy-washy and weak. Clearly Jesus had a different view of love, though. He makes it clear that the entire Bible is summed up in the twin commands to love God and to love our neighbour as ourselves. This is the only command we've been given as followers of Christ! Yet, somehow we would prefer to reduce the Gospel to another set of religious laws, drawing lines to determine who is good and who is bad, who is "in" and who is "out". The law is always the easy way out. Love is much harder and more complex. It requires more of us – more listening, more seeking to understand, more involvement, more time, more energy. But, the law has never been able to heal us or our world. Only love can do that.

How do you feel about the idea that love is our only commandment as Christians? How are you doing in following this one commandment? When are you tempted to replace it with other, simpler laws? How can you allow your worship to reveal God's love to you more? And how can you learn to express your love for others in your worship gatherings?

Pray:
That's it, Jesus? Seriously?
   Only love? No other command;
      no other law?
      nothing else required?

You must know something about love that we don't, Jesus;
   You trust it so much more than we do,
      you believe its power so completely;
      how else could you have allowed it
         to drive you to the cross?

Teach me to trust love the way you do, Jesus,
   to open my heart to your love,
      and to learn to speak and act and think in love
      as you do;
Give me the courage to make the quest for love,
   an essential guiding principle of my life.

Amen.

Day Thirty-Seven:

Read: John 3:1-17

Reflect:
To really encounter God's extravagant, self-giving love can only change us. This change is so complete, so transforming that Jesus calls it a new birth. It's like we leave the old behind

and start a whole new one – a life that is lived in the reality and the principles of God's reign. If there is one word to describe God's reign it is love – the love that did not hesitate to sacrifice itself for the sake of the world. Once you know, in the deepest part of you, that God was prepared to choose death rather than abandon God's love for us, everything changes, and you find yourself striving to live in love in every relationship, every moment and every situation.

How do you feel when you consider that the cross was not too big a price to pay for God to show you God's love? When you hold this love together with the idea of being "born again" (as John does in his Gospel) what do you think this new birth really is? Are there any ways that you are afraid of committing to be a person of love? How can your worship help you to open to God's sacrificial love even more, and inspire you to embrace the cost of being a person who lives out of the love of God? Would you like to be willing to give up your life for the sake of love? If so, offer this as your prayer when next you join a worship gathering.

Pray:
You keep talking about dying, Jesus;
>about how life is found

not by white-knuckled clinging;
>but by a prodigal losing.

We nod and smile, and ponder the deep significance
>of these words,

and then, with a slow sigh of relief,
>we go back to our life-preservers;
>our safe, protected worlds;
>our well-sheltered, comfortable spirituality;

and we turn our eyes away from those who reach out to us,
>those we could touch with Your life,
>if only we would take the risk.

What were you thinking, Jesus?
>Surely faith is about finding life,

not laying it down?
Surely we need to follow You in order to be sure
   that life doesn't end when we die?
There'll be no dying today, Jesus – not if we can help it.
   And if your promise is to be believed;
      no dying at all – ever.

If only we could keep away the images of those others,
   the different, the lonely, the misunderstood,
      and the forgotten,
   the hungry, the abused, the least;
   the ones in whose eyes we glimpse,
      in unguarded moments,
   the outline of Your face;
   the ones in whose silence we hear a sound,
      not unlike Your voice,
      inviting us to carry a cross.

Day Thirty-Eight:

Read: Isaiah 49:13-19

Reflect:

God's people were in ruin – their country conquered, their Temple destroyed, and their people carried away into exile. No wonder they were tempted to believe that God had abandoned them. But, God speaks into their grief and suffering and offers them the image of a mother lovingly nursing the child she has born, protective and unfailing in her love. And, though sometimes mothers fail their children, God assures the people that God's love is sure – their names have been engraved, cut into the flesh, of God's hands. They are part of God's very being. This is a radical love, an excessive, unreasonable love. This love is offered to all of God's children, including you and me. No matter what you may be going through at the moment, God's love is right there with you.

Reflect for a moment in silence on these images of God's love for you. Allow your knowledge of being loved to settle into the deepest parts of your soul. Can you feel anything shift inside you? Do you find yourself relaxing and growing softer, less brittle or stressed? This is what love can do. Now think about the fact that everyone – everyone – is loved like this by God. How does that change the way you see other people, especially those you struggle to love? As you prepare to join your community in worship this week, allow God's love to come to you and try to lean into it – not just for you, but also for all those who are part of your life.

Pray:
It's more than I can take in, God,
   this palm-engraving love of yours,
     this extravagant commitment you have
       to the likes of me.

But, thank you for your love,
   and for your determination
     that I should know it.
I realise that the only way I will ever know
     if your love has really taken root in my heart,
   is when I can be committed to loving,
     even the unlovely,
   in at least a little of the way
     that you love me.

Amen.

Day Thirty-Nine:

Read: John 15:9-17

Reflect:
In Jesus the whole idea of relationship with God changed. From a distant monarch, unapproachable and dangerous to behold, Jesus shifts us to discover God as loving, welcoming

parent. More than that, Jesus calls us friends, close friends, friends for whom the Christ would lay down life! This is a God who is close and intimate, and a love that changes everything. But, of course, the love needs to be spread around – any friend of Jesus must be a friend of ours. That's why Jesus calls us to love one another even as we have been loved, to befriend one another even as we have been befriended.

Think about the people you worship with each week. Who do you consider your friends? Who would you struggle to be friends with? Who is easy to love and who is not so easy? How does it change things when you realise that just as Christ offers to be your friend, so Jesus offers to be the friend of all of these others? Are you willing to try and fulfil the call to love them as Jesus loves you? As you worship this week, ask God to fill you with love for those who gather with you, and seek, in some small way, to show them love.

Pray:
How many ways You have cared for us, O God;
   How many companions You have given
      to share our difficult and joyous journey.
And yet we forget Your care,
   and reject Your messengers.

Forgive us for failing to recognise You
   in those who are different from ourselves.
Forgive us for rejecting other people –
   children of Yours who are equally loved.
Forgive us for believing the lie
   that says we can do it our way, and we can do it alone.

Teach us to love as You have loved us,
   to embrace and welcome others
      as You have welcomed us,
   to enjoy and commit to the family
      which You have given for our comfort and nurture.

In Jesus Name.

Day Forty:

Read: Ephesians 5:21-33

Reflect:
    It is sad to see how this passage has been used to justify the oppression and abuse of women. When we make this passage all about women 'submitting' and men being 'the head' we have completely missed Paul's point. What Paul is really saying is that, in a society in which women counted for less than men, love would call Christ-following men to treat their wives differently – laying down their lives, sacrificing their own needs and desires, their 'leadership,' in order to serve and love as Christ did. When men, and women, love one another as Christ loved us, the world sees the Gospel in action, and they are drawn to its saving power. What a pity that we've allowed our brokenness to turn this passage into a reflection of the oppressive systems of the world! But, here's the mystery: when two people love each other sacrificially, their union reflects the intimacy that God's worshipping people enjoy with God.
    In what ways have human relationships hindered you from receiving God's love? In what ways have they helped? How do you feel about the idea that human sexuality is a metaphor for worship? In what ways can you allow your worship to become more passionate, more 'erotic', in the sense that you totally give yourself over to God? Try to hold this idea in mind when you worship alone or in community today.

Pray:
It feels strange to think of you as a Lover, God;
    to come to you with the vulnerability of intimacy.
Sexuality has been so devalued in our world,
    reduced to bodies and acts,
        stripped of meaning and connection,
    so it seems wrong to think of your love in those terms.

But, when we think of you coming to us,
    like a long-married couple:
        familiar and committed,

　　　　one in every way,
　　　then it begins to make sense,
　　　　and we hear your message.

You love us with passion and longing,
　　even as we long for you,
　　　and want to lose ourselves in you;
　　and, as a good marriage brings life and love to others,
　　　so you want our love to make the world
　　　　a more loving place for all.

Amen.

Day Forty-One:

Read: 1 John 4:7-21

Reflect:

　　The apostle John – sometimes called the 'apostle of love' – is adamant. Our love for God and our love for one another cannot be separated. After living for years with Jesus, and then living the rest of his life as a follower Christ's ways, he knows firsthand what it means to love God, and to love the neighbour as the self. And he knows that these loves cannot be separated. He even goes so far as to say that we lie if we claim to love God, but we don't love other people! This love business is serious stuff, and, according to John, is the defining characteristic of our faith.

　　To what extent would you say that your life is characterised by love? How do you deal with people – especially Christian brothers and sisters – whom you find it hard to love? How do you feel about John's claim that our love for God is not real if we don't love others? In what ways do you express love for God in your worship? In what ways do you express love for others in your worship? Can you find ways to bring these loves together, and make them both a central part of your offering of yourself to God?

Pray:
I do love you, Jesus,
   and I want to show it in my life;
That's why I come to worship,
   why I sing and pray and help out around the church,
   why I spend time alone with you when I can.
But, when you tell me my love must include other people,
   it gets much harder;
Some of these people have hurt me,
   some of them are so different from me,
      and some of them offend me deeply;
   why should my love for you
      be measured by how I treat them?
But, they are your children, and you love them,
   so how can I love you,
      and not love what you love?

Teach me to expand my heart,
      to make the circle of my worship bigger,
   and to include in my love for you
      these others who share your world with me.

Amen.

Day Forty-Two:

Read: John 21:14-22

Reflect:

   The big fisherman, Peter, had failed miserably. In spite of protesting that it wouldn't happen, he had denied Jesus, and now, Jesus wanted to reconcile with him. And so Jesus asks him three times – once for each denial – to affirm his love again. Peter does so gladly and willingly, but there is a hesitation when Jesus asks him to take on the role of shepherd to the community of believers. Looking back at

Appendix A: Guidelines for Daily Devotions

John, Peter asks Jesus about him – he hadn't deserted Jesus, why not choose him to care for the flock? But, Jesus won't hear of it – it's not about what John did or didn't do. It's not even about what Peter did. It's about the love and the calling of Christ, and so ultimately Peter must decide for himself to put his love for Jesus into action by accepting the call.

In what ways do you feel inadequate in your love for Christ? When have you failed, and felt that you are unworthy to serve God or love God? Hear Jesus asking you now, "Do you love me?" Respond honestly, and recognise any hesitation you may have. Now think about the ways that you can share God's love with others, and recognise God's call there. Can you offer yourself in service to Christ, even though you know you have failed – and will probably fail again? Can your discipline of worship help you to continue to commit to love and service? Allow God's love to keep flooding you, and challenging you each week as you worship.

Pray:
I am too aware of my shortcomings, God;
   I know how hard I find it to love,
      and how easily I stray from my commitment to you;
Sometimes I wonder why you would call me.

But, you do ask me to follow you,
   to serve your people,
      to care for the least;
You do trust me to love you,
   and to put that love into action.

And so I offer myself, as a gift of love,
   and as a channel for your love
      to flow to others.

Amen.

Week Seven: Becoming Purposeful

Day Forty-Three:

Read: Genesis 22:11-18

Reflect:

It's easy to miss the profound message of this passage by getting caught up in the moral question of Abraham's attempt to sacrifice his son. It was different world back then, and people did not have the privilege of seeing God in the incarnate Christ. In a world where child-sacrifice was common, the idea that God would step in to stop the sacrifice was radical and completely new. But, the really incredible thing is this – God chooses a human being to fulfil God's purposes in the world! Read that sentence again, and let it sink into your soul. God chooses to partner with us in saving the universe.

How do you feel about the idea that God seeks human partners for God's work? Would you like to be a partner of God, or do you find that thought intimidating? In what ways does worship help you to understand God's purposes in our world? In what ways does worship help you to participate in God's purposes? As you contemplate the miracle of being co-workers with God, respond in praise and thanksgiving, and ask God to show you what your part is in God's purposes.

Pray:

An old man and a young boy,
  a sacrifice stopped and a ram in a thicket,
    these things point to an amazing truth, God:
    that you use us to do your work!

And that means me, too;
  somehow I have a part to play
    in your saving and healing of the world.

It is more than I can understand
   that my daily routines, my ordinary actions,
      have eternal consequences,
   but that's what you tell me.

Help me to live up to your faith in me, Jesus,
   to give each day to you as an offering of worship,
   and as an opportunity to partner with you
      in bringing life and love into the world.

Amen.

Day Forty-Four:

Read: Jeremiah 1:4-10

Reflect:
The young man, Jeremiah, must have been shocked to discover that he had been made with a purpose in mind, that God had formed him for the ministry of a prophet. Clearly he was taken aback – uncertain of his abilities, and possibly of whether he even wanted the job. But his life was centred on this work, and through years of struggle, misunderstanding and persecution, he remained true to his calling. Maybe it was the assurance that he was born for this that carried him through. In some sense, Jeremiah's experience is true for us all – we all have specific gifts and abilities that are useful for God, and God calls us to use them in God's service. God does not call us to become something we are not. God calls us to offer what we are – what God has made us to be – in service of the Gospel.

What are you good at? How are those abilities useful to God? What are you not so good at? Have you ever tried to become good at those things because you thought you weren't what you are supposed to be? What if you let go of that, and offered yourself to God just as you are? As you worship this week, listen for a sense of call, for the place where your gifts connect with the work of Christ in your church and your world.

Pray:
We would never have expected it,
  but you chose us.
We would never have believed it,
  but you have called us to follow you.
We would never have known it could happen,
  but you have given us a place
    in your liberating work of salvation.

We are people of unclean lips,
  sinful men and women,
    weak and unworthy to be called by your name;
  and yet, against all expectations,
    not because we deserve it,
    but because you are gracious and loving,
  we are chosen.

Thank you.

Amen.

Day Forty-Five:

Read: Luke 4:14-21

Reflect:
If ever there was a person who had a sense of purpose, of calling, it was Jesus. At the start of his ministry, he made it clear what he was about – liberation, wholeness, upliftment, justice. It was clear from the very beginning: whoever followed Jesus was joining him in a whole new way of living in the world, a whole new system of relating to one another, of

sharing the world's resources, of deciding who was important and who wasn't. Everything would be different for followers of Jesus, and his purpose was to become their purpose, our purpose.

Read the words Jesus read from Isaiah again. What do those statements mean to you? In what ways do you believe that Jesus is still bringing good news to the poor, liberation to the captives and restoration to the blind? How do you feel about being part of this mission, even if only in a small way? As we worship, we are reminded of this purpose of Christ, and we are called to participate in it. How does your worship teach you to be part of Jesus' mission? Try and put one 'saving' action into practice in your world today.

Pray:
You were not playing games, Jesus;
    this mission of yours was not about cosmetic changes,
        not just reassuring the religious people
        or inviting the non-religious to consider a change;
Your mission was about changing everything;
    about a total overhaul of how people worship God,
        and how people treat each other,
        and how we live in the world.

But, what is so amazing, is that, from the start,
    you invited people to be a part of it,
        you called simple men and women
        to be your co-workers;
    and now you also invite me.

I long to be part of your mission, Jesus;
    I want my worship to show me your vision
        of what the world can be,
    and to inspire me, empower me,
        to loving, liberating action.

Yes, Jesus, I will follow you.
Amen.

Day Forty-Six:

Read: Matthew 5:13-16

Reflect:

Salt, giving the world flavour, and light, giving the world colour. Two simple things that make a huge difference to our lives. This is what we – as individuals and as Church – are called to be. God's mission is not about making the entire world the same – bland and tasteless. Nor is it about making the world black and white. Rather, it is about bringing out the rich and varied tastes, the hues and textures, in people and places and creatures. If the world is not a more flavourful, colourful, vibrant place because of us, we have misunderstood our mission!

What are your favourite flavours and colours? Now imagine that they were taken out of your world. How would that feel? Have there been times when your faith has done that to your life, or to others around you? Now imagine what a faith that adds colour and flavour to the world looks like. Wouldn't you love your faith to embody that more? How can your own personal worship be more colourful and flavourful? And how can you allow worship to teach you to be salt and light in your world?

Pray:

If not for light, the world would be dark and monochrome;
    no colour, no texture, no art, no beauty.
If not for salt, the world would be bland and depressing;
    no joy in eating, no exciting flavours,
    nourishment for the body perhaps,
        but not for the soul.
How two such small things
    can make such a big difference!

I long to be light and salt, Jesus;
    to bring joy and beauty,

richness and vibrancy to the world.
Won't you teach me, Jesus,
to use your words,
to embrace your attitudes,
to imitate your actions,
so that I can be a joy-bringer,
and a life-bringer to my world.

Amen.

Day Forty-Seven:

Read: Matthew 28:16-20

Reflect:

The call to make disciples is sometimes seen as a quest for some kind of global Christian empire. Teaching people to obey Jesus' commands is sometimes thought of as coercing them to become part of the Church. But, what if Jesus had something else in mind? If love was the heart of Jesus' message, perhaps the idea was for us to love people so much that they would want to know the God they saw in us. Maybe the only thing we need to teach is love – and that by example, rather than in words or doctrines. There is no question, though, that following Christ is not a personal, private affair. Following Christ leads us out into the world in a very public, very connected, way.

In what ways have you tried to lead other people to faith in Jesus? How has this worked for you? What do you think a disciple of Jesus is like? How would it be best to invite people to become disciples, do you think? If you were all anyone knew of Jesus, what do you think they would believe about him? How can you allow worship to lead you into deeper discipleship? And how can you carry your worship with you into your 'public' life?

Pray:
Sometimes I wish I could keep my faith to myself, Jesus;
    that I could be free of the pressure
        of people watching me to see how I follow you.
Sometimes I wish you hadn't called me to be part of your work;
    I don't want to be a "Bible-puncher",
    I don't want to sound like I'm judging those
        who find it hard to believe.

But, you ask me to share my faith, Jesus;
    to help people to know you and love you;
        not by 'preaching' or judging,
    not by proving them wrong,
        or threatening them with hell,
    but by allowing your love and grace,
        your wisdom and welcome,
            to be experienced through me.

Help me to be a disciple-maker, Jesus,
    in a way that is worthy of you.

Amen.

Day Forty-Eight:

Read: Ephesians 2:4-10

Reflect:

God made us. Then God remade us in Christ. This, as Paul makes so very clear, is a free gift. We cannot earn it. We cannot make ourselves worthy of it. Good works are neither necessary, nor effective, to receive God's grace. We are "God's Masterpieces", but God made us with a purpose in mind – to accomplish good works, not in order to be saved, but as a result of our love for God. Once we have been touched by God's mercy, and once we have recognised God's love for the world, we can only respond by signing up for God's mission to bring peace, justice, compassion and healing to all people.

What is the difference between trying to earn God's favour through good works, and doing good works because of God's favour? How do good works work out in your life? How do you feel about the idea that you are "God's Masterpiece" created to do certain things that God has planned for you? How can your worship help you to receive God's grace, and how can it help you to live a life of God-planned good works?

Pray:

How is it possible that you should think of me
   as your masterpiece, O God?
How wonderfully you made me,
   and how graciously you recreated me
   in Christ;

Let me always remember that I am yours,
   and that I was made for your purpose;
Let me always strive to do the good
   that you made me for,
   so that in my own small way I may contribute
      to the healing of the world you love.

Amen.

Day Forty-Nine:

Read: Philippians 2:1-13

Reflect:

Paul offers us an amazing promise in his letter to the Philippian church: God is working us, giving us the desire and the power to do what pleases him. As much as we want to love and serve God, God is helping us to fulfil our calling. And what is it that pleases God? The attitude and actions of Christ, demonstrated in his humility, his becoming a servant, his laying his life down. God asks us to follow Christ into this humble, sacrificial life, and God empowers us to desire it and do it. Thanks be to God!

As you read this hymn of the early Church that describes Jesus' attitude and actions, what stands out for you? To what extent do you think you embody the same attitude that Jesus had? What do you need to work on more? As you worship in the next few weeks, allow a vision of Jesus' humility to capture you, and ask God to help you to reflect it in your own life and relationships.

Pray:
Though you are God,
> with all the influence and status that the name implies,
>> you refused to pull rank,
>> and parade your power among us.

Instead, you chose to step down into our experience,
> living among us, as one of us,
>> with all the struggle and suffering
>> that goes with being human.

More than that, you adopted the role of slave,
> washing feet, serving people of no reputation or social standing,
>> and giving of yourself completely.

As incredible as it sounds,
> you are the God who serves,
> and we can respond in no other way
>> than to give ourselves to you in return.

Amen.

Day Fifty:

Read: Romans 8:14-21

Reflect:
Our faith is not just for ourselves. It is not even just for the Christian community. Paul makes a startling proclamation in his letter to the Romans – our faith is important for the whole of creation! The entire universe waits for us to "be revealed" as God's children, for us to stand up and become what God made us to be. This makes sense when you realise that Christ calls followers to continue the work he began – work of saving, healing, restoring. This means that our faith, and our worship, has implications for world economics, politics, climate change, human trafficking, poverty, HIV/AIDS, immigration, health care, education and every other part of our existence. All creation waits...May our worship keep reminding us of who we really are, and the difference that we are called to make.

How do you feel about the thought that your faith, and your worship, can make a difference to some of the big issues of our time? Which are the big questions that most concern you? Is there some contribution you can make to address this need? How can your worship inspire, empower and guide you as you seek to stand up to your full height as a child of God? As the journey of this book comes to an end, what commitment will you make today to continue to go deeper in your worship, and to continue to allow worship to change everything in your life? Won't you make it now?

Pray:
Every word we speak, every thought we think,
    every deed we perform, every situation we influence,
        has an impact on the world,
        for better or worse.

If we will only stand up and be
    the children of God we are,
    if we will only allow God's Spirit to lead us,
        and our worship to challenge and inspire us,
    if we will only give ourselves to you, O God,

>   wholly, intimately and passionately,
> everything can change;

> The world waits for those who will be
>   wholeness bringers,
>   truth proclaimers,
>   beauty imaginers,
>   love sharers,
>   and purpose followers;
> And we offer ourselves, in our worship,
>   and in the lives our worship creates,
>   to be the people you want us to be.

For Christ's sake.

Amen.

Appendix B

Guidelines for Small Groups

A significant part of the Christian journey is sharing with, and learning from, one another. Throughout the Church's history this has often been done in small groups, with great effect. The Wesleyan revival, which employed the "class meeting" is one significant example. As a result, the journey of this book includes guidelines for small group meetings, allowing members to interact with the material on a deeper level, and learn from one another as they wrestle together. Since the journey is fifty days, there are only seven small group meetings; each one built around one of the main chapters in the book. The introduction and chapter one should be read before the first meeting, and then each chapter should be read before the meeting dealing with that chapter. The conclusion can be read after the last meeting as a final, personal commitment to take the journey into the rest of life.

Each week, the structure of the meetings is built around the classic cell group format, and includes an ice-breaker, worship suggestions, and questions for reflection around the chapter and one main Scripture reading. These suggestions are all just guidelines, and small group leaders should feel free to adapt them as necessary. If your group is not comfortable with singing, either just skip the musical suggestions, or just read the words or listen to a recording.

The small group journey will, of course, be much deeper and more effective if each person also commits to following the daily devotional guide in Appendix A, and to worship services over the eight Sundays of the journey. I pray that you find this to be a helpful resource, and that your experience of worship, and of the life that flows from it, is deepened over the next few weeks as a result.

Week One: An Invitation to Intimacy

Ice Breaker:
Can you remember the first time you fell in love, or the first time you noticed someone who was deeply in love? Describe the experience to your group.

Worship:
Begin with an open time of prayer, in which group members are invited to offer prayers of love and devotion to God, either silently or out loud.

When you feel that enough time has been allowed for prayer, read Psalm 63:1-8 (if the members of your group are comfortable to read out loud, ask them to read one verse each in turn). Then spend some time singing two or three hymns of love. Some examples could be *Love Divine, All Loves Excelling, My Jesus I Love Thee, O Love That Wilt Not Let Me Go, I Love You, Lord, Breathe, Here I Am To Worship*.

When the music is finished, spend a few moments in silence inviting God to make you aware of God's love for you, and offer your love in return. Then think about people and situations you know where God's love is needed and lift them to God in prayers of intercession.

Close with a short time of sharing how you experienced God's love during this time of worship, and give thanks together.

Questions for Reflection:
Read John 17:21-23 and discuss the following questions together:

1. What do you think Jesus meant when he prayed that as God was in him, and he was in God, so we would be in God? (Vs.21)
2. When have you been aware of a longing for God within you? What made you aware of it?
3. How have you experienced being one with God?
4. In what ways does worship help you to experience your unity with God, and then live your life out of that unity?

Week Two: Welcome to a New World

Ice Breaker:
When have you experienced a time of great change? What was good and what was difficult about that experience?

Worship:
Start by singing together a hymn or two of praise, like *To God Be The Glory, Amazing Grace, Blessed Be Your Name* or *I Will Never Be The Same.*

In a moment of silence, think of area in your life where God has helped you to change for the better. Give thanks either in silence or, if you are comfortable to do so, out loud. Then move back into silence, and reflect on areas in your life where you feel you still need to change. Silently offer your confession to God, and open yourself to God's Spirit to work in those areas of your life. Close this prayer time with one or more people offering short prayers of thanksgiving for God's gracious work of change in our lives.

Go around the group and speak out people or places that need God's grace and love to bring about healing, transformation, peace or new life. In a time of open prayer, lift these situations to God.

Close with a hymn of thanksgiving like *Give Thanks* or *Now Thank We All Our God.*

Questions for Reflection:
Read Revelation 1:9-18 and discuss the following questions together:

1. What do you learn about Jesus from John's vision in the passage you just read? Try to think of the various elements symbolically rather than literally.
2. How do you feel about the idea that worship is meant to transform us? What transformations do you think God might be seeking to create in you as you worship?
3. What is the main "context" for your life? How would you change if you made living in the context of God's presence your priority?
4. How do you usually think about time and space? What are your happiest moments, and your happiest places to be? How can worship help you to find God in every time and every place?
5. Who are the people you most like to spend time with? Who are the people you most struggle to be with? How can worship help you to be more open to others – especially strangers, people who are different from you, and people with whom you disagree?

Week Three: Becoming Loving

Ice Breaker:
Describe your earliest memory of thinking about God. What pictures of God did you hold in your mind? What words did you use when you first starting speaking or thinking about God?

Worship:
Begin with a moment of silence.

Sing together a hymn of praise like *Immortal, Invisible God Only Wise* or *Indescribable*.

Share in a time of open prayer, encouraging each member of the group to speak out one image or word from the hymn you have just sung as their prayer. Move into a time of confession in which you acknowledge the ways you fail to express those same words and images in your own lives. Give thanks for the assurance of God's grace, forgiveness and wholeness.

Invite the group to think about the events of the world that have been reported in the news this past week. Invite each person to pray silently or out loud for God's wholeness to be manifested in one situation.

Sing together *Make Me A Channel Of Your Peace, God of Justice,* or some other hymn of commitment and service.

Questions for Reflection:
Read Isaiah 6:1-8 and discuss the following questions together:

1. What were the main elements of Isaiah's experience here? How was he changed by experiencing God's holiness?

2. When have you had a new insight into God's glory or holiness in worship? How did that affect you and the way you live?

3. Before you read this chapter, how would you have described "holiness"? How would you explain it now?

4. Where, in the world around you, or in your own life, do you see a need for the "quickening of conscience"?

5. What one thing can you do this week to live a more "whole-y" life?

Week Four: Becoming True

Ice Breaker:
Have you ever lied or been lied to? Share the circumstances when this happened, and how it made you feel. What were the results of the lie for you and others involved?

Worship:

Read Psalm 25:1-10 responsively, then invite the group to pray out loud, in a single sentence or word, one prayer that arises in them from the Psalm.

Sing *Lord, Reign In Me* or *O Word Of God Incarnate* or some other hymn about God's truth and how it touches us.

Spend a few moments in silence inviting God's Spirit to fill you again, and open your mind to the truth of God.

Let each member of the group speak out one word that comes to mind for them when they think about the truth of God, and then offer a short prayer giving thanks for God's truth expressed in all of these different ways.

Close with a song that opens your heart to God in preparation for your conversation. Some possibilities could be *Lord, I Give You My Heart* or *Dear Master, In Whose Life I See* (in some countries this is sung as "Dear Jesus").

Questions for Reflection:

Read John 4:21-24 and discuss the following questions together:

1. What do you understand by the words "in spirit and in truth"? Why is it important to worship like this?
2. How comfortable are you with your mind? Do you live in your mind, or do you find it hard to take time to think, reflect and know?
3. Have you ever confused truth with facts? Have you ever been in a situation in which you came to realize that the truth was more than the facts? If not, can you imagine what this might be like?
4. In what way is Jesus the truth to you? In what ways would you like to live the truth of Jesus' way more effectively?
5. When have you experience being "fed with the truth of God" in worship? How did that happen for you? How can

make being fed with truth a more regular part of your worship?

Week Five: Becoming Beautiful

Ice Breaker:
What would you consider to be one of the most beautiful things you have ever seen or experienced? What impact did this beauty have on you?

Worship:
Start by reading Job 38:1-18 with each member of the group reading one verse in turn. Respond by singing a hymn of praise like *All Creatures Of Our God And King, All Things Bright And Beautiful, Creator King* or *How Great Thou Art.* Then spend a moment in open prayer offering words or sentences of praise for God's beauty and creation.

Move into a time of silent reflection on times when your lives have failed to reflect or appreciate God's beauty and offer your confession. Finish this moment by letting one member of the group speak God's words of forgiveness over you.

In a moment of reflection play a piece of beautiful music, or, if you have the facilities, a short video of great beauty, and invite the group to meditate on the sounds and/or images. Finally, offer a few short prayers for places in your community that need to be beautified in some way.

Questions for Reflection:
Read Philippians 4:4-9 and discuss the following questions together:
1. How good are you at thinking about good things, as Paul describes? How can you be better at making good things your focus?

2. Paul promises that God's peace comes to us when we focus on goodness and beauty. How have you experienced this?
3. How comfortable are you with your imagination? Have you ever allowed your imagination to be a significant part of your prayer or worship experience? What was the result?
4. What is your response to the "three transcendents" of the ancient Greeks (the good, the true and the beautiful). How do they each help you to understand the other two?
5. In what ways does worship help you to be more aware of beauty, and God's presence in what is beautiful? In what ways does worship help you to be a more beautiful person?

Week Six: Becoming Loving

Ice Breaker:
If someone asked you what love is, how would you describe it? Share a story about a time when you felt deeply loved. How did this experience change you?

Worship:
Begin your worship by passing the peace. Then offer prayers of thanksgiving for one another and for the love you are learning to share in your group (you can do this in pairs or small sub-groups if that would work better for your group).

Sing together a hymn or two of thanksgiving like *It Passeth Knowledge That Dear Love Of Thine*, *Great Is Thy Faithfulness*, or *Give Thanks*.

Read 1 Corinthians 13:4-8a responsively, and then spend a few minutes thinking over the last week. Bring to mind any times when you have behaved in a less than loving way to others. Offer your confession, giving thanks for God's forgiveness and grace.

Share any needs of people or situations you know where God's love is needed, and then move into a time of open prayer as you lift these needs to God. Finish the prayer by saying the Lord's Prayer together.

Close the worship time with a hymn celebrating God's love like *Come Let Us Sing Of A Wonderful Love, I Could Sing Of Your Love Forever (Over the mountains and the sea)* or *Forever*.

Questions for Reflection:

Read 1 John 4:7-12 and discuss the following questions together:

1. How do you respond to John's assertion that when we know love we know God, but if we don't know love, we don't know God? When have you experienced this to be the case in your own life?
2. What is your response to the assertion in this chapter that law is the only commandment we have been given as Christians? What are the implications of this for your life, your faith and your worship?
3. How would you describe a closed heart and an open heart? What tempts you to close your heart? What helps you to open it?
4. If loving God's way is about moving from "need love" to "gift love" in all the different loves of our lives, how can you practice doing this with your family, your friends and your companions in church?
5. How does worship help you to receive and give love more freely?

Week Seven: Becoming Purposeful

Ice Breaker:
What do you think of the idea that God has a purpose for your life? In what ways are you cooperating with this purpose already?

Worship:
If you are able to, you may want to share in communion as the central act of your worship this week. Make sure a comfortable space is prepared with the communion elements. Depending on your church's tradition you may need to have the elements consecrated before hand, or invite one of your ministers to share with you that evening. If you can't share in communion, perhaps just share a small love feast, breaking bread together, but without the usual words of consecration and memory.

Begin with a time of silent preparation and thanksgiving. Ask someone in the group to read Psalm 139:1-18, and respond with prayers of thanksgiving and praise. Then sing a hymn or two celebrating God's purpose and calling like *Be Thou My Vision, Guide Me O Thou Great Jehovah* (some hymn books use the word Redeemer), *May The Words Of My Mouth,* or *Shout To The North And The South.*

Spend some time in intercession for others and for the world. Finish by committing to one small thing you can each do to help to answer your own prayers. Share it with the group.

Now move into communion, or the love feast (if you are going to do this). Serve each other as you do, and give thanks for the way Christ has served us in his life, death and resurrection. Invite God's spirit to fill you and empower you as you seek to follow Christ in your life to come.

Close with a prayer of thanksgiving, and a hymn like *Take My Life And Let It Be* or *I Will Offer Up My Life.*

Questions for Reflection:
Read Luke 4:14-21 and discuss the following questions together:

1. Identify all the different elements of Jesus' purpose as found in this passage (good news to the poor etc.). Share what each one means to you.

2. In what parts of your life do you feel that you have a clear sense of purpose? Are there any areas where you feel you lack purpose? What is the impact of this on your life?
3. In what way can you co-operate with Jesus' purpose of "bringing heaven to earth"? How can worship teach you to do this more?
4. How strong is your will? Do you easily make and keep your decisions and commitments, or do you often have crises of "willpower"? Are you willing for God to work on your will?
5. How has worship helped you to become a more purposeful person? How can you allow it to do this work more in your life?

Appendix C

Guidelines for Sunday Worship

It should come as no surprise, after the Introduction to this book, that I believe in the power of Sunday services to open us to God's transforming Spirit. As a result of this, I have included this final Appendix, a collection of suggestions for the eight Sunday services of this fifty-day journey. Each Sunday is based on one of the Chapters of the book, starting at Chapter One. The Eighth Sunday is a final ending for the journey, and so relates loosely to the Conclusion, but is really an opportunity for you to lead your congregation into whatever direction this quest has suggested for you. The best use of these resources is if the whole church is sharing together in reading the book, practicing the daily devotions, and meeting in small groups.

All the resources and ideas listed here are offered not as directives, but as suggestions, as stimulants for your own creativity. As such, they can and should be adapted, used or discarded according to your church's specific needs. All I ask is that the content of the book be kept as the primary guideline.

The prayers can be used as is, or replaced with prayers from the daily devotions or from another source entirely. The liturgies that are suggested are for use, either without the Eucharist as an additional source of prayers, or with Holy Communion, as the basis for the service. They are all from my first book *Food for the Road – Life Lessons from the Lord's Table*, and are available as free downloads from Sacredise.com.

I need to offer an apology to those whose worship does not follow English language customs. In South Africa, in particular, where we have eleven official languages, and a number of different worship traditions, many of the hymns mentioned here will hold little relevance. Likewise, the prayers may need translation of idiom and form as much as of language. I can only offer the following defence: my work arises from my own primary context, which is English, and which employs a worship form that blends traditional and contemporary elements. Further, my work is primarily used by churches that have a similar worship 'culture'. I hope, though, that the suggestions offered here may still provide stimulus for creative practice in worship in whatever context this book is used.

Finally, I pray that your worship may be deep, celebratory and transforming as you journey together in the Hour That Changes Everything.

Week One: An Invitation to Intimacy

Readings:
Ezekiel 16:4-14
Psalm 42
Ephesians 5:21-32
John 17:1-5, 20-26

Sermon Starter:
The key to this week's worship is the availability of union with God. Each of these passages speaks in a different way about how God longs for intimacy with human beings. The Ezekiel prophecy uses the image of an infant girl found abandoned, nurtured and raised into a beautiful woman, who is then claimed by God as God's bride. The Psalm speaks of the longing God has for us, and us for God, in the language of the

depths within us calling out for connection. Paul's letter to the Ephesians uses the metaphor of the marriage union to reflect the union of Christ and the Church, and in Jesus' prayer he prays for us to know God's love, revealed in Christ, and to be one with the Godhead, even as God is one within God's self. This is the invitation to intimacy that God offers.

The worship will flow into the journey of this chapter (which continues through the personal devotions and small group meetings this week) if it is allowed to connect with the longing of God's people for a real, lived experience of God, and if it reassures the worshippers that God does not play "hard-to-get". Try to start the journey off with a real sense of meeting with God, and with a message that creates a sense of expectation and welcome for God's people. Help listeners to know that the adventure of the next few weeks is not simply an academic exercise, but, while deepening understanding, will be an experiential encounter with God. The metaphors of intimacy, of getting married, or of falling in love, can all be used as possible contact points and 'hooks' for driving the message home.

Prayers:
An Invitation To Intimacy

How can it be that you, Great God,
    should long for us?
How can it be that you seek us out,
    longing for connection,
        intimacy,
    for the opportunity to give yourself again,
        freely, recklessly,
    to enfold us in your love?

It seems impossible that we could find such union with you,
    that we could truly know you,
        and experience true connection with you;
But this is what you promise,

this is your invitation,
>   this is what true God-seekers have always found
>   when they have embraced the quest.

We praise you, Great God, for your availability,
> for your humility and hospitality,
>> and with grateful hearts,
>> we accept your invitation today.

Amen.

Intimacy Lost And Found

Though you long for us and we long for you, O God,
> we still wander lost and alone,
>> bringing pain and grief
>> to ourselves and others;

Though you seek us out, and we want to be found, O God,
> we still forget or deny your presence,
>> living as if you did not exist,
>> and becoming addicted to things that do not satisfy;

Though you invite us into intimacy, O God,
> we still choose cold legalism and dry observance,
>> leaving our souls empty and thirsty,
>> and passing our lifelessness on to others;

Forgive us when, through ignorance, neglect or choice,
> we miss the opportunity for union with you,
>> and we fail to receive and share abundant life
>>> because of it;

Teach us to live in this world as lovers of God,
> to move through this world always in your presence,
> and to touch the world always with your healing;

May peace and joy and love be spread
> to every corner of our world,

> as our worship and our lives draw all others
> > into your embrace.

Amen.

Liturgy:
A Liturgy for Communion

Hymn Suggestions:
Love Divine, All Loves Excelling
O Love That Wilt Not Let Me Go
My Jesus I Love Thee, I Know Thou Art Mine
Great Is Thy Faithfulness
I Love You, Lord
Breathe
Here I Am To Worship
Creator King

Week Two: Welcome to a New World

Readings:
Exodus 34:28-35
Psalm 1
2 Corinthians 3:13-18
Mark 9:2-9

Sermon Starter:
The focus this week is on how our world is changed as we worship, because we are changed. In Exodus, Moses, confronted with God's presence, is changed to reflect God's glory – and his world is more glory-filled. Paul, referring to Moses' experience, proclaims that we are changed in a similar way. Psalm 1 celebrates the changes that come to those who are in union with God, and in Mark's account of the transfiguration, it is not only Jesus who is changed, but the

disciples, and their world, as they go back into ministry after this transforming encounter with Christ.

A key moment here is Peter's desire to stay in this place of worship and intimacy with God. We all know this longing, but Jesus' response is to draw the disciples back into the real world – although that world is now changed for them, alive with God's glory and presence – and to lead them into the ministry that will ultimately take his life.

The worship, and the preaching, this week, is centred on how our 'external world' (the way we perceive and interact with the world and the people in it) is changed by our encounters with God. This change is sometimes difficult, even painful, but it ultimately leads us into a world filled with God, and into the abundant life that Jesus offers us.

Prayers:
Amazing God

You're amazing, God,
  The way you paint the sky
    with endless combinations of colours,
  The way you fill the world with countless creatures,
    all so different, all so unique.

You're amazing, God,
  The way you hide in the faces of people,
  How, if we look long enough and carefully enough,
    we see you in the plump smile of the newborn,
      and the loose skin of the elderly,
    the shocking challenge of those who seem
      so strange to us,
    and the comforting familiarity of those
      who seem so normal.

You're amazing, God,
  The way you never stop finding ways to remind us of you,
  How, if we will only let you,

you take our hand and lead us into life,
vibrant and rich and overflowing.

Isn't strange how we so easily choose to listen
to voices other than yours?
to follow guides that lead us away from you?
Isn't it strange how often we search for life apart from you,
and then wonder why we never find it?

Forgive us our foolishness,
and please don't ever stop whispering to us of your love.
In Jesus' Name.
Amen.

Tough Transformation

It's not that we don't want to change, God,
it's just that change is really hard;
the challenges of the world threaten to overwhelm us,
the struggles of living each day
come close to being too much,
and so we are tempted to grab the quick-fix,
the easy solution,
and inevitably, we our disappointed.

So we pray,
reach into our hearts with courage and hope,
to embrace the tough transformations,
to make the real and lasting changes,
to seek the truly good answers;
for the sake of our families and communities,
our countries and our continents,
our people and our planet,
for the sake of our very selves;

May we find, together and alone,
the strength to climb the mountain

and see your glory;
and then to walk to the cross,
through the pain,
until we know the joy and glory
of resurrection.

Amen.

Liturgy:
A Liturgy for the Spiritual Feast

Hymn Suggestions:
To God Be The Glory
Praise To The Lord, The Almighty
Amazing Grace
How Great Thou Art
Hear Our Praises (May our homes be filled with dancing)
How Great Is Our God
Give Thanks
Change My Heart, O God

Week Three: Becoming Holy

Readings:
Isaiah 6:1-8
Psalm 51
1 Peter 1:12-19
Luke 6:27-38

Sermon Starter:
The central focus of this week's worship is the way God's holiness quickens our conscience. Essentially this mean that in worship, we receive a vision of God's holiness, and this makes us people who are more just, more ethical, more compassionate, more hospitable and more filled with integrity. Our conscience – the voice that tells us what's right and

wrong – is formed, shaped and made alive in our worship. The point of contact lies in the crisis of conscience that is evidenced in corruption, falsehood and heartlessness – painful qualities we encounter every day.

Isaiah's vision reveals how God both convicts and heals as we worship. David's Psalm of repentance is a great example of bringing our brokenness into God's presence so we can be made whole. Peter's letter encourages us to be holy as God is holy, placing this in the context of God's call for us to become people who are not focussed on satisfying ourselves, and of Christ's sacrifice on our behalf.

The challenge here is to allow holiness to be shown for what it is – not a legalistic, boring, religiosity, but a vibrant, warm and welcoming life of compassion and wholeness. This means that the worship, and the preaching elements of it, can be quite celebratory this week.

Prayers:
Holy God

We praise you God,
   for you are holy,
      truly God,
      truly whole and consistent and one;

We praise you God,
   for your holiness does not separate you from us,
      but draws you toward us,
      into our brokenness and sin,
         our darkness and division;

We praise you God,
   that you invite us into your holiness,
      that you welcome us into your hospitable kingdom,
      that you make us whole, undivided, one,
      that you embrace us with compassion,
         even as you teach us to be compassionate;

We praise you that in your holiness,
    and in becoming holy,
      we find life and grace and renewal.

Holy God, we praise you and give you thanks.

Amen.

True Whole-iness

I sometimes wonder how it makes you feel, God,
    when we speak of you
      in the hushed tones of fear,
    when we think of holiness
      as rigid rule-keeping,
      and harsh separations;
Forgive us when we reduce your warmth and welcome,
    your compassion and wholeness,
      to cold religion.

Teach us to be people of true holiness;
    of compassion and loving obedience,
      of hospitality and healing,
May we be those through whom the world
    becomes more friendly and flexible,
      more accepting and inviting,
      more caring and protective;
And may holiness – your whole-iness
    flood the world.

In Jesus' Name
Amen.

Liturgy:
A Liturgy for the Agape

Hymn Suggestions:
Immortal, Invisible, God Only Wise

Crown Him With Many Crowns
Praise, My Soul, The King Of Heaven
Holy, Holy, Holy, Lord God Almighty
God Of Wonders
Ancient Of Days
Lord, Reign In Me
Shout To The North And The South

Week Four: Becoming True

Readings:
Isaiah 55:1-11
Psalm 19
John 4:1-26
Romans 11:33-12:3

Sermon Starter:
This week, the challenge is to speak of truth in terms of the person, Jesus, and the way Jesus taught. These readings are designed to lead you into this theme. Isaiah speaks about God's goodness, freely given, alongside the higher perspective of God's thinking and word. Psalm 19 speaks about the wisdom and goodness of God's commands and truth. Romans invites us to renew our minds in worship, and John, while calling us to worship in spirit and truth, tells the story of a woman who's whole way of thinking and being was transformed by an encounter with Jesus. Hopefully our worship will enable us to experience this kind of change for ourselves.

The key activity this week is to try and move truth out of the realm of 'ideas' and 'concepts' and into the realm of 'being', 'living' and 'doing' – away from doctrine and fact, and into behaviour and character. For preachers, the temptation could be to get caught up in explaining the idea of truth, where it would probably be more helpful to invite people into an experience of truth, both in the word and in the prayer and music. If you can offer some practical examples from your own community to illustrate the "way of truth", that would be very helpful.

Prayers:
Word of God

Like bread that feeds us,
    wine that quenches our thirst,
Like fire that warms us,
    a blanket that wraps around us,
Like the nurture of a mother,
    the attention of a lover,
Your Word whispers into our souls,
    nourishing,
    strengthening,
    empowering.

We praise you, Jesus,
    Word of God,
        Bread of Life,
    for your kindness to us;
And for the words you give us
    to speak,
        to live,
    which fill the world with kindness,
        and life.

Amen.

Truth

In every place of power,
    where truth is redefined to mean
        whatever the powerful choose;
In every place of wealth,
    where the price of truth is set
        by the highest bidder;
In every place of lust,

where truth is distorted
    by greed and desire;
In every place of grief,
    where the wounds of broken truth
        are shared by the weak and poor,
        by the bereaved and the discarded;
May your truth continue to feed our minds,
    and change our hearts,
  so that we may, in our own small way,
    know and share
        the nurturing, nourishing light of your kingdom.

Amen.

Liturgy:
A Liturgy for the Sacrament

Hymn Suggestions:
O Word Of God Incarnate
Dear Master In Whose Life I See (Some versions use "Dear Jesus")
Tell Me The Old, Old Story
Come Holy Ghost, Our Hearts Inspire
Shine Jesus Shine
Lord, I Give You My Heart
May The Words Of My Mouth
Thy Word Is A Lamp Unto My Feet

Week Five: Becoming Beautiful

Readings:
Joel 2:23-32
Psalm 96
Philippians 4:4-9
Matthew 6:25-34

Sermon Starter:
Whatever happens in the service this week, strive to make it beautiful. Be as creative as possible, and create space for the artists in your community to shine. Try to include extra displays of natural beauty as well – flowers, plants, water features. Allow the beauty to speak for itself as much as possible. In the sermon try to use stories, metaphors and images as much as you can. Make the whole service a celebration of, and an opening to, beauty.

In terms of content, the readings open the door to explore how beauty speaks to us, challenges us and changes us. Joel's prophecy speaks about God's activity being seen in nature, and in the powerful imaginations of dreamers and prophets. Psalm 96 praises God's beauty, and describes how all of creation joins in the adoration. In Philippians, Paul invites us to find peace by focussing our thoughts on what is good and true and beautiful, and in Matthew's Gospel, Jesus points to flowers and birds as examples of God's love and care – inviting us to allow nature and its beauty to teach us trust and faithfulness.

The heart of the message this week is that imagination is good, is a God-given and God-used gift, and that we need to inspire, purge and empower our imaginations through opening to God's beauty. Seek to challenge your people to become people of imagination, creativity and beauty.

Prayers:
God Speaks

You speak, God – you always speak,
    if we will but listen;

All we need to do is pause, and turn our attention
    to the song singing from the heavens,
        and whispering in the wind;
    to the flight of the dove,
        and the touch of its wings on our heads;

to the giggling of the water,
and the mark it leaves in our hearts;

Your voice comes to us in faithful surround sound,
bekoning us to join the chorus,
share in the dance,
and extend the invitation into all the earth.

You speak, God – you always speak;
and joyfully, we are listening.

Amen.

A Goodness Worth Pursuing

Goodness isn't always popular, Jesus;
There are those who doubt that it has value,
that fear that goodness only leaves us vulnerable
and unable to navigate the complexities
of the real world.
But, we believe that the opposite is true,
that it is goodness that must ultimately prevail,
and that holds the key to the wholeness
and happiness we seek.

And so we pray for goodness to infiltrate every un-good place,
where callous self-interest humiliates
and impoverishes others,
where casual disregard for the common good
undermines security and neighbourliness,
where unexamined or overstated fear addicts us to control,
where our obsession with the immediate
blinds us to the consequences of our actions.

Teach us the power of the good,
the healing of the noble,
the life of the praiseworthy,

and capture our hearts that we may give ourselves to know
   your goodness -
the only goodness that is truly worth pursuing.

Amen.

Liturgy:
A Liturgy for the Eucharist

Hymn Suggestions:
All Creatures Of Our God And King
For The Beauty Of The Earth
All Things Bright And Beautiful
Angel Voices Ever Singing
Angels Praise Him
Let Everything That Has Breath
Creation's King
I Stand In Awe Of You (You are beautiful beyond description)

Week Six: Becoming Loving

Readings:
Deuteronomy 6:4-9
Psalm 133
Luke 10:25-37
1 John 4:7-12

Sermon Starter:
Building worship services around love can be really hard, because it is such a common theme that it is far too easy to become "cheesy" or sentimental. However, with some careful thought and planning, a focus on love can be profound and transforming. The heart of the readings this week is the Great Commandment – the original from Deuteronomy, and Luke's narrative which includes the parable of the Good Samaritan. Psalm 133 celebrates the unity of God's people, and the life it

brings, while John's letter reminds us of how our relationship with God and our love for one another are related.

Alongside this exploration of love, it is important that our need for open hearts is also examined. Placing the call to love in the context of all the things that tempt us to close our hearts can make this service relevant and healing. The challenge to give up our self-protectiveness, and remain open and welcoming, is not a small thing to ask, but it is the key to following Christ's loving example. In the worship, and the message, then, it is important that people are drawn into an experience of God's love – for them and for the world – and not just invited to think about love abstractly.

Prayers:
The Measure of Faith

We celebrate a faith that is measured
   not by the usual signs of greatness,
   but by the marks of love;
And we celebrate the God who gives it.

We celebrate a love that is measured
   not by romance or emotion,
   but by acts of compassion and service;
And we celebrate the God who gives it.

We celebrate a life that is measured
   not by the trappings of wealth or power,
   but by the lives that are healed and enriched;
And we celebrate the God who gives it.

God, who measures every heart and life,
   we praise you for the life that is revealed in Christ,
   and for the Spirit who empowers us to follow
     Christ's example.
And we praise you for the love and grace

which we find in you, receive from you,
and against which we shall ultimately be measured.

Amen.

The Influence Of Love

How easily we forget your love, God;
    and in our forgetting,
        how alone we feel,
        and how disconnected from you,
            from everything;
How easily we discard love as an option, O God;
    and in our discarding,
        how much pain we cause,
        how much violence is done,
        what poverty and injustice results;

How easily we deny love's power, O God;
    and in our denying,
        how corrupt we become,
        how addicted to power, and wealth, and applause,
        how quick to justify our greed, consumption and expediency;

Forgive us for allowing anything else to come before your love,
    and for the brokenness that we have brought
        on ourselves and our world;
    teach us to love as you do,
        wholeheartedly,
        vulnerably,
        openly,
        unconditionally;
    and use us to nurture and expand
        the influence of love in your world.

Amen.

Liturgy:
A Liturgy of Compassion

Hymn Suggestions:
Come Let Us Sing Of A Wonderful Love
It Passeth Knowledge That Dear Love Of Thine
What Shall I Do My God To Love
Blessed Assurance
The Power Of Your Love
Here Is Love Vast As The Ocean
I Could Sing Of Your Love Forever (Over the mountains and the sea)
Forever

Week Seven: Becoming Purposeful

Readings:
Jeremiah 1:4-12
Psalm 139:1-18, 23-24
Luke 4:14-21
Philippians 2:5-13

Sermon Starter:
The idea of purpose – of being called – is both an exciting and a tricky one. This week the service is meant to draw us into a personal and collective sense of call, while taking seriously the example of Jesus, and the message of God's reign that define and direct every Christian's purpose. It is important to avoid the temptation in the worship to get too "triumphalist" as if we are the solution to all of the world's problems. In one sense we are – as are all people – but our calling is not best fulfilled in arrogance. Rather, as the Philippians reading indicates, it is Christ's humility that must characterise our lives.

All of the readings invite us into a sense of call in different ways. Jeremiah gives us a glimpse of God's call of one of the great prophets. The Psalm reminds us of God's purpose for, and empowerment of, each one of us. The Gospel reading is both Jesus' personal mandate, and the plumb line against which all callings are measured.

This week might also be a good one to invite people into areas of service and ministry within your church, offering them opportunities to find and fulfil their calling within a community of faith. The prayers and music should inspire us and remind us that God's grace toward us is not just for ourselves, but that we are saved for service.

Prayers:
This Hidden Kingdom

We don't see it, but it's everywhere we look;
We don't hear it, but its message is constantly whispered
   throughout the world;
We can't touch it, but its energy flows
   through every interaction,   every connection.

This Kingdom of Yours, God, is hidden in the ordinary stuff
   that makes up our everyday lives;
It's like yeast in a loaf of bread, like a tiny seed that
   imperceptibly sprouts and grows
     in the secret, unseen place;

And while we may miss it, or doubt it,
   or wonder why it appears weak in the face of evil,
This Kingdom of Yours exerts an inexorable influence on us
   calling us to be more than our selfishness and pride
     would lead us to believe we are
   leading us to love and serve and connect in ways
     that leave us and our world different,
       more alive, more real, more whole.

And so, God, we celebrate this hidden Kingdom of Yours
   we praise You for its gentle power,

and we open ourselves, once again,
>   to its life-giving influence.

Amen.

Your Kingdom Come

The Kingdom of God is at hand – You proclaimed it, Jesus;
>   But, it often feels like it's a million miles away.

You demonstrated its grace and showed its power,
>   but the signs often appear faded or absent in our world.

We need Your Kingdom to come, O God,
>   in all its fullness, in all its glory;

This waiting, this "now and not yet" experience of Your reign
>   is hard and frustrating.

And so we pray for Your Kingdom to be revealed in our lives,
>   turning our sickness and sin, our brokenness and fear
>   into friendship and compassion, wholeness and joy.

May Your Kingdom come to us now.

We pray for Your Kingdom to be revealed
>   in our neighbourhoods,
>   turning our division and suspicion, our judgement
>   and our competition
>   into fellowship and care, compassion and service.

May Your Kingdom come to us now.

We pray for Your Kingdom to be revealed in our world,
>   turning our war and our disparities, our consumption
>   and our self-interest
>   into peace and collaboration, stewardship and reverence.

May Your Kingdom come to us now.

Your Kingdom is here, and it is coming, O God.
Make us faithful heralds of its message

and tireless practitioners of its ways.
For Jesus sake.
Amen.

Liturgy:
A Liturgy for the Foretaste of the Heavenly Banquet

Hymn Suggestions:
Be Thou My Vision
Guide Me, O Thou Great Jehovah (Some version use "Redeemer")
O For A Thousand Tongues To Sing
A Charge To Keep I Have
Take My Life (Can be sung to the tune of "The Rose" which gives it a more contemporary feel)
I Will Offer Up my Life
Song For The Nations (May we be a shining light)
God Of Justice
What I Have Vowed (Lord, I am not my own)
I, The Lord Of Sea And Sky

Week Eight: Living the Change

Readings:
Genesis 18:1-19
Psalm 16
John 20:19-23
2 Corinthians 2:14-3:3

Sermon Starter:
This final Sunday of the fifty-day journey you may want to lead into whatever is next in your liturgical planning. It may well be helpful, though, to pause for a moment, and allow the quest into a deeper worship life to get solidly rooted in the ministry of your community, and strongly connected to the big issues of our day. It is important to make the point that worship is not an escape from the world and its troubles, but is rather a way of engaging the world from a divine

perspective. This means that we are driven back into our communities and homes as life-bringers, peacemakers and healers.

The worship this week is a celebration of the end of the journey, but is also a commissioning to live out the transformation that has happened during the last seven weeks. The Genesis reading takes us back to the very beginning – God's promise through Abraham that all nations would be blessed through his offspring. Psalm 16 reminds us that God shows us the paths of life, and provides glorious companions to travel those paths with. John's Gospel remind us that we are "Sent Ones" even as Jesus was, and Paul tells us what the result of that sending is – a world filled with the fragrance of Christ.

Have fun with this service, but also ensure that the calling to be transformed by worship, and to carry God's presence, purpose and character into our world, is proclaimed strongly and invitingly. Try to create links with specific ways that your church is involved in the big issues of your neighbourhood and country, and once again, don't be shy about giving people clear opportunities to commit to service.

Prayers:
A New World

In the quiet moments, in the still places,
    I can sometimes hear it;
An urgent voice, echoing through the wildernesses
      of the world,
      and of my heart
    calling me to prepare and to participate
      in the new world that wants to be born.

How can I be part of something that I haven't seen,
    that I struggle even to conceptualise, let alone understand?
Yet, still the voice calls, and my heart stirs.

I begin to imagine a world of joy and creativity,
   a world where the poor are always cared for
     and the rich are always generous;
   a world where justice guides,
     and where mourning is always temporary;
   a world where the highest values are valued most highly
     and where priorities and agendas are set
       with the greatest good in mind.

This world exists, Jesus, in the Gospel you preached,
   in the stable and the cross and the empty tomb,
   in Baptismal waters and Eucharistic meals
   in your constant calling, and your constant coming.

And so we praise you for this world,
   and for the dream that we can learn to know it
     here and now
       even as you do.

Amen.

Building A New World

Here, in the society we have created for ourselves,
   we have honoured the great,
     the wealthy,
     the visible,
     the first,
     the best;
   and we have forgotten the quiet power of humility.

And so now, we face the fruits of our misplaced values:
   our leaders falter and we feel betrayed,
   our wealth slips away, and we wonder how we will survive,
And across the world people find it harder to buy food,
     to stay safe, and to find shelter.

So now we pray for a new heart, for a new way of being,
   for the courage and vision to build our world
      on different values;
   humility,
   service,
   compassion,
   generosity,
   integrity.

Perhaps it's a dream, O God, but we believe it is Your dream,
   and it's the only true hope we have.
So, may Your will be done here among us,
   within us,
   through us.
Amen.

Liturgy:
A Liturgy for the Celebration of Sacrifice

Hymn Suggestions:
O Loving Lord, Who Art Forever Seeking
God Of Almighty Love
They Who Tread The Paths Of Labour
O Master Let Me Walk With Thee
I Believe that God Appeared In Human Form
Servant Song (Brother let me be your servant)
When It's All Been Said And Done
My Life Is In You, Lord
History Maker

Additional Resources

The Sacredise web site is filled with resources to enhance and deepen your worship, not just through this journey, but every week. Go to www.sacredise.com for more information, or to sign up for the free monthly ezine.

If you follow the Revised Common Lectionary, weekly resources are posted, about four weeks ahead, to the Lectionary Worship Resources blog (www.sacredise.com/lectionary) based on each week's readings.

If you need resources to connect your worship more strongly with God's call to justice and mercy, you may be interested to explore *Every God-Beloved Life – Song, prayers and readings of worship and justice.* This CD offers new Kingdom-of-God based worship songs that have been designed especially for congregational worship. Many of the songs would fit well into the worship services in this book. For more information, or to find out how you can purchase a copy, go to www.god-beloved.com.

Notes

[1] From the Foreword to Kimball, Dan; *Emerging Worship – Creating Worship Gatherings for New Generations* (Grand Rapids: Zondervan, 2004), p.vi.

[2] Significant research into this was done by my friend and colleague Rev. Dr. Dion Forster, and presented in the Hugh Price Hughes lecture, *Revolution or Evolution? Considering the impact of 'emerging church' conversations on the mission and ecclesiology of established churches,* that he delivered at the Hinde Street Methodist Church in London, England in March 2009. I have received a transcript of the lecture from Dion (it can also be downloaded from this url: http://www.hindestreet.org.uk/Groups/14858/Hinde_Street_Methodist/Thinking/Hugh_Price_Hughes/Hugh_Price_Hughes.aspx - scroll down for the 2009 lectures), and it makes disturbing, but challenging and hopeful, reading.

[3] Kevin Light, a former Methodist minister, and the founder and director of *Labyrinth – The Movement* in Cape Town, in private communication.

[4] As the authors note on p.15: *"In fact, the title of this book,* unChristian, *reflects outsiders' most common reaction to the faith: they think Christians no longer represent what Jesus had in mind, that Christianity in our society is not what it was meant to be."* Kinnaman, David & Lyons, Gabe, *UnChristian* (Grand Rapids: Baker Books, 2007).

[5] Kimball, Dan; *Emerging Worship – Creating Worship Gatherings for New Generations*, p.2-3.

6. See Isaiah 58.
7. Isaiah 58:13.
8. Amos 5:21-24.
9. 1 Corinthians 11:17-32.
10. Foster, Richard J., *Celebration of Discipline* (London: Hodder and Stoughton, 1989), p.207.
11. White, Susan, J.; *The Spirit of Worship – The Liturgical Tradition* (London: Darton, Longman and Todd, 1999), p.15.
12. Ibid. p.16.
13. This statement was made as part of a sermon that Bill Hybels preached at the Willow Creek Arts Conference in June 2000, at which I was a delegate.
14. Although I have encountered it before in other places, this quote is drawn from this Wikipedia article: http://en.wikipedia.org/wiki/William_Temple_%28archbishop%29.
15. From the hymn, *When I Survey The Wondrous Cross*, written by Isaac Watts (1674-1748). Public Domain.
16. This story, and more detail on William Temple's life, can be found in this article by James Kiefer: http://satucket.com/lectionary/william_temple.htm.
17. This particular version of Temple's definition is taken from Foster, Richard J., *Celebration of Discipline*, p.199.
18. Matthew 13:44-46.

Chapter One – An Invitation to Intimacy

19. Quoted in a Time Magazine article in Vol.149, No.2 (13 January 1997). I sourced the quote from the WikiQuote web site at this url: http://en.wikiquote.org/wiki/Bill_Gates.
20. Morgenthaler, Sally, *Worship Evangelism* (Grand Rapids: Zondervan, 1995), p.17.
21. This sense of frustration and disappointment was expressed in an article that Sally wrote for the May/June issue of REV! Magazine, called *Worship as Evangelism: Sally Morgenthaler rethinks her own paradigm*. The whole article can be found on the REV! Magazine site here: http://www.rev.org/article.asp?ID=2409.
22. Kirvan, John, *Silent Hope: Living With The Mystery Of God* (Notre Dame: Sorin Books, 2001), p.20.

[23] Psalm 42:1-2.
[24] Jeremiah 2:13.
[25] Micah 6:8.
[26] Philippians 3:10 (KJV).
[27] The testimony of Augustine's conversion has been recorded in a number of works with which I have engaged over the years. I am particularly grateful, though, for the simple and concise way it is described in Susan J. White's book *The Spirit of Worship* (London: Darton, Longman & Todd, 1999) p.13.
[28] See Nash, Wanda, *Gifts from Hildegarde* (London: Darton, Longman & Todd, 1997), p.27.
[29] See Brother Lawrence, *The Practice of the Presence of God,* edited and paraphrased by Donald E. Demaray, (Grand Rapids: Baker Book House, 1975).
[30] It is beyond the scope of this book to give a historical overview of writings about encounter with God in the various spiritual traditions of the Church. There are many helpful resources to pursue further study. One book that I have found particularly helpful and concise is Kenneth Leech's manual for spiritual direction *Soul Friend* (London: Sheldon Press, 1977). See especially pp.139-154.
[31] Borg, Marcus, *The Heart of Christianity* (San Francisco: HarperSanFrancisco, 2004), p.157.
[32] Psalm 2:12a (NIV). Other versions use words like "submit" to express the intent of this verse, but the original word is best translated by the NIV's "kiss".
[33] 1 Corinthians 6:16,17.
[34] Ephesians 5:31,32.
[35] Bell, Rob, *Sex God* (Grand Rapids: Zondervan, 2007), p.15.
[36] See, for example, Wilson-Dickson, A., *The Story of Christian Music* (Oxord: Lion Publishing plc, 1992), p.85.
[37] Blume, F., *Protestant Church Music* (New York: W. W. Norton & Company, 1974), p.14.
[38] Lewis, C.S., *Mere Christianity* (Glasgow: Fount Paperbacks (Thirty-sixth impression) 1982), p.129.
[39] Rollins, Peter, *How (Not) To speak Of God* (Brewster: Paraclete Press, 2006), p.17.

[40] Smith, James K. A., *Desiring The Kingdom* (Grand Rapids: Baker Academic, 2009), p.80.
[41] Psalm 42:7 (NIV).
[42] Webber, Robert E., *Worship is a Verb* (Peabody: Hendrickson Publishers, 1992), p.45.
[43] One good example of this is Psalm 136.
[44] Webber, Robert E., *Worship is a Verb*, p.110.
[45] Groeschel, Craig, *The Christian Atheist: Believing in God but living as if he doesn't exist* (Grand Rapids: Zondervan, 2010), p.34.
[46] Labberton, Mark, *The Dangerous Act Of Worship* (Downers Grove: IVP Books, 2007), p.168f.
[47] Webber, Robert E., *Worship is a Verb*, p.213.
[48] Foster, Richard J., *Celebration of Discipline* (London: Hodder and Stoughton, 1989), p.203f.
[49] John 4:21-24.

Chapter Two – Welcome to a New World

[50] The full quote, from his book *Walden* (published in 1854) is: "The mass of men lead lives of quiet desperation." This quote was sourced from the WikiQuote web site at this url: http://en.wikiquote.org/wiki/Henry_David_Thoreau.
[51] Peck, M. Scott, *The Road Less Travelled* (London: Rider, 1988), p.15.
[52] Fox, Matthew, *Creativity: Where the Divine and the Human Meet* (New York: Tarcher Putnam, 2002), p.24. This statement is part of a wider discussion of the general sense we share today that we have somehow lost ourselves. In a powerful and helpful way, Fox begins with exploring some of the illusions we have developed about ourselves that have led to our sense of 'lostness' and to the devastation of our world. He prophetically negates these illusions by using them to speak about what we are not. The rest of the book, then, explores creativity as an inherent, and healing, part of who we are.
[53] John 10:10b.
[54] Driver, Tom, F., *The Magic of Ritual – Our Need for Liberating Rites that Transform Our Lives & Our Communities* (San Francisco: Harper Collins, 1991), p.172.

55 Eugene Peterson does an expert job of describing the worship that is pictured in, and that would have been built upon, this vision in the fourth chapter, *The Last Word on Worship,* in his book *Reversed Thunder* (San Francisco: HarperSanFrancisco, 1991), pp.57-71.
56 2 Corinthians 3:16-18 (Emphasis mine).
57 Foster, Richard J., *Celebration of Discipline* (London: Hodder and Stoughton, 1989), p.214.
58 This quote is usually attributed to Nin, but without citation. It has also been attributed to the Talmud, but again, without confirmation of the specific source. In this case the quote has been sourced from the WikiQuote web site at this url.: http://en.wikiquote.org/wiki/Anais_Nin.
59 Rohr, Richard, *Hope Against Darkness* (Cincinnati: St. Anthony Messenger Press, 2001), p.125.
60 See Smith, James K. A., *Desiring the Kingdom* (Grand Rapids: Baker Academic, 2009), p.32f.
61 Quoted, without reference, by Trevor Hudson in his book *Signposts to Spirituality* (Cape Town: Struik Christian Books, 1995), p.19.
62 Richard Rohr describes what he calls our *Theism* – the idea that God is outside of our world – and explains how it fails to embrace the biblical Christian understanding of *Incarnation*. He writes *"The vast majority of Christians I have met worldwide are actually theists, but not Incarnational at all. God is still out there, invited into things, and they are all inviting God to come to them. Theism, the most common form of religion, is still a split worldview. True Christianity is totally integrative."* See *Hope Against Darkness*, p. 126.
63 Brian McLaren describes what he calls the 'prosperity system' in terms very similar to this, forcefully arguing that the way we have structured our relationships with the world and one another, especially in terms of economic realities, is destructive and unsustainable. See *Everything Must Change* (Nashville: Thomas Nelson, 2007), pp.187-224.
64 In a similar way, McLaren also addresses the problem of our 'separateness' and the violence and factions it creates in the section on 'the security system' in *Everything Must Change*, pp. 149-185.

65 This shocking reality is well-documented in David Kinnman and Gabe Lyon's book *UnChristian* (Grand Rapids: Baker Books, 2007), particularly in Chapter Three. They write: *"For instance, based on a study released in 2007, we found that most of the lifestyle activities of born-again Christians were statistically equivalent to those of non-born-agains. When asked to identify their activities over the last thirty days, born-again believers were just as likely to bet or gamble, to visit a pornographic website, to take something that did not belong to them, to consult a medium or psychic, to physically fight or abuse someone, to have consumed enough alcohol to be considered legally drunk, to have used an illegal, nonprescription drug, to have said something to someone that was not true, to have gotten back at someone for something he or she did, and to have said mean things behind another's back."* p.47.

66 *Desiring the Kingdom*, p.33.

67 *Hope Against Darkness*, p.130.

68 Fox, Matthew, *Original Blessing* (Santa Fe: Bear & Company, 1983), p.90.

69 Acts 17:28.

70 Ephesians 1:21-23.

71 Colossians 1:17.

72 Matthew Fox offers a powerful depiction of what 'living in a machine-like world' does to us in *Creativity: Where the Divine and the Human Meet*. He writes: *"But if we live in a machine, then we are mere cogs in it, mere pieces that just happened to show. Our main duty is to shut up and obey – obey the economic machine, the political machine, the military machine, the religious machine, the educational machine. To live inside a machine is scary business. Fear takes over. Anxiety increases. Numbness multiplies. Meaninglessness becomes more widespread than meaning. Coldness dominates. Sterility reigns. Creativity dies. Passivity becomes a virtue.* (p.23). In a similar way, Brian McLaren speaks about a conversation he had with Leonard Sweet in which Sweet referred to the society we have created as a "suicide machine" (See *Everything Must Change*, p.52).

73 Genesis 1:28.

74 See Revelation 21:1-3 and Romans 8:19-21.

75 White, James, F., *Introduction to Christian Worship* (Nashville: Abingdon, 1990), p.88.

76 McLaren, Brian, *Everything Must Change*, p.143.

Notes

[77] Psalm 139:7-10.
[78] Exodus 3:1-4.
[79] My thoughts on the different ways we view time are strongly influenced by Susan J. White's thinking in *The Spirit of Worship* (London: Darton, Longman & Todd, 1999), p.80.
[80] White, James, F., *Introduction to Christian Worship*, p.52.
[81] Luke 8:41-56.
[82] Peterson, Eugene H., *Working The Angles* (Grand Rapids: William B. Eerdmans Publishing Company, 1987), p.68.
[83] There are many Bible verses that can be quoted to challenge the idea that we are first and foremost individuals in God's eyes, but one simple reference will suffice here. In the account of the creation in Genesis 2, the newly created man is placed in the garden which is to be his home, and God immediately remarks that "it is not good for the man to be alone" (vs.18). The resulting search for a mate among the animals fails, although in the naming of the creatures there is an indication that companionship and connection is found there to some extent. However, ultimately the man needs someone like him, and so the woman is created. The point is clear. Human beings are only fulfilled in relationship.
[84] M. Scott Peck, in his book *The Different Drum* (London: Rider & Co., 1987), argues that the rampant individualism (as he calls it) of American (and by extension Western) society, is only half of what makes human beings alive and whole. If this is made out to be the whole need, he says, then it results in the brokenness and loneliness that we all know only too well. Rather, he argues, human beings need to find themselves in a simultaneous experience as individuals and as connected. See pp.53-58.
[85] McLaren, Brian D., *A New Kind of Christianity* (New York: HarperOne, 2010), p.207.
[86] This is not an exaggeration. McLaren points out that the three great monotheist religions in the world today comprise more than half of the world's population. As he points out, if they are in conflict, then no one in the world is safe, especially when we consider the weapons that people of these religions possess. (*A New Kind of Christianity*, pp.207f).
[87] *Signposts to Spirituality*, p.71.
[88] Matthew 6:5-6.
[89] Matthew 6:9.
[90] Matthew 18:19-20.
[91] 1 Corinthians 12:12-27.

92 Hacker, George, *The Healing Stream* (London: Darton, Longman & Todd, 1998), p.17.

93 Mark 3:16-19.

Chapter Three – Becoming Holy

94 It was not really surprising that the debates on BBC television between the leaders of the three major parties in Britain (Gordon Brown, David Cameron & Nick Clegg) referenced, more than once, the abuse of public office and the recently exposed misuse of public funds by members of parliament (See this highlights video as an example: http://news.bbc.co.uk/2/hi/uk_news/politics/election_2010/8624100.stm). The fight against corruption in public office seems to be a fairly regular and widespread phenomenon, as witnessed by similar revelations that have come to light in South Africa over the last few years. The famous arms deal and the 'Travelgate' scandal are but two examples, but they are certainly not the only issues, as evidenced by this 2008 Mail & Guardian article: http://mg.co.za/article/2008-11-07-an-open-cookie-jar. The United States is also not free from the problem of corruption, as reported in this Wikipedia article: http://en.wikipedia.org/wiki/Political_scandals_of_the_United_States.

95 The post in question can be found at this url: http://rockinthegrass.blogspot.com/2007/02/everyone-is-doing-it.html

96 See Isaiah 6:1-8.

97 Fox, Matthew, *Original Blessing* (Santa Fe: Bear & Company, 1983), p.110.

98 See Luke 8:41-56.

99 See John 4:1-26.

100 See John 8:1-11.

101 See Mark 15:1-9.

102 See Luke 14:1-6.

103 See Luke 5:29-32.

104 See Mark 11:15-18.

105 Fox, Matthew, *Original Blessing*, p.110.

106 1 Peter 1:15-16.

107 See, for example, Vine's Expository Dictionary article here: http://www.antioch.com.sg/cgi-bin/bible/vines/get_defn.pl?num=1394#B1.

108 McClung, Floyd, *Holiness and the Spirit of the Age* (Cape Town: Struik Christian Books, 1991) p.11.

109 Isaiah 55:8-9.

110 John 14:9-11.

[111] Exodus 25:8-40.
[112] See, for example, Romans 1:7; 1 Corinthians 1:2; 1 Peter 2:9.
[113] Matthew 5:48.
[114] Fox, Matthew, *Original Blessing*, p.111.
[115] See the New Oxford American Dictionary (Oxford University Press, 2005) entry for the word' holy'.
[116] Luke 6:36.
[117] *The Works of John Wesley*, Jackson Edition, "Preface to 1739 Hymns and Sacred Poems", vol. 14:321.
[118] See John Wesley's Sermon No. 76 – *On Perfection*.
[119] *Original Blessing*, p.113.
[120] Borg, Marcus J., *The Heart of Christianity* (San Francisco: HarperSanFrancisco, 2004), p.127.
[121] Willimon, William H., *Worship as Pastoral Care* (Nashville: Abgindon Press, 1979), p.48.
[122] 1 Samuel 16:14-23.
[123] Groeschel, Craig, *The Christian Atheist: Believing in God but living as if he doesn't exist* (Grand Rapids: Zondervan, 2010), p.43.
[124] White, Susan J., *The Spirit Of Worship – The Liturgical Tradition* (London: Darton, Longman & Todd, 1999), p.101.
[125] Matthew 6:12-15.
[126] Williams, Rowan, *Resurrection* (New York: Morehouse Bralow, 1977), p.52, quoted in White, Susan J., *The Spirit Of Worship*, p.111f.
[127] White, Susan J., *The Spirit Of Worship*, p.105.
[128] James 1:22-25.
[129] White, Susan J., *The Spirit Of Worship*, p.110.

Chapter Four – Becoming True

[130] For a more detailed explanation of this video and the problems with it see the Snopes.com urban legend website. The article can be found at this address: http://www.snopes.com/politics/religion/demographics.asp.
[131] Gladwell, Malcolm, *Blink: The Power of Thinking Without Thinking* (London: Penguin Books, 2005), p.56f.
[132] The whole post can be found at the entry for 19 April 2010. The permalink is here: http://julieclawson.com/2010/04/19/what-is-emerging/
[133] John 18:38.
[134] John 4:24.

[135] Romans 12:1,2 NIV.

[136] In 1980 popular conservative writer, Tim La Haye (best known for his *Left Behind* series of Christian novels) wrote a book called *The Battle for the Mind*. More recently, popular television preacher and writer, Joyce Meyer, released her book *Battlefield of the Mind*, in 2002.

[137] One example is this comment from James C. Coleman, James N. Butcher and Robert C. Carson's book *Abnormal Psychology and Modern Life* (Dallas: Scott, Foresman and Company, 1984): *"The fundamental unity of mind and body is perhaps nowhere better documented than in health and illness. The development of psychophysiological disorder... is only one example of this enormous influence of mental factors on bodily functioning."* (p. 275).

[138] *Thayer's Greek Definitions*. Definition of *Strong's Exhaustive Concordance of the Bible* number G3563.

[139] 1 Corinthians 2:16.

[140] As with most legends this one has more than one version. Two versions of this tale, and many other legends from the first people of North America, can be found at the First People web site at this address: http://www.firstpeople.us/FP-Html-Legends/TwoWolves-Cherokee.html

[141] For the factual explanation of this urban legend see http://www.snopes.com/religion/lostday.asp.

[142] Again, this urban legend is well examined and explained at Snopes.com: http://www.snopes.com/photos/odd/giantman.asp.

[143] Please note: I am *not* saying that there is nothing factual in the Bible. On the contrary, I believe that much of the Bible is based upon historical fact. What I am saying is that the factuality of the Bible has little bearing on the truth it proclaims, because Biblical truth is far deeper and far more important than facts can ever be.

[144] Borg, Marcus, J., *The Heart of Christianity: Rediscovering a Life of Faith* (San Francisco: HarperSanFrancisco, 2003), p.43.

[145] John 14:6.

[146] McLaren, Brian, *A Reading Of John 14:6;* Brian McLaren, 2006. As Brian explains, this article was originally written for his book *The Secret Message Of Jesus*, but was ultimately left out. The full article is well worth reading, and is an important exploration of this widely misunderstood text. It can be downloaded from this url on Brian's web site: http://www.brianmclaren.net/emc/archives/McLaren%20-%20John%2014.6.pdf.

[147] John 15:26; 1 John 5:6.

[148] John 16:13-16.

[149] Bell, Rob, *Velvet Elvis* (Grand Rapids: Zondervan, 2005), p.82f.

[150] John 8:31-32.

[151] Titus 1:1b.
[152] Romans 1:18; 2:8.
[153] 2 Corinthians 4:2.
[154] 2 Thessalonians 2:11-12.
[155] 1 Corinthians 13:6.
[156] A few examples are: Matthew 4:4; 15:6; Hebrews 4:12; James 1:22.
[157] John 5:39.
[158] Borg, Marcus, J., *The Heart of Christianity*, p.47.
[159] Colossians 3:16.
[160] Matthew 13:10-13.
[161] One example of this is the conversation between Jesus and a religious lawyer in Luke 10:25-37. This is a great example of both Jesus' use of questions, and his teaching through parables.
[162] Borg, Marcus, J. *The Heart of Christianity*, p.59.
[163] van de Laar, J., *Food for the Road – Life Lessons from the Lord's Table* (Knysna: Sacredise, 2008), p.141.

Chapter Five – Become Beautiful

[164] Fox, Matthew, *Creativity: Where the Divine and the Human Meet* (New York: Tarcher/Putnam, 2002), p.210f.
[165] Some examples are the visions and enactments of Ezekiel (e.g. 12:1-16, 37:1-14, 47:1-12), the song of Habbakkuk (3:17-19), the Songs of the Suffering Servant in Isaiah (42:1-9, 49:1-13, 50:4-9, 53:1-11) and Jeremiah's book of Lamentations.
[166] It is interesting to note how oppressive regimes often seek to control and censor the arts in order to silence this prophetic voice. Frequently this is accomplished through two movements. First, the art that represents the dominant regime is applauded as aesthetically 'superior' to that produced by others, essentially raising the voice of pro-regime art above dissenting artistic voices. Second, the art of protest or of dissent is censored, essentially making the creation or enjoyment of such art illegal in an attempt to eradicate the 'status quo disrupting' message of these artists. This movement can be clearly identified in both Nazi Germany, where Jewish art was treated in this way, and apartheid South Africa. A short, but informative, article that explores this historical movement in music is written by Philip A. Songa and can be found at http://www.allaboutjazz.com/southafrica/lifetimes.htm. See also, John De Gruchy's book *Christianity, Art and Transformation – Theological Aesthetics in the Struggle for Justice* (Cambridge University Press, 2001), especially pp. 89-90, pp.139-143, pp.203-212.

[167] A moving 2006 article about the renaming ceremony which retells Sophiatown's story can be found on the City of Johannesburg web site here: http://www.joburgnews.co.za/2006/feb/feb13_sophiatown.stm.

[168] Genesis 6:5 KJV.

[169] 2 Corinthians 10:5 KJV.

[170] Matthew Fox quotes these exact words in the case of a teacher who was forbidden by her school board (the majority of whom were Christians) to use the word "imagination" in the classroom, in *Creativity: Where the Divine and the Human Meet*, p.58f.

[171] Augustine's ambivalence toward the 'passions of the flesh' is widely documented, and easily explained by the indulgent life he led before his conversion, as John De Gruchy explains. De Gruchy also gives a very helpful overview of the great Reformers and their cautious attitudes to the arts in his book *Christianity, Art and Transformation*.

[172] Genesis 1:31.

[173] Genesis 1:27.

[174] Genesis 1:1.

[175] Fox, Matthew, *Creativity: Where the Divine and the Human Meet*, p.228.

[176] John De Gruchy describes how Dietrich Bonhoeffer pointed to the incarnation to support this view: "There are not two realities, but *only one reality*, and that is God's reality revealed in Christ in the reality of the world." *Icons As A Means Of Grace* (Wellington: Lux Verbi.BM, 2008) p.100, quoting from *Ethics*, in *Dietrich Bonhoeffer Works*, vol.6 (Minneapolis: Fortress, 2005) p.58.

[177] Psalm 19:1.

[178] Romans 1:19-20a The Message.

[179] Fox, Matthew, *Original Blessing* (Santa Fe: Bear & Co., 1983), p. 90.

[180] 2 Corinthians 11:14.

[181] John De Gruchy summarises the relationship between the three transcendents very helpfully in his book *Christianity, Art and Transformation* pp.104-107. He particularly notes: "*Truth without goodness and beauty degenerates into dogmatism, and lacks the power to attract and convince; goodness without truth is superficial, and without beauty – that is without graced form – it degenerates into moralism. Alternatively, we could say that truth and goodness without beauty lack power to convince and therefore to save...The true and the good are not primarily perceived by the rational faculties as propositions and principles: they are experienced through hearing and seeing, through intuition and imagination. Hence the fundamental importance of the arts for Christian faith and life. (p.107).*

Notes

[182] A March 25, 2008 article from ABC News tells the story of a young cheerleader who died under anaesthetic undergoing breast surgery, and relates the growing trend toward cosmetic surgery among teenage girls. See the article here: http://abcnews.go.com/GMA/Parenting/story?id=4520099.

[183] Rob Bell explores this idea, in a slightly different way, in his book *SexGod* (Grand Rapids: Zondervan, 2007). In his discussion of lust and its effects he explains: *"It isn't just what lust does, it's where lust leads. God made us to appreciate aesthetics: taste, smell, touch, hearing, sight. Shape, texture, consistency, color. It all flows from the endless creativity at the center of the universe, and we were created to enjoy it.* **But when lust has us in its grip, one of the first things to suffer is our appreciation for whatever it is we're fixated on.**" (p.75f . Emphasis mine).

[184] Pastor and theologian Chris Seay offers some great insights into what true beauty is, and the role of beauty in the Church. He says, *"When people ask me what I'm most encouraged about in the state of the Church, it's the fact that we're finally talking about beauty. My biggest fear is that we're probably still missing what beauty is. There's a reason that Thomas Kinkade is the most well known artist in the Christian community - it's because he paints pictures of things that aren't real, they're landscapes that don't even actually exist - where things that are really beautiful always reflect reality. That's part of our struggle with the Scriptures. These people are far too real...Good art and beauty is always a reflection of something that goes on in real life. That's why even the most wholesome art, like Norman Rockwell, has this tension that it holds of beauty...and pain is always present there, right? The suffering of a small child...This beautiful picturesque world and yet it's not all right...What I hope for in a sermon, or a photograph or a painting is something that touches me deep inside and, I don't necessarily say 'that's pretty' but I say 'that's true'."* (This is from a video called *Art & Beauty* which can be found at: http://www.theworkofthepeople.com/index.php?ct=store.details&pid=V00084).

[185] Philippians 4:8-9.

[186] De Gruchy, John W., *Christianity, Art and Transformation*, p.200.

[187] I have heard this quoted a number of times over the years (as I'm sure you have as well). The source which I used to confirm the attribution, though, was http://www.wisdomquotes.com/000796.html.

[188] Smith, James K. A., *Desiring the Kingdom: Worship, Worldview and Cultural Formation* (Grand Rapids: Baker Academic, 2009), p. 54.

[189] John De Gruchy offers a thorough and very helpful exploration of the link between the art of our sanctuaries and the ethical values by which we choose to live. In doing so, he argues persuasively for a theological approach to aesthetics in our worship and to the process of choosing what art gets used in worship. See *Christianity, art and Transformation*, p.242-243.

[190] Of course, this is part of the reason that the word has come to be associated with the ideas of destruction and the end of the world. It is believed that this is the heart of the content of the book of Revelation. While this is not the place to offer a commentary on John's vision, it must be noted that to interpret Revelation simply as a prophecy of the end times (which, as some authors assert, is to happen in our lifetimes) is to miss the point. More than being about the end of the world, it is a book about God's Kingdom breaking into and saving the world – which is, of course the heart of Jesus' Gospel message. More than being a book of judgement, Revelation is all about God's grace. The images are common ones drawn from the apocalyptic literature of the Old Testament, and the primary revelation in the book is not of destruction, or even of the end of the world, but of Jesus Christ, as John notes in Chapter 1:1.

[191] The story of *Sacred Space* can be read at this address: http://seeward.com/sspace.php, or can be heard, as told by Clint Kemp himself, on a video from *The Work of the People* here: http://www.theworkofthepeople.com/index.php?ct=store.details&pid=V00305.

[192] One of my favourite Old Testament passages reflects this playfulness of God beautifully. Proverbs 8:22-31 speaks of Wisdom as present with God and as the worker at God's side during creation. Verse 31, speaks of Wisdom's happiness with the world God created, using a word which literally refers to play.

[193] Fox, Matthew, *Creativity: Where the Divine and the Human Meet*, p.179.

[194] Ibid. p.155.

Chapter Six – Becoming Loving

[195] Peck, M. Scott, *The Road Less Travelled* (London: Rider, 1988), p. 83.

[196] Matthew 22:36-40 and Mark 12:28-31.

[197] The historical basis for this is from a March 20, 2007 article *Collision Course – Jesus' Final Week* at the Christian Century website, written by two prominent Jesus scholars, Marcus Borg and John Dominic Crossan: http://www.christiancentury.org/article.lasso?id=3091.

[198] According to Franciscan priest Father Richard Rohr, 90% of Jerusalem's economy was tied into this corrupt system, which fleeced the poor and lined the pockets of the priests. I first heard this mentioned in a series of lectures, which he presented around his book *Hope Against Darkness*. The tapes of these lectures were given to me on loan from a colleague. An online search has indicated that he also refers to this in his book *Things Hidden: Scripture as Spirituality*, although I have not read this particular work of his and therefore have no page reference.

[199] By whose authority did Jesus do what he did – Matthew 21:23-27; Mark 11:27-33.

[200] Paying taxes to Caesar – Matthew 22:15-21; Mark 12:14-17.

[201] The story of the woman who, by the custom of levirate marriage, marries seven husbands as they each die in turn and the question of marriage in heaven – Matthew 22:23-33; Mark 12:18-27.

[202] In Mark's Gospel Jesus is quoted as saying, "No other command is greater than these." In Matthew it is worded even more strongly: "On these two commandments hang all the law and the prophets" (KJV). The Apostle Paul agrees with this assessment of the Great Commandment as well. In Galatians 5:14 he writes: *"For the whole law can be summed up in this one command: Love your neighbour as yourself."*

[203] Luke 10:25-28.

[204] A particularly impressive passage where this happens is the extended narrative and discourse running from the feeding of the 5000, to Jesus walking on water, to his statement, "I am the bread of life" and the conversation about Moses and manna in the wilderness in John 6:1-59.

[205] Nouwen, Henri, J.M., *Intimacy: Essays in Pastoral Psychology* (San Francisco: Harper & Row, 1969), p.29.

[206] Borg, Marcus J., *The Heart Of Christianity*, p.151

[207] 1 John 2:7-8.

[208] See Matthew 15:22-28 and Mark 7:25-30.

[209] This comment was made in an article entitled *Blogging toward Sunday: Faith to fire back* on *Theolog* the blog of *The Christian Century* journal written by Trygve David Johnson. Find the article here: http://theolog.org/2008/08/blogging-toward-sunday-faith-to-fire.html

[210] The open-hearted capacity for change that Jesus demonstrates in this encounter is described by Peter S. Hawkins in his article Dogging Jesus which first appeared in The Christian Century in the August 9, 2005 issue. The article is reprinted online at Religion Online: http://www.religion-online.org/showarticle.asp?title=3231. Note particularly this section: "By and large, the Gospels sidestep the issue of what we might call Jesus' psychological development; instead, they depict other kinds of variability that result from having a body and an emotional life... There is one occasion, however, that stands out among these human moments – an occasion when we see him learn something new and, as a result, become someone different; As recorded by Mark as well as Matthew, Jesus is brought up short by an unexpected truth. Not only does he change his mind, but does so in a breathtaking 180-degree turn. Most astonishing of all, it is a pagan woman who makes him do it."

[211] Luke 19:1-10.

[212] John 8:1-11.

[213] Luke 23:39-43.

[214] Marcus Borg speaks about the opening of the heart as the primary task of spirituality, and describes what the open heart looks like in terms of being open to wonder, compassion, justice, awareness and gratitude. See *The Heart of Christianity* pp.161-3.

[215] See John 13:35.

[216] As in 1 John 4:7.

[217] As in Ephesians 5:25.

[218] As we have seen in the Great Commandment in Matthew, Mark and Luke's Gospels.

[219] See Matthew 5:43-48 and Luke 6:27-36.

[220] Brian McLaren's exegesis of Jesus' encounter with the Canaanite woman profoundly makes the point that the love we are called to express is not an "in crowd" love, but must ultimately extend even to those we would be tempted to hate, exclude, or judge. See *Everything Must Change* (Nashville: Thomas Nelson, 2007), pp. 155-9.

[221] Again, see the passage that is quoted at the start of this chapter: 1 John 4:8 (Emphasis mine).

[222] My thoughts in this section have been influenced by my reading of, and reflection on, C.S. Lewis's book *The Four Loves* (Glasgow: Fount, (Reprint) 23rd Impression), 1982.

[223] Bell, Rob, *Sex God* (Grand Rapids: Zondervan, 2007), p.58.

[224] See Romans 8:15.

[225] See John 14:16 & 15:15.

[226] See Ezekiel 16:1-14; 1 Corinthians 6:16-17; Ephesians 5:31-32.

[227] 1 Corinthians 13:4-8.

[228] Rollins, Peter, *How (Not)To Speak Of God* (Brewster: Paraclete Press, 2006), p.72.

[229] Acts 2:42-47.

[230] Psalm 133.

[231] 1 Corinthians 11:17-30.

[232] Matthew 25:40.

[233] Romans 9:1-3.

[234] *What The World Needs Now Is Love*, lyrics by Hal David, music by Burt Bacharach. © Imperial Records 1965.

Chapter Seven – Becoming Purposeful

[235] Smith, James, K. A., *Desiring the Kingdom: Worship, Worldview and Cultural Formation* (Grand Rapids: Baker Academic, 2009), p. 47f.

Notes

[236] Shaw, George Bernard, in the Epistle Dedicatory to his play *Man and Superman* written in 1903. The quote itself was sourced from this web page: http://www.quotationspage.com/quote/27168.html. Details of Shaw's play can be found at Wikipedia: http://en.wikipedia.org/wiki/Man_and_Superman. The full text of the Epistle Dedicatory can be found on this web page: http://www.bartleby.com/157/100.html.

[237] Zander, Benjamin and Rosamund Stone, *The Art Of Possibility* (New York: Penguin Books, 2000), pp.40-41.

[238] See, for example, the account of Samuel anointing David as king in 1 Samuel 16:1-13.

[239] Jeremiah 1:4-8.

[240] Psalm 139:14-16.

[241] See Galatians 1:15.

[242] See, for example, Romans 12:4-8; 1 Corinthians 12:1-31; and Ephesians 4:11-16.

[243] In United States, George W. Bush, and the United Kingdom, Tony Blair, both came under fire for statements in which, it was claimed, they ascribed their actions, particular in relation to the Iraq war, to have been guided by God. See the following news sites for articles that illustrate this: The Washington Post, 2005: http://www.washingtonpost.com/wp-dyn/content/article/2005/10/13/AR2005101301688.html; Guardian, 2003: http://www.guardian.co.uk/world/2003/nov/02/usa.religion; and the BBC, 2006: http://news.bbc.co.uk/2/hi/4772142.stm. In a similar way, public statements made by TV Evangelist Pat Robertson about the destruction caused by Hurricane Katrina on New Orleans, blaming it on America's abortion policy, illustrate what a distorted view of God and of the individual's purpose can do. See the "Controversies and criticisms" section of this Wikipedia article for details: http://en.wikipedia.org/wiki/Pat_Robertson. In South Africa we have seen similar dynamics creeping into the public communication of President Jacob Zuma. He has been quoted as claiming that the ruling African National Congress will rule South Africa "until Jesus comes again" and that God and Jesus are on the side of the ANC. See this article for more details: http://www.africanews.com/site/SA_ANC_to_rule_till_Jesus_comes/list_messages/23648.

[244] See Matthew 6:9-13.

[245] These thoughts are drawn from a video interview with Brian McLaren which can be found at The Work Of The People web site: http://www.theworkofthepeople.com/index.php?ct=store.details&pid=V00248.

[246] See Luke 4:1-13.

[247] Luke 4:18,19.

[248] See Wilcock, Michael, *The Message of Luke* from the *The Bible Speaks Today* commentary series edited by John R.W. Stott (Leicester: IVP, 1979), p.61.

[249] Luke 4:21.

[250] This seems to be quite widely recognised, but for reference, see the article *The Proclamation* at *Religion Online*, which was originally published in *The Christian Century* January 7-14, 1998, p.13 by John Stendahl: http://www.religion-online.org/showarticle.asp?title=650, and the commentary by Roy Harrisville for January 24, 2010 at *Working Preacher.org*: http://www.workingpreacher.org/preaching.aspx?lect_date=1/24/2010.

[251] See Leviticus 25:10-17.

[252] McLaren, Brian D., *A New Kind Of Christianity* (New York: HarperOne, 2010), p.140.

[253] Another very helpful examination of the Jesus' message and purpose is found in Marcus Borg's wonderful book *The Heart of Christianity: Rediscovering a Life of Faith* (San Francisco: HarperSanFrancisco, 2004), pp.126-148.

[254] Quoted from a personal communication with Rod Washington in *A New Kind of Christianity*, p.138.

[255] McLaren Brian D., *Everything Must Change* (Nashville: Thomas Nelson, 2007), p.144.

[256] Philippians 2:5-11 (Although, this passage really needs to be read all the way from verse 1).

[257] Romans 8:1-2.

[258] Romans 8:14, 17, 19, 28-30.

[259] Philippians 2:13.

[260] Willard, Dallas, *The Divine Conspiracy* (London: Fount, 1998), p. 299.

[261] Matthew 3:1

[262] Romans 10:14

[263] For a more detailed explanation of this word, see the Wikipedia article at this url: http://en.wikipedia.org/wiki/Kerygma.

[264] For a brief, but helpful, treatment of the *kerygma* and its role in shaping the life of the Christian community, see Pass, David B., *Music and the Church: A Theology of Church Music* (Nashville: Broadman Press, 1989), pp.66-69.

[265] 1 Corinthians 14:23-24.

[266] See, for example, Psalm 7:17; 9:2; 13:6; 22:25; 43:5; 86:12; 104:33; 108:3; 119:164; 138:1; 145:1-2; among others.

[267] White, Susan J., *The Spirit of Worship* (London: Darton, Longman & Todd, 1999), p.41.

[268] Foster, Richard J., *Celebration of Discipline* (London: Hodder and Stoughton, 1989), p.212.

[269] Ibid. p.214.

[270] Buechner, Frederick, *Telling The Truth: The Gospel As Tragedy, Comedy & Fairy Tale* (New York: HarperCollins, 1977), p.21.

[271] *The Methodist Worship Book* (Peterborough: Methodist Publishing House, 1999), p.110.

[272] Willimon, William H., *Worship as Pastoral Care* (Nashville: Abingdon Press, 1979), p.154.

Conclusion – Living the Change

[273] Sourced from the WikiQuote website here: http://en.wikiquote.org/wiki/Martin_Luther_King,_Jr.

[274] Wendell Berry, *What Are People For?* (New York: Farrar, Straus, and Giroux, 1990), 95-96. Quoted in McLaren, Brian D., *Everything Must Change* (Nashville: Thomas Nelson, 2007), p.141f.

[275] Labberton, Mark, *The Dangerous Act of Worship* (Downers Grove: IVP Books, 2007), p.13.

Made in the USA
Lexington, KY
30 January 2011